FEMINISMS AND DEVELOPMENT

Disrupting taken-for-granted assumptions, this expert series redefines issues at the heart of today's feminist contestations in a development context. Bringing together a formidable collective of thinkers from the Global South and the North, it explores what it is that can bring about positive changes in women's rights and realities.

These timely and topical collections reposition feminism within development studies, bringing into view substantial commonalities across the countries of the Global South that have so far gone unrecognized.

Series editor

Andrea Cornwall

Forthcoming title

Women in Politics: Gender, Power and Development
Mariz Tadros

About the Editor

Charmaine Pereira is a feminist scholar-activist who has worked extensively on the themes of feminist thought and practice, sexuality, gender and university education, and civil society and the state. Based in Abuja, she coordinates the Initiative for Women's Studies in Nigeria (IWSN), which strengthens capacity for teaching and research in gender and women's studies. As IWSN national coordinator, Pereira has developed and led programmes on the politics of sexual harassment and sexual violence in universities, gender justice and women's citizenship, and women's empowerment. She is the author of *Gender in the Making of the Nigerian University System* (2007) and co-editor of *Jacketed Women: Qualitative Research Methodologies on Sexualities and Gender in Africa* (2013).

Changing Narratives of Sexuality

Contestations, Compliance and Women's Empowerment

edited by
Charmaine Pereira

Zed Books
LONDON & NEW YORK

Changing Narratives of Sexuality: Contestations, Compliance and Women's Empowerment was first published in 2014 by Zed Books Ltd, 7 Cynthia Street, London N1 9JF, UK and Room 400, 175 Fifth Avenue, New York, NY 10010, USA

www.zedbooks.co.uk

Designed and typeset in Monotype Bembo by Kate Kirkwood
Index by John Barker
Cover designed by www.alice-marwick.co.uk
Printed and bound by CPI Group (UK) Ltd, Croydon, CR0 4YY

Distributed in the USA exclusively by Palgrave Macmillan, a division of St Martin's Press, LLC, 175 Fifth Avenue, New York, NY 10010, USA

A catalogue record for this book is available from the British Library
Library of Congress Cataloging in Publication Data available

ISBN 978-1-78360-013-7 hb
ISBN 978-1-78360-012-0 pb

Contents

Acknowledgements

To all the women, and men, whose experiences and lives form the backbone of the accounts in this book, I am grateful. This collection has been a long time in the making. It grew out of the work of the sexualities theme group of the Pathways of Women's Empowerment research consortium coordinated by Andrea Cornwall, then at the Institute of Development Studies (IDS) at the University of Sussex. Andrea's enthusiasm and support, to the consortium in general as well as to the thematic group members whose writing is featured here, has been invaluable.

I am grateful to the UK Department for International Development (DFID) for financial support for the research. Thanks are also due to the IDS, the Swedish International Development Cooperation Agency (SIDA) and the Norwegian Ministry of Foreign Affairs for support for two visits to the IDS under the auspices of Visiting Fellowships held between 2011 and 2013, which enabled me to complete the editing of the book.

I would like to thank Bibi Bakare-Yusuf, Takyiwaa Manuh and Firdous Azim for their inspiration and generous encouragement at different stages of the work. Immense thanks go to all the contributors in this collection for their willingness to rewrite drafts and their patience in seeing this project through to the end. Jenny Edwards has always been there to sort out queries and finalized the preparation of the manuscript for the publisher. Any weaknesses or inaccuracies in the text remain my responsibility.

Preface

Andrea Cornwall

The stories we tell and those that are told about sexuality shape our experiences of the world in powerful ways. And yet sexuality – and especially its positive, pleasurable dimensions – is all but absent from discourses of women's empowerment in development. Sexuality is seen at most as a source of harm, danger and trouble; rarely do we get to hear women's stories of the ways in which their sexual lives, identities, desires and relationships shape their experiences of agency and power.

Changing Narratives of Sexuality draws attention to the significance of sexuality for an understanding of women's transformative agency. Juxtaposing case studies from a rich diversity of cultural contexts and domains of representation, the book expands possible readings of the relationships between sexualities, gender and empowerment. The contributors take us from studies of women's storytelling in Egypt to the stories that are told about women's bodies and desires as part of religious education classes in Bangladesh, to the refugee camps in Palestine where young women navigate their sexual agency in a context of multi-layered repression. We move from an analysis of an instance of lurid reportage in Nigeria that speaks volumes about the prevailing societal contradictions and moralizing discourses shaping and constraining women's sexual agency, to contexts of sexuality activism and organizing in China that are opening up spaces for contestation and change. Nuanced and insightful,

Charmaine Pereira's introduction provides us with an account that simultaneously locates these studies against a conceptual backdrop and provides us with a compelling account of the workings of institutionalized normative heterosexuality through dominant modes of representation.

Changing Narratives of Sexuality forms part of a series, Feminisms and Development, which has grown out of an international research and communications programme, Pathways of Women's Empowerment. Established in 2006 as a network of researchers and research institutions spanning five continents, with regional hubs in the Middle East, South America, South Asia and West Africa, a cross-hub research initiative on global policy discourse, and a coordinating and communications hub in the UK, Pathways sought to trace positive change in women's lives and understand how such change comes about – through intentional action, such as activism, policies, projects and programmes, and through broader dynamics of societal, cultural, economic and political change. A key dimension of this work was a focus on the 'hidden pathways' of women's empowerment, those dimensions of women's experience that are absent, obscured or simply invisible in the framings and foci of mainstream development. Three entry-point themes representing key lines of analysis and action within feminist enquiry and activism shaped our programme: body, voice and work. The thematic working group on the body sought to look outside readings of women's bodies that focus on subjection and subjugation, peril and pain towards an approach that sought a more holistic understanding of women's experiences of sexuality, and of the dynamics of power and empowerment in women's intimate lives.

Changing Narratives of Sexuality seeks to make sense of flux in narratives of sexuality in mainstream public institutions, such as the media, religious groups, legal institutions and the development industry, as well as in the spaces of everyday sociality. But it seeks to do more than this. There is in this work an activist concern with knowing more about what it takes to bring about positive change for women: in challenging normative constrictions that dominate public and popular narratives of women's sexuality, in confronting the limits set on women's enjoyment of sexual rights, agency and pleasure, and in constructing new stories that re-present women's experiences of their bodies in ways that are positive and empowering. It is in its interweaving of academic enquiry and activism that this book makes such a unique and important contribution to understanding women's empowerment in all its dimensions.

INTRODUCTION
Changing Narratives of Sexuality

Charmaine Pereira

In Nigeria, nude photographs of a young up-and-coming actress are published in 'respectable' newspapers, an event that a decade earlier would have been unthinkable. Newspaper versions of this sex scandal remain at odds with the actress's own narrative, as it unfolds in successive updates of the story. In divorce cases in Egypt's new family courts, the story of the denial of women's legal rights to sexual pleasure is not told even as courts construct a different narrative which undermines women's pursuit of divorce, on the basis of their emotionality and lack of rationality. In Palestine, young women recount stories about their hopes and aspirations for the future in a context where their bodies have become the site of the immobilities and insecurities of the body politic. The narratives of bodily vulnerability and restriction that the young women tell, as well as those told about them, are juxtaposed against the stories in which they resolve to transcend restrictive boundaries and expectations. What do these different narratives of women's sexuality, by and about women, tell us about tensions and contradictions in the constructions of women's bodies and sexualities? And what scope is there for women to change repressive norms and conceptions of sexuality?

These questions are central to a thematic focus on changing narratives of sexuality, which is one of the research themes addressed by the international consortium Pathways of Women's Empowerment (Pathways). This collection brings together essays written by consortium members from across Pathways' regional hubs located in South America, the Middle East, South Asia and West Africa. Working collectively, we have explored the use of narratives as a way of understanding sexualities in the context of change, and the possibilities for women's empowerment.

The contemporary world is forged out of change on multiple and dynamic fronts. Rising religiosity is a mark not only of social relations but also of political affairs; economic insecurity affects labour markets and access to resources; and all of this is set against a backdrop of political flux and struggles against repressive rule and for democratization. All these changes affect gender relations and have varying implications for the ways in which sexuality may be 'read'. How might these readings of sexuality be recounted and engaged with by different actors in diverse cultural and institutional arenas? The politics of sexuality has generally been problematized with regard to sexual orientation and the normative character of heterosexuality, that is, the sense in which heterosexuality is generally accepted as the way social and sexual relations 'ought to be'. This collection addresses primarily the ways in which heterosexual women are themselves affected by normative heterosexuality (see Jackson 2006) and how women act to try and change the norms involved.

Sexuality has been described as a term referring to 'the way(s) in which human sexual energy becomes part and parcel of psychological, social, cultural and political life' and as 'a realm of political, social and cultural organization, in which knowledge, norms, meanings and possibilities are constructed, contested and controlled' (African Gender Institute 2009). This highlights the multiple and contextual meanings of sexuality (Tamale 2011). There are many ways of becoming sexual and thus not only one form of sexuality but several (Gagnon 1977). We begin from the premise that sexualities are themselves gendered, an understanding that is the outcome of considerable feminist analytical and political work in this sphere, but at the same time, there is no singular theorization of the relations between sexualities and gender. Yet the theoretical and political significance of such relations for domains such as the body, relations of intimacy, subjectivity, and the workings of power and agency, demands exploration (Richardson 2007).

We are interested in narratives as a way of approaching the study of sexualities for a number of reasons. Narratives allow us to explore cultural patterns of representations and action (Squire 2005) whilst opening up the theme of what social role stories can be said to play. Thus we may ask about the extent to which stories perform conservative functions by maintaining dominant orders. Alternatively, there is the question of how stories might be used to transform lives and cultures (Plummer 1995). The focus on changing narratives of sexuality is simultaneously a focus on the multiple changes shaping women's relations to sexuality and power, and on the ways in which women exercise their agency by taking up particular narratives of sexuality, using them to destabilize restrictive social and sexual norms.

The rest of this chapter begins with an analysis of sexual politics in terms of the relations between heteronormativity and sexualities, followed by an exploration of the ways in which women's empowerment has been conceptualized with regard to sexualities. The significance of context and change are highlighted before I examine the ways in which diverse representations of sexuality, in different realms, may be understood as narratives. The chapters in this collection present a wide array of changing narratives of sexuality, with varying implications for women's empowerment.

Heteronormativity and sexualities

The politics of sex and sexualities has sometimes but not always been addressed under the rubric of institutionalized heterosexuality. Most analysts have treated it primarily in terms of the control of homosexuality, leaving the character of normative heterosexuality itself relatively unquestioned (cf. Jackson 2006). More recently, there has been greater interest in the ways in which heterosexuals are themselves affected by normative heterosexuality. Feminists working in this field have drawn on the work of earlier writers such as Adrienne Rich (1980), who linked heterosexuality to the entrenchment of gendered divisions of labour and the ways in which men take possession of women's productive and reproductive capacities.

Jackson (2006) argues that Rich's concept of 'compulsory heterosexuality' could be read as a precursor to 'heteronormativity' but that there is an important difference. The notion of 'compulsory heterosexuality' encompasses the sense in which 'institutionalized, normative heterosexuality regulates those kept within its boundaries as well as marginalizing and sanctioning those outside them' (Jackson 2006: 105). 'Heteronormativity' as a concept, she points out, has not always included this dual character of social regulation. It is the focus on what goes on *within* heterosexual relations that Jackson (2006: 105) considers of particular interest, given its role in how 'heterosexuality depends upon and guarantees gender division'.

Heterosexuality is quite diverse, with different configurations being associated with varying degrees of respectability and status. Jackson (2006: 107) elaborates further:

> Heterosexuality ... should not be thought of as simply a form of sexual expression. It is not only a key site of intersection between gender and sexuality, but also one that reveals the interconnections between sexual and non-sexual aspects of social life. Heterosexuality is, by definition, a gender relationship, ordering not only sexual life but also domestic and extra-domestic divisions of labour and resources ... Thus heterosexuality, while depending on the exclusion or marginalization of other sexualities for its legitimacy, is not precisely coterminous with heterosexual sexuality.

The value attached to the 'normative' character of heterosexuality is that accorded to a very specific form based on traditional gender arrangements and monogamy. Jackson (2006: 105) argues that 'the analysis of heteronormativity needs to be rethought in terms of *what* is subject to regulation on both sides of the normatively prescribed boundaries of heterosexuality: both sexuality *and* gender' (emphasis in the original).

Within structures of regulation and subordination, the workings of human agency have been the focus of work in the humanities and social sciences since the 1970s. Drawing on this body of work, feminists have pursued the question of 'how women resist the dominant male order by subverting hegemonic meanings of cultural practices and redeploying them for their "own interests and agendas"', with the latter identified as the site for women's agency (Mahmood 2005: 6). The early work on women's agency was of critical importance in rethinking the portrayals of women beyond the West as passive and submissive beings bound by patriarchal structures.

Dominant feminist tendencies in conceptualizing agency have treated it primarily in terms of resistance to normative structures. The notion of agency most often invoked by feminist scholars is rooted in liberalism, however, and locates agency in the political and moral autonomy of the subject (Mahmood 2005). Charting a different trajectory, Mahmood explores the women's mosque movement in Egypt which emerged in the 1970s, as part of the Islamic Revival. Women started to organize weekly religious lessons, first in their homes and then in mosques, to read the Quran, the Hadith and other religiously inflected literature. The women's mosque movement was a popular movement that spread rapidly across most neighbourhoods in Cairo, offering lessons on the teaching and study of Islamic scriptures, social practices and forms of bodily comportment considered necessary for the development of the ideal virtuous self.

In the context of feminism's privileging of those forms of agency that subvert and resignify hegemonic discourses of gender and sexuality, other forms of agency are generally ignored. Mahmood's focus is simultaneously on 'the different meanings of agency as they emerge within the practices of the mosque movement' in Egypt and on 'the kinds of analytical questions that are opened up when agency is analyzed in some of its other modalities – questions that remain submerged ... if agency is analyzed in terms of resistance to the subordinating function of power' (2005: 153–4).

> ... if the ability to effect change in the world and in oneself is historically and culturally specific (both in terms of what constitutes 'change' and the means by which it is effected), then the meaning and sense of agency cannot be fixed in advance, but must emerge through an analysis of the particular concepts that enable specific modes of being, responsibility and effectivity. Viewed in this way, what may appear to be a case of deplorable passivity and docility from a progressivist point of view, may actually be a form of agency – but one that can be understood only from within the discourses and structures of subordination that create the conditions of its enactment. In this sense, agentival capacity is entailed not only in those acts that resist norms but also in the multiple ways in which one *inhabits* norms. (Mahmood 2005: 14–15; emphasis in the original)

Miriam (2007) elaborates heterosexual norms through a re-theorizing of the connection between heteronormativity and male supremacy, by revisiting Adrienne Rich's (1980) notion of compulsory heterosexuality. Miriam goes further to discuss her notion of agency within this framework. Her argument is interesting because of its illumination of ways of thinking about agency, sexualities and empowerment. Whilst feminists have contested Rich's notion of male power on the grounds that it promotes a discourse of women as victims, Miriam's counter-argument to this view is that whilst it is necessary to include an account of women's and girls' sexual agency in order to understand heteronormativity, this does not mean that a theory of 'sex-right' is therefore obsolete and inadequate. Instead, she argues, women's agency needs to be understood in terms of 'the sexual antinomies in late modernity' (Jackson and Scott 2004). Analysis of these, she points out, would help us demystify the hidden and entrenched character of the compulsory dimension of heterosexuality.

In making her argument, Mariam draws on Catherine MacKinnon's (1989) theory of sexuality, which developed Rich's notion of sex-right in significant ways. MacKinnon has been criticized for theoretical determinism on the grounds that she posits causal relations between sex, gender, domination and heterosexuality: 'Sex is gender is sexual positionality' (Butler

1994, cited in Miriam 2007: 214). However, Miriam argues that, rather than providing a causal analysis, MacKinnon poses questions such as what sexuality is understood to be, what sex means, and what is meant by sex. MacKinnon's conclusion was that sexual meaning, by which she understood heterosexual meaning, was constructed in the interests of male sexuality: 'It is these interests that construct what sexuality as such means, including the standard way it is allowed to be felt and expressed and experienced, in a way that determines women's biographies, including sexual ones' (MacKinnon 1989: 129).

The term 'determines' used by MacKinnon above has been interpreted by many feminists to refer to causal relations between sexuality and gender, with gender being the causal condition for sexuality. Contesting this interpretation, Miriam (2007: 215) states that MacKinnon is referring here to the way in which gender is produced by sexuality:

> ... we can see that the contents of normative feminine behaviour – what is allowed and disallowed – shows evidence of men's interests ... which is to say that the 'gender definition of "female"' coheres with 'the social requirements for male sexual arousal and satisfaction' ... Thus (hetero)sexuality itself *is* this process of putting into play the contents of gender, the process through which meanings of gender are embodied, and are thus constituted and organized in socially determinative/compulsory ways.

Rather than precluding agency, MacKinnon can be seen to be theorizing the conditions under which women's sexual agency is 'enabled'. Agency is understood here in an ontological sense to mean the ways in which an embodied female subject lives through (hetero)sexuality: the latter thus becomes the ground of women's agency. However, to say that women are agents is not synonymous with saying that they are empowered or free. Freedom connotes the capacity to co-create and transform one's situation. MacKinnon's theory of (hetero)sexuality points to a situation in which women's agency is only enabled within an interpretive and power schema based on men's sex-right. Agency therefore cannot be conflated, in and of itself, with 'transformative' agency. Instead, women's agency may be exercised in ways that 'reproduce or re-entrench, rather than overcome, domination, coercion or victimization' (Miriam 2007: 213).

McNay (2000: 4) makes a similar point about the need to contextualize agency within power relations, 'in order to understand how acts deemed as resistant may transcend their immediate sphere in order to transform collective behaviour and norms'. The basis for her refusal to equate agency with transformation is different from that of Miriam's (2007), however. McNay is critical of the notion of agency as resistance and as therefore inherently subversive, on the grounds that such a notion has no impact if the interplay between individual behaviour and social norms is ignored. She notes that 'analysis of the way in which certain subversive practices may get taken up and collectivized is important if resistance is to mean anything other than the truism that individuals do not reproduce social norms in a straightforward fashion' (McNay 2000: 129).

The question of women's sexual agency is particularly salient in the context of sexual violations. Miriam (2007: 222) points out that 'In order to understand women's sexual agency, we have to shift our attention from the liberal model of individual choice to the meaning of the situation in which women make choices.' Here she is recalling Frye's (1983: 56) point that: 'The elements of coercion lie not in [the coerced individual's] person, mind or body but in the manipulation of the circumstances and manipulation of the options.' Relations of power precede any time-bound decision to consent to sex.

The tensions between sexual fear, occasioned by the realities of rape and numerous other forms of sexual abuse for many women, and the notion of sexual freedom as an ideal have been addressed in a variety of ways. Focusing on African women, Patricia MacFadden (2003) puts forward the viewpoint that the notions of 'pleasure' and 'choice' are rarely recognized as being among the most contentious aspects of female sexuality. The fear of sexual pleasure is directly linked to the construction of women's sexuality as 'filthy', arising as it does out of the recognition of an intimate relationship between sexuality and power. Moreover, the non-recognition of pleasure as fundamental to women's rights has led to debates and activism around sexuality, reproduction and rights being confined to 'safe' zones within culturally sanctioned understandings of women's roles and bodies.

In a response to this piece, I have pointed out that MacFadden erases significant complexities and contradictions in African women's lives, making claims that rest on problematic assumptions (Pereira 2003). It is possible to argue for the need to enhance the value of female sexuality and to promote basic sexual freedoms without assuming, as MacFadden does, the universal suppression of female sexualities. More important, it is necessary to understand how sexual pleasure and sexual power are lived and made sense of by diverse categories of women and men, just as there is a need to understand changing constructions of sexuality and the relations among sexualities and economic, political and social arenas.

Sexualities and women's empowerment

Early texts that address the political economy of sexuality provide some fascinating perspectives on how women's empowerment in relation to sexuality might be conceptualized. Writing in Russia at the turn of the twentieth century, Alexandra Kollontai had as her ultimate aim the complete liberation of working-class women and the establishment of the foundation of a new sexual morality. In 'The Social Basis of the Woman Question', Kollontai (1977a) argued that the solution of 'the family question' was no less important than the attainment of political equality and economic independence for women. Women's liberation ultimately encompassed freedom in love, an ideal that was unattainable without transformation of the social and economic conditions defining the obligations of working-class women, fundamental change in all social relationships between people, and a thorough change of moral, psychological and sexual norms.

Kollontai developed these ideas further in 'Sexual Relations and the Class Struggle' (1977b), pointing to the sexual crisis of the time and the hypocrisy of relegating sexual matters to the 'private' realm, beyond the consideration of the social collective. Her point that a social group works out its ideology, and thus its sexual morality, in the process of struggle with hostile social forces is as relevant today as it was in her time. Kollontai's autobiography (1971) is an illuminating example of the battle she experienced against the intervention of the male into a woman's ego, a struggle that revolved around a complex of decisions: work or marriage or love. Her novel *Red Love* (1927) is a psychological exploration of sexual relations in the post-war period, the period of civil war that followed the revolution, against a backdrop of changes in the contexts of women's engagement in public affairs and work outside the home.

Around the same time as Alexandra Kollontai was working and writing in Russia, the anarchist Emma Goldman was active in the USA. Goldman's two-part autobiography (1986) focuses on her passionate commitment to the political ideals of anarchism and her accompanying personal search for love and intimacy. Goldman's political aims concerned the quest for women's economic self-determination and for women's right to sexual freedom. Candace Falk's (1990) biography explores the intersection of Goldman's public and private lives, offering a critical analysis of anarchism and Goldman's relation to it through the trajectory of her personal experiences.

More recently, women's rights in the arena of sexuality have been vigorously pursued under the rubric of sexual rights. At the transcontinental level, considerable work has been carried out on the relationship of sexualities to reproduction, health and rights (Correa and Parker 2004; Cornwall and Welbourn 2002). Correa and Parker examine the controversies related to sexualities that have been expressed in United Nations negotiations and unravel the challenges inherent in different modes of conceptualizing sexual rights. They argue that it is crucial to debate the unintended implications of choices in terms of the philosophies underlying human rights approaches.

A critical task, in addition, is the identification of human rights principles that would be appropriate for defining entitlements in relation to sexualities.

> In conceptualizing sexual rights it is ... necessary to clarify the implications of such rights. Do they mean full legal protection with the risk of paternalism and intrusion? Or, on the contrary, do they fundamentally imply the right to privacy and intimacy, which in many circumstances increases the vulnerability of those less empowered in sexual matters? Or, instead of these two options, is the conceptualization of sexual rights to be viewed as a discursive platform for processing conflicts in relation to existing rights, in other words, as a political framework for creating the conditions for people themselves to be the subjects of their sexual rights? (Correa and Parker 2004: 25)

Some of the challenges involved in framing a positive approach to sexual rights, that is, one that goes beyond protection from fear and abuse, require the rethinking of the boundaries between public and private. Correa and Parker (2004: 26) point out that the debate on sexual rights has 'matured enough to begin to openly advocate for sexuality as a practice of freedom', that is, as a valid space for the search for pleasure, based on principles such as equality, responsibility and choice. This requires conceptual definitions and political strategies that will effectively 'prevent and punish sexual abuses that occur in the private domain and, at the same time, enhance the possibility of pleasurable sexual experiences in privacy and intimacy' (2004: 26). The authors point out that fostering a deeper sense of entitlement and responsibility in relation to sexualities will require cultural and social transformation to enhance change at the subjective, household, community and institutional levels.

Conceptualizing the articulation among sexualities, inequality and freedom has provided a different kind of challenge. Prior to the International Conference on Population and Development in Cairo in 1994, feminists had spent considerable time debating the relevance and meaning of reproductive rights in developing regions, and among marginal groups in wealthy societies. In these diverse locations, women's ability to make reproductive choices was restricted primarily by socio-economic constraints. In conceptual terms, the problem was resolved by stating that the realization of reproductive rights required an enabling environment which comprised democratic conditions, material support and women's empowerment. Correa and Parker (2004) argue that this framework should be used in the conceptual development of sexual rights too.

With regard to freedom, new inroads have been made to seeing freedom as a precondition for and an objective of social and economic justice (Correa and Parker 2004). Amartya Sen (1999) has gone beyond the mainstream understanding of freedom as political liberty in order to reconsider it as empowerment. For Sen, empowerment means greater individual and collective autonomy; this requires opportunities that contribute to development, broadly conceived, and which also serve to expand freedom in the public sphere. In addition, the *Human Development Report 2000* (UNDP 2000) refers to different types of freedom in the context of sustainable livelihoods: freedom from want, freedom for the realization of one's full potential, and freedom from fear with no threats to personal security. These broadened notions of freedom, as Correa and Parker (2004) point out, can be usefully explored in further refining sexual rights.

In the context of HIV and AIDS, understandings of women's empowerment are often associated with the negotiation of safer sex (see, for example, Holland *et al.* 1992). Holland *et al.* show that conceptualizing women's empowerment in this framework is restricted by prevailing assumptions and thought categories which cast the defining feature of heterosexual sex as a dominant masculinity. At the same time, the individual men and women engaging in sex are conceived of as free, rational agents. Safer sex thus becomes the responsibility of these individual men and women, who are freely able to make rational choices for their own protection. Holland *et al.* argue that there is a tension here between the conception of empowerment as a matter of individual assertiveness and choice and a more collective conception of empowerment as a challenge to dominant masculinity. In a similar vein, McNay (2000) argues that female sexual agency cannot change without concurrent changes in masculine sexual identity. Moreover, there must be both social and individual uptake of subversive practices for these to have any impact on women's lives.

During the AIDS conference in Barcelona in July 2002, UNIFEM took up the slogan 'Empower women, halt HIV/AIDS' (cited in Silberschmidt 2005). Silberschmidt argues that the promotion of women's empowerment and women's rights is 'often based on simplistic solutions to complex socio-economic problems'. Drawing on the politics of equal rights to dismantle men's advantages over women 'would be to abandon our knowledge of how those advantages are produced and defended. Ironically, empowering women may free men from taking responsibility, in particular in sexual matters' (2005: 200–1).

Placing sexual rights and sexual pleasure in context ultimately affords a more nuanced understanding of the dynamics of sexuality in a given social setting. Musallam (1983) analyses, in some depth, women's right to sexual pleasure among the four main schools of Muslim jurisprudence of the Sunni, and the tensions inherent in the dominant form of birth control, coitus interruptus. He also discusses Arabic erotica – popular literature comprised largely of anthologies of popular material on sex, which included specific birth control prescriptions. The place of birth control in Arabic erotica, as Musallam points out, is far more prominent than in either ancient Indian or Chinese erotica.

Fatema Mernissi (2001) confronts the question of whether cultures manage emotions differently when it comes to structuring erotic responses. Her book *Scheherazade Goes West* is an exquisitely crafted exposition of Western men's fantasies of Muslim harems, juxtaposed against actual lived experiences of Muslim women in harems. She illustrates how women's erotic power in many Arab cultures relies on their brainpower, particularly their capacity to communicate and to work at the level of the mind. The aim is to arrive at an intense sharedness of the imagination that is expressed in dialogue. Mernissi's analysis highlights not only particular historical dimensions of cultural difference in erotic responses and sexual relations but also the character and gendered implications of women's erotic power in the Arab cultures she discusses.

On context and change

Our understandings of sexualities as well as of gender are likely to be deepened by recognizing that they are the products of particular social and historical contexts (see, for example, Mernissi 2001; Richardson 2007; Tamale 2011). The significance of context is its delineation of 'broad conditioning factors – political, social and economic' – which shape gendered 'structures of constraint' (cf. Kabeer 2008: 7). It is the context that provides the frame within which 'the particular importance of rules, norms and practices' (Kabeer 2008: 7) derive their meaning, in terms that are relational. Just as the meaning of a word resides neither in the word itself nor in its relationship to its referent but is embedded in the social context of its usage (see Ryle 1949, cited in Crossley 2001; Pereira 2008) so too, one might posit, the meanings of rules, norms and practice are contextually arrived at. The relations between context and empowerment are made explicit by Cornwall and Edwards (2010: 2):

> Context is crucial in making sense of empowerment. Historical shifts in societal and cultural norms and practices, as well as in institutions in politics and the economy, current and previous political conjunctures, the density of donor engagement and the nature of the state, the broader landscape of organizations and social movements, and a number of other contextual factors impinge on the possibilities for women's empowerment – facilitating and enabling but also blocking and restricting possibilities.

An example that highlights the importance of context is provided by Micaela di Leonardo and Roger Lancaster (1996), who trace the contours of Western historical political-economic work on gender and sexualities. The authors show that the taboo on homosexual relations in Europe was implicated in, among other things, the rise of capitalism, the fanning of religious and political intolerance, the emergence of the modern nation-state and the discourses and forms of colonialism. John D'Emilio (1997) refutes the myth that self-identified gay men and lesbians have always existed in all societies at all times. Instead, he argues that gay men and lesbians are a product of history and have come into being in a specific era. This is not the same as arguing that same-sex relations do not exist in societies outside the West. D'Emilio shows how the historical development of capitalism, specifically its free labour system, has allowed large numbers of men and women aggregated in urban settlements to call themselves 'gay' and 'lesbian' and to organize politically on the basis of that identity.

Constructions of women's sexualities are embedded in multiple and simultaneous changes being played out on global, regional, national and more local levels. Together, they establish the hallmark of the end of the twentieth and beginning of the twenty-first century. The growing movements of ideas, trade, money and peoples across the world – what has come to be referred to as globalization – are associated with a variety of changes in social, economic and cultural spheres. Within this period, diverse political regimes and administrations have experienced crises of legitimacy whilst economies have simultaneously become more closely interwoven. The technological revolution that has transformed the possibilities for communicating among individuals, and within and across social groups, has in many ways accelerated the pace of change (Correa and Parker 2004). At the same time, the traditional structure of gender relations has increasingly become contested, and 'accepted notions of the relationship between family and sexuality have fragmented, broken down and been reinvented in societies around the world' (Correa and Parker 2004: 19).

Altman (2004) argues that globalization has a bearing on sexualities in a number of interrelated ways. The common thread, he suggests, is the growth of consumerism and individualism, characteristics that seem more easily transferable with economic growth than particular political values. New media images, through cinema, television and particularly the internet, present hugely divergent ways of imagining sex and gender arrangements and identities. Whilst new styles in music, clothes and hair may travel relatively easily, however, the meanings they acquire in different contexts are likely to vary. The distance between these representations and those thought to be more grounded within society mean that people increasingly 'live in a world rich in conflicting and hybrid imagery' (Altman 2004: 64).

At the same time, globalization is leading to deepening forms of inequality on the economic front. The imposition of market economies and the withdrawal of state services have left many people increasingly pauperized. Radical differences in the opportunities that people have to benefit from rapid social change mean that whilst some have been able to move into middle-class lifestyles, many more have had to resort to petty crime, begging and sex work (Sassen 1998). One of the less obvious repercussions of this scenario then is that 'just as globalization is sharpening a sense of economic inequality in the world, so too it is ensuring that very different conceptions of the sexual will become politically contested' (Altman 2004: 65).

The seemingly uncontrolled and uncertain change enveloping much of the world has gone hand in hand with increasing revivalism in religious, ethnic and national identities. The profound threats presented to the security of social life by ethnic and theocratic struggles, as well as terrorist militias, have come under serious scrutiny in recent years (Imam, Morgan and Yuval-Davis 2004). Many of the same factors shape the increasingly complex relationship between social and economic change and radical changes in sexualities in cultures and countries around the world. The broader contours of such changes are to be found in formal political arenas, such as the state-sanctioned persecution of homosexuals as well as in less visible processes of social and sexual change:

> These processes range from the trans-local movement of sexual traditions and systems of meaning across previously impermeable cultural and political borders, to the emergence of feminist and lesbian and gay political movements outside their traditional base in the Anglo-European world, to the incorporation of conceptual frameworks related to gender, sexuality and health within development discourse and practice, and to complex struggles around sexuality at both local level (in disagreements about abortion, violence against the expression of sexual difference, and so on) and in debates at the level of the United Nations and international relations ... (Correa and Parker 2004: 19–20)

Revivalism in the spheres of religion, culture and tradition is both a characteristic of and a response to a convergence of several interrelated processes. The diverse gendered and sexualized changes brought about by tremendous shifts in the economic and political order give rise to situations of angst and uncertainty in which moral order is perceived to be compromised and in need of restoration. In such contexts, women's bodies often become the targets of control and policing (see Huq 2005; Bakare-Yusuf 2009; Pereira and Ibrahim 2010). Women's recognition of their embodied experiences of deprivation and discrimination was a key feature of the formation of Naripokkho, a feminist organization in Bangladesh, informing as it does their work on body politics. This includes making violence against women visible, advocacy on better services for women who have suffered violence, and defending the rights of sex workers (Huq 2005). In Nigeria, the displacement of social anxieties is evident in a conflation of public morality with women's bodies. This constitutes the common ground for the religious right among Christians as well as Muslims (Pereira and Ibrahim 2010), at the same time as it informs efforts to enact legislation controlling women's dress (Bakare-Yusuf 2009).

Changing narratives of sexuality

The changes referred to above give rise to tensions and contradictions in the constructions of women's bodies and sexualities. These constructions may form the basis for mainstream narratives of sexuality produced by institutions such as the law, religion and the development industry, and by cultural arenas such as television and print media; they may also form the basis for counternarratives produced by women. What form do these different narratives and counternarratives take? How might they be contextualized against the backdrop of the multiple changes taking place in a society at any given time?

The question 'What is a story?' may be addressed from several perspectives (Squire 2005). Squire discusses ways in which stories have been studied as replayed events, expressions of identities, cultural traces or a trace of something that is not there. What a story says and does can be similarly varied. Stories can be taken as cognitive or aesthetic re-enactments, as efforts at personal understanding, as social inscription, and as emotional defences. A story may be read as addressed to its present audience or to a much broader audience of past, present and future figures, whether real or imagined. The common conceptual ground of the approaches referred to, however, is limited.

Beyond the early focus on narratives in terms of their internal organization, there has since been considerable interest in life stories and the light that these might throw on the self in relation to everyday life and lived experience (e.g. Faraday and Plummer 1979; Personal Narratives Group 1989; Abu-Lughod 2008). The more recent narrative turn in ethnography goes beyond stories themselves to address the environments – the occasions and practices – surrounding which stories are told and not told (see Gubrium and Holstein 2008). Squire (2005) makes the point that it is in the potential diversity of narrative readings that their political importance lies. The concept of a narrative offers broad access to a range of disciplinary traditions and is salient for fields within and beyond academia. Moreover, a focus on narratives provides space for the convergence of varied concerns and interests. These include interpreting and improving individual experience, concerns about representation and agency, as well as questions to do with subjectivity, the unconscious and desire. Placing the spotlight on narratives makes it possible for the content of stories to be brought into focus as well as the context of storytelling. The latter includes the real and assumed audiences of stories as it does their social, cultural and fantasy contexts (Squire 2005).

Narratives have the potential to bring together diverse representations that foreground the range of different dimensions of the social identified by Jackson (2006). These are institutional mechanisms such as the law; arenas for the making of meaning, such as language, discourse and everyday social interaction; the routine social practices through which gender and sexualities are constituted and reconstituted in given contexts and relationships; and the sexual and gendered selves who construct, enact and make sense of gendered and sexual interaction. It is these multiple dimensions of the social that constitute the terrain on which the complexity of heteronormative social relations needs to be explored. The salience of narratives may thus be understood in their potential for not only depicting diverse representations of sexuality but also for making connections across representations in a plurality of social arenas.

Narrative analysis takes a number of different forms (e.g. Gubrium and Holstein 2008; Andrews *et al.* 2008). Whilst the content of stories may be of particular significance in some instances, in others it may be the context that is more important. The question of how narratives might be contextualized – how one might understand the relationship of stories to the world in which they circulate – is a critical one. Gubrium and Holstein (2008) point out that the meanings of stories are poorly understood without a grasp of the conditions under which the stories were produced and received, that is, their narrative environments. Plummer (1995) provides us with a useful way of thinking about the analysis of stories, one which acknowledges change, history and culture. His focus is on sexual stories, but he points out that his general approach may be applied to any storytelling process.

> for me, a sociology of stories should be less concerned with analysing the formal structures of stories or narratives (as literary theory might), and more interested in inspecting the social role of stories: the ways they are produced, the ways they are read, the work they perform in the wider social order, how they change, and their role in the political process ... Although recent developments in literary theory and cultural studies will prove useful, and there is indeed a need for analysing the formal properties of stories, I will constantly return to the social work they perform in cultures. *It is time to go beyond the text*. (Plummer 1995: 19, italics in the original)

In going beyond the text, we are interested in the question of what links exist between stories and the wider social world. Plummer puts it this way: '[what are] the contextual conditions for stories to be told and for stories to be received?' Plummer's question highlights two interrelated issues: what makes it possible for some stories to be told at a particular moment; and what interpretive communities exist in the social world which make it possible for stories to be heard at particular historical moments. In a similar vein, Andrews *et al*. (2008: 1–2) point out that:

> By focusing on narrative, we are able to investigate, not just how stories are structured and the ways in which they work, but also who produces them and by what means; the mechanisms by which they are consumed; and how narratives are silenced, contested and accepted.

Going beyond the narrative material is also important for addressing questions such as, Where are particular kinds of narratives likely to be encountered? Under what circumstances are certain stories more or less accountable? and Which interests publicize stories? (Gubrium and Holstein 2008). The critical question of what social role stories can be said to play has been aptly framed by Plummer (1995: 25): 'How might stories work to perform conservative functions maintaining dominant orders, and how might they be used to resist or transform lives and cultures?' It is questions such as these, with particular reference to heteronormativity, that animate the chapters in this collection.

The chapters in this collection examine the theme of *changing narratives of sexuality* in at least one of two ways. The first has to do with the multiple changes that are occurring in all our societies, and the implications of such changes for the ways in which sexualities may be 'read'. Have changing practices and representations of women's bodies and sexualities been associated with new narratives of sexuality, and if so, what space do these narratives provide for women's empowerment? The second dimension of *changing narratives* is about the different ways in which women are exercising their agency to change restrictive narratives of sexuality. What are the sexual politics within which these struggles are taking place? To what extent are women able to produce counternarratives that broaden the possibilities for women's empowerment? Our aim is to identify where women's transformative agency and uses of power for positive change can be found.

Most of the authors treat narratives as manifestations of social and cultural patterns. Since stories are not told in isolation from hearings, the question of how a story is heard is of key significance. How are diverse readings connected to the social world in which they are read? What do women make of the narratives on offer, and what bearing do they have on women's relations to sexuality? Dominant narratives may be challenged by alternative versions – what Andrews (2008: 100) calls 'counter narratives' – or 'how those stories we know best might be retold'. Institutions tell stories too, or have narratives embedded within their ways of working. Of interest here are the narratives of sexuality that may be discerned from an analysis of their practice, or which are consciously told as part of the ways in which institutional and cultural formations present or represent themselves to the world. Why are particular institutional narratives told and not others? In a context where there may be multiple narratives in circulation, which institutional narratives get 'heard' and which ones are silenced?

Organization of the book

There are three sections to the book. Part One, 'Negotiating Desire?', addresses the theme of desire in the diverse realms of storytelling (Mona I. Ali), religion (Samia Huq) and sexual risk (Deevia Bhana). Women's orientations towards desire in these different realms take on varied configurations, including elements of elimination, expression, submergence and reframing. Part Two, 'Body Politics and Sexualities', begins with the contested narratives surrounding the exposure of an actress's nude photos in newspapers (Charmaine Pereira and Bibi Bakare-Yusuf). The next two chapters address a feminist's experience of ageing (Cecilia M. B. Sardenberg) and the inscription of the body politic on to the bodies of single women (Penny Johnson). This part highlights the lived experience of women's bodies and the need for analyses of body politics in understanding sexualities. In conclusion, Part Three of the book, 'Changing Institutions?', engages the challenges and complexities of institutional change regarding perspectives on sexuality in law courts (Mulki Al-Sharmani) and in development institutions (Susie Jolly).

The rest of this chapter traces key strands in the individual chapters. Mona I. Ali explores, through the work of the Women and Memory Forum (WMF), the relations between the ability to write one's body as a woman and the deconstruction of stereotypes of women's and men's sexualities. On the basis that folk tales contribute to the construction of the collective public memory, WMF endeavours to reconstruct representations of women in popular memory by *re*writing and *re*telling stories from the *One Thousand and One Nights*. Ali examines the ambiguity, ambivalences and contradictions in the rewriting of these tales by two generations of writers from the WMF. Many of the WMF's first generation of rewritten stories depict women's sexualities as repressed, if not erased, in their writers' efforts to revise the representations of women as hypersexual in traditional folk tales. The new generation of writers, unlike their predecessors, were able to participate in training by more experienced writers, which exposed them to the stereotyping of women in popular culture and the media. Many of the new writers were more able to represent women in their rewritten stories as expressing sexual agency, and some even wrote about women's sexual desires in relatively explicit ways. Arguing that writing and creativity are key routes to expanding women's awareness of their bodies and sexual desires, Ali highlights the views of most of the second generation of writers that the processes involved in rewriting were empowering for them as well as for their audiences.

Samia Huq discusses the reconfiguration of sexuality at the heart of changing worldviews in urban Bangladesh. Until recently, the modernity of the state had been predicated on the notion of a 'modern woman', which Islamists have sought to unravel. Given this fusion of religion with politics in recent political history, and the subsequent control of women's bodies and sexuality that has ensued, Huq poses the question of whether women's sexuality may be understood in ways other than as oppressed. Exploring how sexuality is configured within the religious worldviews of different categories of women, Huq analyses the narrative conventions women use to discuss relations between men and women, namely premarital relations; marriage and divorce; and polygyny. From listening to how women talk about experiencing their gendered and sexual existence, the author shows how different ways of engaging with norms – negotiation as well as appropriation – produce varying results. It is through their engagement with norms that women are able to highlight change and agency in their lives, invoking religion to authorize or condemn practices relating to their sexuality. Huq concludes by arguing that the two models of agency that foreground religion differently, either at the centre or at the margins of social life, should be brought together in reconsidering the normative meanings and goals of empowerment.

Deevia Bhana explores young women's expressions of

sexuality in post-apartheid South Africa, in a township context marked by historical inequalities, violence and vulnerability to HIV. Bhana shows that whilst the women's understandings of sexuality are not entirely centred on poverty, violence and disease, their perspectives are nevertheless embedded in social and economic relations of power. Two key narratives of sexuality emerge from her discussions with the young women. The first is one in which sexuality is constructed as a domain of love and desire, where young men's capacity to provide material goods is experienced emotionally as love. Provider love is contrasted with a second narrative, one in which the dangers of sexual violence and the pre-eminence of fear remain in the foreground. Although young women are vulnerable to manifestations of coercive male sexual power, they still express agency in terms of resisting sexual pressure and rejecting men's violence. The conflicted character of young women's relations to coercive masculinity are surfaced in the ways in which sexual violence remains a pervasive form of domination but one which gives shape to desire, attraction and love. Bhana points to the emergence of an alternative narrative of sexuality, one in which 'showing patience is showing love'. Creating space for this would require changing gender norms and notions of love, whilst affording the possibility for young women of expressing their agency in more empowering ways.

Charmaine Pereira and Bibi Bakare-Yusuf's chapter is a study of a sex scandal in which nude photos of a Nigerian actress, Anita Hogan, appeared in print media in 2006. The publication of the photos transgressed legal and normative social prescriptions about what constitutes legitimate exposure of the female body in the public arena. The authors point to the role of technology in making this transgression possible, as the pictures were transferred from Hogan's personal computer by a third party who subsequently sent them to the media when his attempts to extort money from the actress were unsuccessful. Through textual analyses, the chapter explores the ways in which the publication of the pictures was represented as female transgression. Readers' and editors' acceptance as well as condemnation of the pictures was expressed in terms that surface the tensions between 'legitimate' bodily exposure, women's vulnerability and the potentially 'contaminating' influence of the expression of a 'free woman's' sexuality, as determined by the character of her relationship with a man. The chapter points to the redrawing of boundaries between 'public' and 'private', through the use of technology, in a context where sexual transgression is read in conflicted and ambivalent ways. The authors argue that analysis of such processes is critical in opening up the space for more open exploration and debate around issues of sexuality, power and gender in the politics of representation.

Cecilia M. B. Sardenberg's chapter is an essay on the control over the body that a culture of eternal youth imposes on ageing white middle-class women in Brazil. Sardenberg draws attention to the ideals of femininity inherent in media representations, the products, services and body technologies geared towards women's beautification and the fight against ageing. She writes about the challenges of being caught between the dominant narrative of ageing as decline and the narrative propagated by the cosmetics industry of a denial of decline. Sardenberg warns against the appropriation of feminist discourse when the pursuit of plastic surgery, implants, liposuction and the like are cast as women's 'autonomy' over their bodies and therefore their 'empowerment'. Challenging hegemonic representations of female beauty, sexuality and ageing, Sardenberg argues, requires systemic critiques of the politics of the body, femininity and sexuality as well as the production of feminist counternarratives.

Penny Johnson makes connections between the narratives of two generations of unmarried women and matters of embodiment, sexuality and (dis)empowerment. Marriage is a key institution through which heterosexuality as well as gender may be understood as being constituted and potentially reconstituted. Johnson's essay shows that what it means for women to be unmarried has to be understood in a contextualized manner, one in which heterosexuality is interwoven with different dimensions of the social. At the same time, however, these meanings may be contested in different ways, whether through the experiences of older women in lives of service, or the focus of young women on education or on rethinking the ideal age of marriage. The comparative dimension introduced by including the stories of young women from two different refugee camps highlights specificities as well as commonalities within the category of 'young unmarried women', showing that it cannot be homogenized. Threats to women's and girls' personal security from potential heterosexual encounters were defined and responded to, by those around them, in explicit bodily terms. Johnson discusses how, in the moment of the second intifada, the insecurities and immobilities of the body politic are enacted on the bodies of young unmarried women. At the same time, the young women resolve to expand boundaries, through education and more recently through film, in a bid to bring about change.

Mulki Al-Sharmani critically examines the institutional narrative of marriage constructed and sustained by substantive family laws, juxtaposed against the lived experience of marriage for many women in Egypt. Based on the doctrines of classical schools of Islamic jurisprudence, Egypt's family laws uphold a contractual model of marriage in which a husband acquires the right to a wife's physical and sexual availability in the conjugal home in return for the obligation to provide for her and their children. Despite much-acclaimed legal reforms, the received model of marriage remains unchanged in the family laws. Al-Sharmani shows how the tensions and contradictions inherent in this institutional narrative of marriage are experienced in the lives of women. The author's analysis of the gendered legal process highlights a particular discourse on women's rationality, women's sexuality, the sexual rights and obligations of husbands and wives, and the intricate interplay of sexual with financial rights and obligations. Al-Sharmani argues that whilst some women are able to gain the legal remedies they seek, the conservative force of the legal narrative is actively strengthened through the repeated performance of courtroom practices and the support from social norms governing gender relations and rights within marriage.

The overall effect is to disempower women both individually and collectively.

Susie Jolly's chapter is a nuanced account of how Chinese activists have drawn on the possibilities afforded by international forces, agendas and discourses, to broaden openings available in the flux and ambivalence of processes nearer to home. Jolly highlights the great overlap among donors, government and activists, showing that, rather than being partitioned from one another, all these institutional spaces have boundaries that are porous. Institutional positioning, however, is a significant force in shaping the views of activists, government figures and donors. Considerable movement across institutional spaces makes it possible to produce overlap as well as dynamism in agendas and discourses in activism around gender and sexuality. Yet work on gender and sexuality is marked more by schism than by collaboration. Development discourse and research on sexuality have tended to ignore power relations and gender, while work on gender has been more likely to emphasize poverty reduction and development than sexuality. Nevertheless, Jolly points to connections between changing discourses on gender and new narratives of sexuality. The implications for women's empowerment are less clear, however. In post-economic-reform China, the pursuit of individual desires for the expression of sexuality appears to be more legitimate than challenging structural barriers which limit how and with whom one may express those desires.

How women and empowerment are configured in the various narratives of sexuality in this collection is a critical question. On the basis that feminism combines both analytical and prescriptive agendas, the authors' analytical explorations are separated from the demands of political judgement and action (cf. Mahmood 2005). Our approach to understanding power and empowerment in the narratives is one that does not assume at the outset that an action, practice, text or any other entity is necessarily empowering or disempowering for women. All authors were asked to address the following questions: (1) What narrative/s of sexuality are you focusing on? (2) How is power implicated in the representations and discourses that your narrative/s draw upon? (3) How will your chapter address the 'changing narratives' dimension of this theme? and (4) What are the implications of the relations between women and the narrative/s of sexuality that you have addressed, for women's empowerment? In addition, authors addressed questions such as, How is empowerment being understood and by whom? What is the context for all this? Which categories of women are involved? What forms of gender and sexual politics are implicated? What are the short-term and the long-term implications? and What is left out?

Sexuality will always be more than stories or narratives can express. Moreover, the sexualities expressed in stories are often likely to be covers for processes that are much deeper and more complex. The relationship between sexualities and narratives is such that sexuality may at times be revealed by stories, and at other times be concealed by them. The narratives identified by the authors draw on discourses relating to sexualities in complex ways. In some instances, dominant discourses are offered as templates for the construction of acceptable stories. Narratives may be organized around cultural scripts and discourses that participants invoke and use for their own ends (cf. Day Sclater cited in Andrews *et al.* 2008). This raises the question of how diverse discourses of sexuality are related to or drawn upon in the particular narrative in focus. What patterns may be identified in a given narrative of sexuality? In telling one particular story, what other stories are not being told?

The chapters in this book afford a rich understanding of the potential for narratives of sexuality to explore cultural patterns of representations and action in different dimensions of the social and to express the multiple changes impinging upon women in relation to sexuality and power. The narratives in which they feature may perform conservative functions by maintaining dominant orders or alternatively might be used to transform lives and cultures (cf. Plummer 1995). As they circulate in culture and are taken up by different actors, different stories have the potential to expand or restrict the space for women's empowerment in ways that may be unanticipated. What has been most compelling for us in this collection are the ways in which certain narratives of sexuality are taken up and become vehicles for the expression of women's agency in breaking with repressive social and heterosexual norms.

References

Abu-Lughod, L. (2008) *Writing Women's Worlds: Bedouin Stories*, University of California Press, Berkeley.

African Gender Institute (2009) 'Review Essay: Teaching Gender and Sexualities Part 2'. http://agi_media.s3.amazonaws.com/linking_concepts_of_gender_with_sexualities.pdf

Altman, D. (2004) 'Sexuality and Globalization', *Sexuality Research and Social Policy*, Vol. 1, No. 1, pp. 63–8.

Andrews, M. (2008) 'Never the Last Word: Revisiting Data', in M. Andrews, C. Squire and M. Tamboukou (eds.), *Doing Narrative Research*, Sage, London.

Andrews, M., C. Squire and M. Tamboukou (eds.) (2008) *Doing Narrative Research*, Sage, London.

Bakare-Yusuf, B. (2009) 'Nudity and Morality: Legislating Women's Bodies and Dress in Nigeria', *East African Journal of Peace and Human Rights*, Vol. 15, No. 1, pp. 53–68.

Butler, J. (1994) 'Against Proper Objects', *Differences: A Journal of Feminist Cultural Studies*, Vol. 6, No. 2–3, pp. 1–27.

Cornwall, A. and J. Edwards (2010) 'Introduction: Negotiating Empowerment', *IDS Bulletin*, Vol. 41, No. 2, pp. 1–9.

Cornwall, A. and A. Welbourn (eds.) (2002) *Realizing Rights: Transforming Approaches to Sexual and Reproductive Well-being*, Zed Books, London.

Correa, S. and R. Parker (2004) 'Sexuality, Human Rights and Demographic Thinking: Connections and Disjunctions in a Changing World', *Sexuality Research and Social Policy*, Vol. 1, No. 1, pp. 15–38.

Crossley, N. (2001) *The Social Body: Habit, Identity and Desire*, Sage, London.

D'Emilio, J. (1997) 'Capitalism and Gay Identity', reprinted in R. N. Lancaster and M. di Leonardo (eds.), *The Gender/Sexuality Reader*, Routledge (first published in 1979), New York.

di Leonardo, M. and R. Lancaster (1996) 'Gender, Sexuality, Political Economy', *New Politics*, Vol. 6, No. 1, p. 21.

Falk, C. (1990) *Love, Anarchy and Emma Goldman*, Rutgers University Press, New Brunswick, NJ.

Faraday, A. and Plummer, K. (1979) 'Doing Life Histories', *Sociological Review*, Vol. 27, No. 4, pp. 773–98.

Frye, M. (1983) *The Politics of Reality: Essays in Feminist Theory*, Crossing Press, Freedom, CA.

Gagnon, J. (1977) *Human Sexualities*, Scott Foresman, Glenview.

Goldman, E. (1986) *Living My Life* (two vols.), Pluto Press, London.

Gubrium, J. and J. Holstein (2008) 'Narrative Ethnography', in S. N. Hesse-Biber and P. Leavy (eds.), *Handbook of Emergent Methods*, Guilford Press, New York.

Holland, J., C. Ramazanoglu, S. Scott, S. Sharpe and R. Thomson (1992) 'Pressure, Resistance, Empowerment: Young Women and the Negotiation of Safer Sex', *AIDS: Rights, Risk and Reason*, Vol. 5, pp. 142–62.

Huq, S. P. (2005) 'Bodies as Sites of Struggle: Naripokkho and the Movement for Women's Rights in Bangladesh', in N. Kabeer (ed.), *Inclusive Citizenship: Meanings and Expressions*, Zed Books, London.

Imam, A., J. Morgan and N. Yuval-Davis (eds.) (2004) *Warning Signs of Fundamentalisms*, Women Living under Muslim Laws, Dakar.

Jackson, S. (2006) 'Gender, Sexuality and Heterosexuality: The Complexity (and Limits) of Heteronormativity', *Feminist Theory*, Vol. 7, No. 1, pp. 105–21.

Jackson, S. and S. Scott (2004) 'Sexual Antinomies in Late Modernity', *Sexualities*, Vol. 7, No. 2, pp. 233–48.

Kabeer, N. (2008) *Paid Work, Women's Empowerment and Gender Justice: Critical Pathways of Social Change*, Pathways Working Paper No. 3, Pathways of Women's Empowerment, Brighton.

Kollontai, A. (1927) *Red Love*, Seven Arts Publishing Company, New York (transcribed in 1998 by sir@marx.org; http://www.marxists.org/archive/kollonta/works/r100.htm).

—— (1971) *The Autobiography of a Sexually Emancipated Communist Woman*, translated by Salvator Attansio, Herder & Herder, New York (first published in 1926).

—— (1977a) 'The Social Basis of the Woman Question', in A. Holt (trans.), *Selected Writings of Alexandra Kollontai*, Allison & Busby, London (first published 1909 as a pamphlet).

—— (1977b) 'Sexual Relations and the Class Struggle', in A. Holt (trans.), *Selected Writings of Alexandra Kollontai*, Allison & Busby, London.

MacFadden, P. (2003) 'Sexual Pleasure as Feminist Choice', *Feminist Africa*, Vol. 2, pp. 50–60.

MacKinnon, C. (1989) *Toward a Feminist Theory of the State*, Harvard University Press, Cambridge, MA.

Mahmood, S. (2005) *Politics of Piety: The Islamic Revival and the Feminist Subject*, Princeton University Press, Princeton.

McNay, L. (2000) *Gender and Agency: Reconfiguring the Subject in Feminist and Social Theory*, Polity Press, Cambridge.

Mernissi, F. (2001) *Scheherazade Goes West*, Washington Square Press, New York.

Miriam, K. (2007) 'Toward a Phenomenology of Sex-right: Reviving Radical

Feminist Theory of Compulsory Sexuality', *Hypatia*, Vol. 22, No. 1, pp. 210–28.

Musallam, B. (1983) *Sex and Society in Islam*, Cambridge University Press, Cambridge.

Pereira, C. (2003) 'Where Angels Fear to Tread? Some Thoughts on Patricia MacFadden's "Sexual Pleasure as Feminist Choice"', *Feminist Africa*, Vol. 2, pp. 61–5.

—— (2008) *Changing Narratives of Sexuality – Concept Paper*, Pathways Working Paper No. 4, Pathways of Women's Empowerment, Brighton.

Pereira, C. and J. Ibrahim (2010) 'On the Bodies of Women: The Common Ground between Islam and Christianity in Nigeria', *Third World Quarterly*, Vol. 31, No. 6, pp. 921–37.

Personal Narratives Group (1989) *Interpreting Women's Lives: Feminist Theory and Personal Narratives*, Indiana University Press, Bloomington, IN.

Plummer, K. (1995) *Telling Sexual Stories*, Routledge, London.

Rich, A. (1980) 'Compulsory Heterosexuality and Lesbian Existence', *Signs*, Vol. 5, No. 4, pp. 631–60.

Richardson, D. (2007) 'Patterned Fluidities: (Re)imagining the Relationship between Gender and Sexuality', *Sociology*, Vol. 41, pp. 457–74.

Ryle, G. (1949) *The Concept of Mind*, University of Chicago Press, Chicago.

Sassen, S. (1998) *Globalization and Its Discontents*, New Press, New York.

Sen, A. (1999) *Development as Freedom*, Random House, New York.

Silberschmidt, M. (2005) 'Poverty, Male Disempowerment and Male Sexuality in Rural and Urban East Africa', in L. Ouzgane and R. Morrell (eds.), *African Masculinities: Men in Africa from the Late Nineteenth Century to the Present*, Palgrave Macmillan, New York and University of KwaZulu-Natal Press, Durban.

Squire, C. (2005) 'Reading Narratives', *Group Analysis*, Vol. 38, No. 1, pp. 91–107.

Tamale, S. (ed.) (2011) *African Sexualities: A Reader*, Pambazuka Press, Cape Town, Dakar, Nairobi and Oxford.

UNDP (2000) *Human Development Report 2000: Human Rights and Human Development*, United Nations Development Programme, New York.

PART I
Negotiating Desire?

1

Rewriting Desire as Empowerment in the Women and Memory Forum's Storytelling Project

Mona I. Ali

> To write – the act that will 'realize' the uncensored relationship of woman to her sexuality, to her woman-being giving her back access to her own forces; that will return her goods, her pleasures, her organs, her vast bodily territories kept under seal; that will tear her out of the superegos, over Mosessed structure where the same position of guilt is always reserved for her (guilty of everything, every time: of having desires, of not having any; of being frigid, of being 'too' hot; of not being both at once; of being too much of a mother and not enough; of nurturing and of not nurturing …). Write yourself: your body must make itself heard. (Cixous 1989: 103)

This chapter aims at exploring the role of re/writing or not being able to re/write, desire in the dis/empowerment of women, and the deconstruction of contemporary stereotypes pertinent to male and female sexuality. Diverse bodies of folktale are analysed in the light of Cixous's quote above with the purpose of making the connection between the ability to write one's body and to challenge predominant stereotypes of women's sexuality and the empowerment of women. The new folktales are part of the work of the Women and Memory Forum (WMF) and its Storytelling Group, which has been involved in rewriting old Egyptian folktales and tales from the *One Thousand and One Nights* in its 'Said the Female Storyteller' project.

Said the Female Storyteller is one of many projects of

the Women and Memory Forum, an Egyptian feminist non-governmental organization (NGO). The main concern of this NGO is with the rewriting of history from a feminist perspective for the purpose of 'the empowerment of women through information generation and dissemination'. In other words, the main objective is 'fill[ing] in the blank pages and mak[ing] the silences speak' (Greene and Kahn 1985: 13). The project is based on the supposition that women's role in creating history has long been neglected in favour of that of men. The Women and Memory Forum is of the view that this process has greatly influenced the formation of the collective public memory and the reinforcement of certain beliefs about women's inferiority to men. Hence there is a need to exert efforts to trace the origin of these beliefs 'in order that, their origin and tendency known, they may be consciously adopted, rejected or modified (…) a necessary aspect of the struggle for a better world' (Popular Memory Group 1998: 79). This quotation succinctly summarizes the objectives of the Women and Memory Forum's project of rewriting the collective public memory from a feminist perspective.

The Said the Female Storyteller project deals with one component of popular memory, which is folktales and tales from the *One Thousand and One Nights*. The purpose of this project is the rewriting of the tales from a gender-sensitive perspective; for, although storytelling has always been a woman's sphere, a quick look at several collections of Arab folktales and at the *One Thousand and One Nights* will show that the tales in these works present the same stereotypes of women present in Arab cultures and societies.[1] This can be attributed to the fact that women storytellers have internalized the images of women prevalent in the patriarchal societies to which they belong.[2] These stereotyped images, in their turn, help to preserve the status quo of women in their societies. In 1998, the Women and Memory Forum initiated the project of writing/rewriting new gender-sensitive tales and performing them in storytelling evenings attended by audiences in different venues. The aim was to prompt the audiences to reconsider the validity or otherwise of the stereotypes of women in the collective memory of Arabs.[3]

A completely new phase of the project began in 2007 under the Pathways of Women's Empowerment Programme. Training workshops for young men and women were organized to facilitate rewriting of the stories.[4] In these workshops, the more experienced writers of new stories who had started the rewrite project guided a group of young writers and bloggers through a process of discussing the gendered character of selected readings and audio-visual materials. The trainees were then introduced to the idea of the rewriting of folktales. At the end of the second day of a three-day workshop, the trainees wrote their own gender-sensitive tales. On the third day, the new tales were then critiqued for their gender perspectives and artistic quality by the trainers and by their colleagues. Part of the training focused on the stereotyping of women in popular culture, illustrated by representations of women in the media. Some of the most common representations were found to be relevant to women's sexuality. As the coordinator of the workshop and one of the first members of the WMF's rewriting project, I noticed a great change in some of the new stories in tackling the issue of sexuality – whether that of men or that of women. I think the change is very significant for women's empowerment on both macrocosmic and microcosmic levels, that is, on the level of the writers of the stories as well as on the level of the characters in the stories. It is a change that is worthy of study as it addresses important questions in the field of feminist writing and feminist activism.

The methods I use in this study are based on literary analysis and comparison of three bodies of work: the old folktales and tales from the *One Thousand and One Nights* as rendered in published collections of those stories; the stories of the first generation of writers in the WMF's Said the Female Storyteller project; and the stories written by Egyptian young men and women in the Pathways three-day workshop. Additionally, I conducted telephone interviews with five of the new writers – four women and one man – whose stories deal explicitly with the issue of sexuality. The choice of interviewees was based on the visibility of issues pertaining to sexuality in their stories. Telephone interviews were utilized in order to avoid embarrassment, whether in directing the questions or in answering them. I have not sensed the need to conduct similar interviews with my colleagues in the WMF Said the Female Storyteller project as I attended almost all the discussions about the stories we produced. However, questions were addressed, as the need arose, to some of my colleagues about the meanings of certain expressions and feelings they expressed in their stories.

Rewriting the oversexual, writing the asexual

In most of the old folktales and tales from the *One Thousand and One Nights*, women's sexuality is depicted as a great menace to the honour of men and to their status in society, whereas men's sexuality is one of the defining signs of their masculinity. In the frame story of the *One Thousand and One Nights* (Kamal 1999: 211–16), both Shahryar and his brother are cuckolded by their unfaithful wives who betray them with black slaves. Additionally, Shahzaman, Shahryar's younger brother, discovers that all the concubines in the palace engage in sex parties led by Shahryar's wife in the palace garden. This 'calamity' is the reason given in the old book for Shahryar killing all the virgins he marries on their wedding nights. This continues for quite a long time till he gets married to Shahrazad, who would have suffered the same destiny had it not been for her resourcefulness and great storytelling skills.

In their flight at the discovery of their wives' betrayals, Shahryar and his brother meet Sit el-Hara'ir, a woman who has been kidnapped by the Genie on her wedding night. On meeting this woman, Shahryar and Shahzaman have their belief in the unfaithfulness of women reconfirmed. According to them, Sit el-Hara'ir proves to be as loose as their wives. She invites, even forces them, to have sex with her, threatening to wake the hulky Genie if they do not do so, in an attempt to avenge herself on the

Genie by forcing passers-by to have sex with her. According to her, and to the long chain of rings she has obtained from those who sleep with her, Shahryar and Shahzaman come after more than seven hundred men, while the Genie presumes he has her in his grip. She even quotes a male poet saying, 'Do not ever trust women or women's vows/Their contentment and their anger are flanking their vaginas' (Kamal 1999: 215).

A statement about women's sexuality is thus made, stereotyping women as wayward beings whose sexual drives control their actions, leading them to constitute a threat to men's honour and to the social peace in their societies. This interpretation, supported by the lines of poetry at the end of the story, seems to ignore the real reason for the woman's so-called unfaithfulness, namely retaliation. In fact, the woman takes revenge on her kidnapper who deprived her of her wedded husband on her wedding night. Additionally, the characters of Sit el-Hara'ir as well as the wives of Shahryar and Shahzaman are utilized to stereotype women as unfaithful creatures whom nobody, even the huge Genie, can prevent from obtaining the sexual gratification they seek. This in turn justifies Shahryar's killing of all his one-night wives. Worse still, the women of the frame story are not the only ones with threatening sexuality. The *One Thousand and One Nights* and Egyptian folktales teem with such women – women who would do anything for their own sexual pleasure, including betraying husbands in their homes, eloping with their lovers, and killing co-wives and female competitors.

This depiction of women in the frame story of the *One Thousand and One Nights* seemed to provoke the writers of the WMF Storytelling Group. The story had two rewrites, both of which try to present women in a better light. In Somaya Ramadan's 'The Tale of King Shahryar and His Brother: Another Story, Unpublished', it is Shahryar and his brother who try to seduce the woman, who implores them to save her from the Genie and to return her to her family. Although she hates the Genie for kidnapping and imprisoning her, she rejects their attempts to seduce her, 'touching the collar of her dress to make sure nothing is revealed' (Kamal 1999: 82). Additionally, she threatens to wake up the Genie to defend her. Nevertheless, when the brothers enter one of the bars to spend the night during their journey, Shahzaman tells a fake story about the woman in which he claims that she was totally under the spell of their sexual prowess, cuckolding the Genie who was asleep in the same place. Shahzaman even cites the lines about women's infidelity in the old story in order to impress his audience further. Meanwhile, Shahryar is infatuated with the beautiful woman bartender who also rejects his advances; she smiles tiredly saying, 'I don't have time for such things' (Kamal 1999: 86).

As we can see from the above story, Somaya Ramadan, one of the first members to join the WMF Storytelling Group, chooses to present the women in her story as very conservative, their sexuality being completely silenced. In her comment on the story and her discussion of female sexuality in the storytelling project, Ramadan admits: 'The result [of the first experience of rewriting], as I see it, is a story that is missing something; there was still a dominant voice between the lines of my story. The women's voices were also loaded with all the elements of a voice that is raised against oppression, instead of creating a free voice that makes its own destiny, i.e. without enough rebellion and challenge. It might have been because I felt I was doing something totally new, or maybe because I haven't been completely liberated yet' (Said the Female Storyteller 1999: 16–17).

The other rendition of the same story by a member of the WMF Storytelling Group was that of Sahar el-Mougy. El-Mougy's story takes the form of a letter by Shahrazad to her sister Doniazad in which she attempts to defend Shahryar against her sister's accusations that he is a 'serial killer'. The major point in Shahrazad's argument is to reveal to her sister the real reason behind the killings, which is his impotence. According to el-Mougy's Shahrazad, Shahryar has killed those women not to avenge himself with regard to his unfaithful wife and her like; he simply wanted 'to cover up his own shame' (Kamal 1999: 115). Hence, in her rewriting of the frame story, el-Mougy adopts a strategy that is used to varying degrees by Ramadan in her story as well as by other members of the group, namely blaming male sexuality – or the lack of it – for the plight of women. For, while Ramadan casts the immense sexual desire of the Genie and the two brothers as responsible for the agonies of Sit el-Hara'ir and the bartender, in el-Mougy Shahryar's sexual impotence is the basis for women suffering death at his hands. In el-Mougy's story, Shahrazad is said to obtain sexual gratification during their intercourse although the impotent Shahryar cannot.

> I was fulfilled. I became the woman I have never been before ... But he is not fulfilled except after hours and hours of exhausting attempts in which the flow of silenced desire is mixed with following what my eyes reflect in each moment, fearing a look of boredom or maybe haughtiness. (Kamal 1999: 116)

El-Mougy's story is thus an attempt at presenting a more sympathetic image of Shahryar who is 'a man in trouble and the trouble is related to his masculinity' (el-Mougy 2008: 221). What el-Mougy's story ignores is the fact that, apart from Shahrazad, tens of other women have suffered and have been killed selfishly because of Shahryar's sexual problem. Strangely enough, no comment is made on Shahrazad's unhesitating show of love and understanding upon realizing that Shahryar has killed all the other women to 'chop off the head of the secret after one night with each virgin' (Kamal 1999: 115). This can be attributed to el-Mougy's being the product of a patriarchal culture in which men's sexual prowess is increasingly valued as the defining sign of masculinity. Consequently, el-Mougy understands, on both macrocosmic and microcosmic levels, the agony experienced by a man who is not sexually competent. Goldberg puts it this way: 'Men have been put on the defensive and often torture themselves with anxiety about so-called impotence [...] the subject has become an almost maniacal preoccupation. Some writers have termed impotence a contemporary male plague' (Goldberg 2000: 34).

In the old story 'The Tale of the Concubine about Men's Wiles', the concubine tells the story of a jeweller who sees a picture of a very beautiful woman whom he knows is a concubine of one of the ministers in India (Kamal 1999: 225–30). He then travels all the way from Persia to India to find her and to take her for himself. His journey proves a success and he returns with the woman after playing a trick on her and on the minister. The story ends when the jeweller 'takes her at once and leaves. He marches fast till he reaches his country after he has fulfilled his aim' (Kamal 1999: 230). Although the tale gives a first impression of being supportive of women, for the concubine who tells the story tries to show that men can be much more cunning than women, who are usually accused of being the sly and wily ones, the story fails to present the woman in a positive light. The concubine is represented as a 'desired object' (Koolen 2007: 402): she is completely passive even when exposed to great danger as a result of the jeweller's trick. Portrayed as a sex object who enjoys a certain status at the palace because of her rare beauty, the beautiful woman does not seem to have any sexual preferences since she leaves the minister's palace and travels with the jeweller with no sign of resistance.[5] The jeweller, on the other hand, is enchanted with her beauty, travels a long way to get her, and invents the trick that enables him to take her with him to his country.

The tale is rewritten by Hala Kamal, the founder of the WMF Storytelling Group, in 'The Tale of the Woman and the Picture'. Here, the woman in the picture is said to be the owner of the Palace of the Arts and Sciences where a group of female artists and scientists live peacefully. They are claimed by the spice man in their town to be a group of loose women who 'do whatever they want without surveillance from men'. Worse still according to the spice man, the owner of the palace, Gameela, who is also a painter, paints only portraits of women not men. Like the jeweller in the old story, the jeweller in Kamal's story takes advantage of Gameela when she volunteers to show him around the palace. He molests her, but with the help of the other female inhabitants of the palace she narrowly escapes being raped by him. The tale, therefore, is consistent with the stereotypical representations of sexuality, both male and female, that are prevalent in Arab societies.[6] The sexuality of the man is dangerous, leading to cunning and sexual violence, while the good women of the tale seem to be asexual, showing no interest in men even on the artistic level. The paintings of Gameela are all of women and she is claimed to say that 'she cannot find in men any sort of beauty' (Kamal 2000: 104). No hint at lesbianism is made in the story either; the inhabitants of the palace are representations of women who are too preoccupied with their work, whether artistic or scientific, to have any interest in sex.

Women's sexuality in most of the new stories of the WMF Storytelling Group seems to reflect the image of the good women in the old stories.[7] The female protagonist in 'The Tale of Ne'am and Nei'mma' (Kamal 1999: 108–13) by Sahar el-Mougy and Dalia Basiouny is similar to the women in Kamal's story. In 'The Tale of Ne'am and Nei'mma', Nei'mma is depicted as the beautiful girl who is the dream of most of the men in her neighbourhood. Ne'am, on the other hand, has no interest in any of them; she is a woman of learning who spends her time in the library and despises the neighbourhood men for gossiping in the coffee shop, talking about their sexual adventures instead of trying to use their time more beneficially. Female sexuality is again completely silenced here. No attempt at denial is presented, but there is a hint at the possibility of the total disposal of men altogether in the lyric at the end:

> Living without you
> And without your love, lad.
> Stop talking about your infatuation
> You're ridiculed by the whole town
> Do you love her? Yea, you love her
> But she, with or without you, is
> ...
> By herself, happy and content. (Kamal: 1999: 113)

In Soha Raafat's 'Horreya in the Diplomatic Field', the wife Horreya hints at her desires by romantically asking her husband Mahmoud for a kiss. He immediately denies this wish for the very unromantic reason that he is busy eating watermelon with his hands, causing 'the blood of the watermelon to run between his fingers' (Raafat 2003: 116). Horreya does not despair; she gives it another try but in vain, as Mahmoud announces that her attempts at getting a kiss have upset him and spoilt his already bad mood.

Horreya then decides to suppress her desire and even her femininity. She patiently 'lets her moustache and beard grow and wears men's clothes or clothes that are wide enough to cover the curves of her body'. This seems to satisfy Horreya for some time until Mahmoud suddenly decides one day that he wants her to return to her old feminine self. Only then does Horreya declare her rebellion; she has accepted rejection but will never accept inconsistency. She insists on denying her femininity as 'she prays to God to preserve her present condition'. Even when Mahmoud insists that it is a matter of 'either regaining her femininity or separation', she plays a song by the famous Egyptian singer Om Kolthoum in which she sings that regaining the past is impossible.

'Romantics' by the present writer, a member of the WMF Storytelling Group, is another story that depicts the female protagonist, the Fairy, as a woman who is in no need of sex. The tale is a story within a story; it is a dialogue between Shahrazad and Shahryar in which she tells him the story of Hasan and the Fairy. Hasan, who claims to be a romantic man, falls in love with the Fairy whom he sees swimming in a lake. He is alerted to her presence by her feathers which he finds lying on the bank of the lake. Falling in love at first sight with the Fairy, Hasan decides to hide the feathers in order to force her to stay with him and marry him, as she would not be able to return to her people. The Fairy politely rejects his request, arguing that she is not really thinking about marriage, let alone an offer of marriage from a total stranger. Hasan, on the other hand, insists on marriage, claiming that he is infatuated by everything about the Fairy, including her soul. When Hasan then burns the Fairy's dress to force her to stay with him rather than return to her home in the World of Fairies, she plays a trick on him that makes him impotent. Complaining about the cruelty of the Fairy's revenge, Hasan is faced with the her apt reply: 'You say that you want me for my Self, not for my body. I too want you for your Self and not your body. Where's the problem then?'

No questions are asked as to how the woman would handle her sexual desires with an impotent husband. Sexual potency in such stories seems to be a problem for men only, not women – at least not good, respectable women. This supports many of the cultural stereotypes about women and their sexuality. The tale seems to 'demonstrate the pervasiveness and insidiousness of patriarchy, the ways that women internalize sexist and misogynist beliefs and, in turn, how women's sexual desires are shaped by living in patriarchal environments' (Koolen 2007: 400).

Rewriting women's sexual agency

Earlier, we saw how the frame story in the *One Thousand and One Nights* focuses on men's dismay at women's sexual desires and their conviction that such desires lead almost inevitably to women's infidelity. We also saw how the new versions of this story produced by members of the WMF Storytelling Group focused on male sexuality in different ways. In one, male sexuality was represented as a kind of oppression that is inflicted on almost asexual women; in the other, it featured as impotence that women should tolerate. This perspective on male and female sexuality is contrary to that expressed in 'Humps' by Mariam Al-Nakr, one of the young women who attended the Pathways workshop.

In 'Humps', Sit el-Hara'ir seduces Shahryar who refuses to assist her in her attempt to escape from the Genie. She manages to get pregnant which seems to have been the aim of the seduction attempt in the first place, rather than getting assistance. Immediately after having sex with Shahryar and showing him her long chain with all the rings on it, she smiles nonchalantly and heads off to the sea, while the puzzled Shahryar mumbles in utter amazement, 'You cheated on the Genie with all those men?'

It is discovered afterwards that the seduction has been a purposeful act through which Sit el-Hara'ir manages to conceive many daughters who inherit her liberated soul. Their large silvery-white wings carry them all above the crowded city, helping them to find one another and eventually to unite with their mother. Al-Nakr's story thus emphasizes a very important aspect of female sexuality, namely, women's reproductive ability. It is this ability that has been exploited by others for their own purposes; now it is used by Sit el-Hara'ir to help her beget daughters who enjoy the liberation and solidarity she has longed for.[8]

Male sexuality as a source of danger for women is one of the themes underlying 'The Musk of the Night (Misk el-Leil)' by Nesma Idris, another WMF writer. Misk el-Leil, the female protagonist of the story, is a coquettish woman as presented by Idris herself in many performances of the story. Being a published writer in her own right, Idris feels freer than the other writers. She renders Misk el-Leil as a woman who is outspoken about the way she wants to be loved; she informs her lover explicitly that she wants him to approach her only at night: 'I hate the day and melt in the night' (Kamal 1999: 197). The ignorant man chooses to ignore Misk el-Leil's direct statement about her sexuality and insists on visiting her during the day when she is in her worst mood. After several rejections, the man decides to surprise her one night. When he sees the beauty of the house and smells the lovely fragrances, he immediately jumps to the conclusion that the woman must be with another man for whom she wears her best perfumes. He jumps at her with an axe and cuts her throat. He is shocked to find out that she has been alone; he discovers that 'he cut a branch of Misk el-Leil who is a tree, a tree whose scent does not appear except in the middle of the night' (Kamal 1999: 198).

Although Idris renders her female protagonist as sexually active, the woman is punished by her lover and the punishment is death. The story confirms the claims of Muhawi and Kanaana about the concept of honour in relation to women's sexuality in Arab cultures: 'Women's inability to maintain this quality [suppressing their sexuality and hence preserving the honour of the family] by being involved in an illegitimate sexual relation is a grave sin and serious betrayal of the family's honour. This used to lead to violent punishment that (up till the recent past) might have been honour killing' (Muhawi and Kanaana 2001: 41).

Fatma Ismail, one of the young Pathways writers, highlights the sexual oppression women are exposed to in a marital relationship. In her story 'A Moony Night', Ismail completely reverses the stereotypical roles of husband and wife in a marital relationship. The story is based on the tracing of several minor details of everyday life in an Egyptian family, thus exposing the injustices and suffering endured by women in the stereotypical roles assigned to them by Egyptian culture and society. The aim of this endeavour, says Ismail, is to urge men to realize the unfairness of certain practices that they perform.[9] One of these practices is the initiation of the sexual act by the man. In 'A Moony Night', Motei' (the Obedient), the male protagonist of the story, prepares himself for sleeping with his wife, waiting for her to initiate sex. When she is gratified, she turns her back on Motei' and falls fast asleep, not caring whether he was satisfied or not. This is a common complaint of many wives about their husband's behaviour during sexual intercourse, said Fatma Ismail in a personal interview. Yet, the problem is not usually discussed in public, asserts Shams Yehia, one of the attendees of the workshop.[10] Wives are often told that this is one of the secrets of the bedroom that should not be revealed even to the most intimate of friends. Writing about it in clear terms is therefore very daring. It has proved more daring than expected; even when the story was told in a storytelling evening, stifled coy laughs by women and angry comments by men could be heard.

In her story 'Don't You Have Any Shame', Yasmine Adel, another young Pathways writer, approaches women's sexual desires in a more explicit manner. Rewriting the famous tale of Aladdin and the magical lamp, Adel gives the leading role to Aladdin's mother, Mounira, an impoverished and lonely widow who spends the best part of her life raising her son without remarrying. When Mounira gets the chance to make the three wishes for herself that the lamp's genie promises to grant, her last wish is a daring request that she insists on being granted. This is clear from the following dialogue:

> Mounira: You know Mr Mohsen, you are a strong man and I'm a lonely pretty woman. You see?
> Genie: I'd rather you make yourself clear. I don't want to understand you wrongly.
> Mounira: Nothing is wrong. I mean exactly what you are thinking of.
> Genie: No, no, not that thing. Look 'baby', I'll say it to you flatly: My work ethics won't let me.
> Mounira: But this is my command, and you are not leaving without fulfilling it.

When asked whether she had any inhibitions about her story being told to a large audience and whether that caused her any embarrassment, Yasmine Adel replied in the negative. She has also answered my questions about the use of comedy as a sort of buffer by declaring that she is now writing a more open work in which female sexuality occupies a larger part and it is not a comic work. Answering another question about the performance and whether she can say her words herself or not, she confirmed that she can do that as she thinks it is the right of women to express their sexual needs freely. For her, the presence of men in an audience is never an issue, as it is women she has in mind. She thinks not of how men would think of her but only of empowering other women by encouraging them to talk. As for her male friends, she says that she has three very intimate male friends with whom she shares her cares and concerns, and sexuality is one of them. According to her, the three male friends are very sensitive to women's needs. Answering a question about the attitude of the male friends towards women exercising the right to sexual pleasure and whether they feel threatened by it, she asserts that they usually express joy at being made aware of whatever might please or upset women and they are generally happy to learn more about this issue.

When I directed the same question to Ahmad Abou el-Waffa, one of two young men who attended the workshop, he replied using exactly the same words, adding that he had felt threatened before when he had known for a fact that women had sexual desires, the nature of which were completely unknown to him. Being influenced by the tales, Abou el-Waffa used the image of the genie and the lamp, saying, 'Women's sexuality was a genie in a lamp; now the genie is out of the lamp, I find it easier to handle him.' This image, for me, however, is an indication of a hidden fear of women's sexuality which for ages has been silenced and dealt with as taboo. Another indication is Abou el-Waffa's anger at the comic treatment of the theme. He considers it commercialization and trivialization of a very serious issue that deserves more serious treatment. Apart from a derogatory attitude towards comedy, this view shows some apprehension towards this newly discovered terrain on the part of some young men who share the same interests and are part of the same cultural milieu as the young women who attended the workshop. In my interview with her, Yasmine Adel supports this view, saying that individually her male friends seem to accept her frankness when talking about her own desires, but they still advise her not to talk that way in front of other males in the same group lest they should misunderstand her motives or lose respect for her. This is a clear statement that women's sexuality is not yet as normalized a theme for discussion among young men as it is among young women.

Shams Yehia, another young woman who attended the workshop and wrote a story that explicitly deals with female sexuality, seems to agree that men still have to undergo some training if they are really to accept women's openness about their sexuality. Yehia belongs to a group of political activists who work with Palestinian children in the camps in Lebanon during the summer. The group is composed of about fifteen young women and men who are all students of the American University in Cairo. Yehia maintains that the females in the group are very outspoken about their sexual needs and that the men seem to listen attentively and to respect their right to express their needs, yet she often gets the feeling that they are not sincere and that deep down they would prefer to mingle with girls who are shy and timid. This does not seem to deter Yehia at all since she believes that her sexual needs have to be met for her to be happy, and for this to be achieved she has to speak explicitly in order to realize this right.

This point of view is bluntly stated in Yehia's story 'Anne', which was described by the other attendees of the workshop as shockingly explicit about sex. In her story, Anne, who has six brothers, is the one who inherits her father's business, being the most efficient of all the siblings. She also marries off her brothers but does not show interest in an early marriage for herself. When asked the reason, she declares that happiness lies not in joining the married club as much as in acquiring the gratification she aspires to; meeting sexual needs is confirmed to be one of the most important means of reaching happiness in a marriage. Anne thus decides to make love to each suitor who proposes to her in order to ensure fulfilment and gratification. She eventually meets the man of her dreams, Kahraman, and they live happily for some time till she notices that Kahraman's performance is becoming stale and that it lacks the spark that she used to enjoy. Kahraman, however, refuses to listen to her complaints and insists on continuing with a relationship that is one-sided without exerting any effort to rectify the situation. After a while, he starts to lose interest in her and to cheat on her with the concubines in their palace. When Anne discovers this, she loses hope in him and starts to search for a more satisfying partnership. It is with the slave Osman that she finds her needs met. Kahraman knows about the affair, catches Anne with her lover, and stabs her with his knife, killing her on the spot.

Like Shams Yehia's story 'Anne', 'Steps towards the Light' by Samar Ali deals with the issue of women's infidelity, resonating with the frame story of the *One Thousand and One Nights*. Yet, as is evident in these two stories, women's infidelity is usually a reaction to men's total obliviousness to their needs and men's indifference towards women. In 'Steps towards the Light', Sara's mother, a medical doctor, is killed by Sara's father in her clinic when he catches her having sex with her lover. According to the law, the murder of the mother is a crime of honour and so the father is released a short time afterwards. Meanwhile, the dead mother, the narrator of the story, keeps visiting Sara to ease her pain and to explain her apparent infidelity, but this is of no avail. Sara shuts her ears to her mother's desperate attempts until the day her father decides to remarry. Only then does Sara go to her mother's clinic to complain to her. The mother seizes the opportunity to tell her the whole story of how Sara's father's recurrent vows to divorce her made her believe she was already divorced, despite a sheikh's fatwa that she was not, so long as her husband did not really mean to divorce her. She tells Sara that deep down she was confident that that man was no longer her husband. When she meets Hashem, one of her patients, and starts to have feelings for him, she does not feel the inhibitions of a married woman but remembers her right to happiness and fulfilment. She tells Sara, 'I was not cheating on your father, I was defending me.' Sara believes her mother and sympathizes with her to the extent that she decides to live and work in the clinic in order to enjoy her mother's company.

Conclusion

It is clear from the analysis of stories by the WMF's storytellers that the writers treat sexual desire as something that women can easily dispose of, if the need arises. If desire is the reason a woman loses her dignity, compromises her pride or is exposed to physical or psychological harm, she can just boycott it altogether, along with men. This has been seen as a sort of resistance that women resort to, in order to prove their strength and self-sufficiency. Yet by so doing, they conform to the stereotypical values of the culture which assign men the role of the aggressor, treating men as subjects of desire and women as its object.

While oppressed wives or wives who do not find sexual gratification in the WMF stories decide just to live and forbear, suppressing their sexual desires, such wives in the young women's Pathways stories decide to defend their rights to sexual pleasure. The change in the new stories of the Pathways group, where women pursue their desires and their own sexual pleasure, can be construed favourably as a sign of liberation. In these stories, young women declare their sexual desires to be rights that they will fight for. The first step in the struggle is to talk openly about these desires, to let both men and society at large recognize their needs.

Many of the new stories, such as 'Humps' and 'Don't You Have Any Shame', however, fall into the trap of 'othering' men in the sense that men are simply represented as the objects of desire. They are sought after by women for the women's purposes. Men who are real partners, sharing the same needs and desires with women, are rare in the stories. Even where this model exists, as in the character of Hashem in Samar Ali's 'Steps towards the Light' or Kahraman in the early years of marriage in Shams Yehia's 'Anne', there exists also, in a rather apologetic manner, the negative model of male sexuality. This model is stereotypical too and is used as an excuse for women's infidelity, another stereotype that recurs in the new stories.

Eleven years of advocacy for the rights of women through writing and creativity in Egypt have achieved a real leap in women's awareness of their bodies and their desires. Direct engagement with rewriting that has a focus on sexuality is also very important in enhancing both women's and men's awareness of issues pertaining to female sexualities. Almost all the Pathways writers interviewed insisted on the role played by the sessions around stereotypes of women and women's sexuality in helping them overcome their inhibitions about writing explicitly on female sexuality and creating female characters that can articulate their needs and desires. The Pathways gender training workshops definitely show what Laan and Both (2008: 511) maintain in 'What Makes Women Experience Desire?', namely that 'Probably the best cure for women's sexual problems is helping women to allow themselves to be sexual, and to work on the circumstances that may help them to be so.'

Yet more work needs to be done for women to avoid falling into the trap of stereotyping the sexualities of others in the same way that their own sexualities have been stereotyped. Additionally, this chapter suggests that more methods should be used to involve men in the work of advocacy through creativity. Greater effort should be exerted to hold rewrite workshops where more young men are invited to participate; follow-up sessions on these workshops should take place to guarantee the sustainability of the results. The work presented here shows that new feminists are not willing to forsake their rights to pleasure, and so it is necessary for feminist activism to educate men too about their own desires and those of women. It is clear also that young men realize the importance of knowledge about women's desires.

The Pathways project of rewrite workshops highlights the importance of creative writing, and the arts in general, in the work of advocacy. All the writers interviewed stressed the key role played by the arts in alerting them to issues of sexuality in a subtle but very effective manner. They also emphasized the space that creative writing allows them to express their feelings and desires. For most of them, writing is empowering at both ends of the spectrum; it is empowering for writers themselves and for their audiences as well. Writers believe they were empowered by reading works of creative writing and they believe that their own works in turn will encourage other women to be more outspoken about their own sexuality.[11] It is this act of writing and outspokenness that is claimed by many writers to be the main tool to 'challenge the structural foundations of patriarchy' (Amiruddin, quoted in Marching 2007: 233).

Notes

1 See Aboueleil (2008: 51–4); Goodman *et al.* (1996: 84); and Muhawi and Kanaana (2001: 8) for the tales being a women's sphere and see Kamal (1999: 27–30 and 36–40) for the negative stereotypes.

2 An analysis of this phenomenon is presented in Vandecasteele-Shweitzer and Voldman (1984: 45–6).

3 For an extensive discussion of this project, see Kamal (1999: 7–74).

4 Twenty-three trainees attended the workshop, comprising two young men and twenty-one young women. They were chosen using multiple recruitment methods: an announcement in the English Department, Cairo University; the Young Women Forum of the New Women Foundation (an NGO); young people's literary clubs; a small circle of young writers on Facebook; and word of mouth. A newspaper announcement was deliberately avoided due to the lack of financial and human capacity needed to screen the hundreds of candidates who were expected to apply if such media were used. The two people responsible for the choice of candidates – the coordinator and one assistant – would not have been able to handle such numbers. The candidates were required to be between 18 and 35 years of age and to present a specimen of their writing, preferably published. Of all those who attended the workshop, only two did not manage to write stories. Some wrote as many as four stories. The final output was thirty-one stories and one poem.

5 For evidence of her special status, see the description of her bed and her jewellery (Kamal 1999: 227).

6 For a discussion of an extensive analysis of these representations, see Muhawi and Kanaana 2001, in which they maintain that 'in the sexual relation between a man and a woman, the society considers the man as the one who takes or gains something while the woman is the one who gives or loses something ... It is clear that social discrimination between men and women in the Palestinian society, and other Arab societies, is mainly based on the sexual instinct' (2001: 41–2).

7 For an analysis of the meanings of 'the good woman' as the woman who has no interest in sex or sexuality, see Muhawi and Kanaana (2001: 36, 41–4) and Herb Goldberg's angry rejection of this female stereotype in 'the woman had denied her sexuality. Sex was supposedly his need, not hers. She took no responsibility for her sexuality so that he often was left feeling degraded and selfish for acknowledging his needs. She could also wait for him to lust and to cheat and then point an accusing finger. She was 'clean' and he was 'dirty" (2000: 29).

8 For a discussion of the reproductive role of women's sexuality in Arab

societies, see Muhawi and Kanaana (2001: 40–1, 43).

9 Personal interview with Fatma Ismail on 8 January 2009.

10 Personal interview with Shams Yehia on 8 January 2009.

11 Personal interviews with Mariam Al-Nakr and Yasmine Adel on 8 January 2009.

References

Aboueleil, K. (2008) *The Woman and the Tale: A Study of the Creativity of the Egyptian Woman in the Egyptian Folktale*, Dar Al-'Ein Publishing House, Alexandria.

Cixous, H. (1989) 'Sorties: Out and Out: Attacks/Ways Out/Forays', in C. Belsey and J. Moore (eds.), *The Feminist Reader: Essays in Gender and the Politics of Literary Criticism*, Macmillan Press, London.

El-Mougy, S. (2008) 'From the Folktale to the Feminist Tale: A Testimony', *Alif*, No. 28.

Goldberg, H. (2000) *Hazards of Being Male: Surviving the Myth of Masculine Privilege*, Wellness Institute, Gretna, LA.

Goodman, E., K. Boddy and E. Showalter (1996) 'Prose Fiction, Form and Gender', in E. Goodman (ed.), *Literature and Gender*, Routledge, London and New York.

Greene, G. and C. Kahn (1985) 'Feminist Scholarship and the Social Construction of Women', in G. Greene and C. Kahn (eds.), *Making a Difference: Feminist Literary Criticism*, Routledge, London and New York.

Kamal, H. (1999) *Kalat Al-Rawwyya* (Said the Female Storyteller: Tales from the Perspectives of Women Inspired by Arabic Folktales), Women and Memory Forum, Cairo.

Koolen, M. (2007) 'Understanding Desires: Sexuality as Subjectivity in Angela Carter's The Infernal Desire Machines of Doctor Hoffman', *Women's Studies*, No. 36, pp. 399–416.

Laan, E. and S. Both (2008) 'What Makes Women Experience Desire?' *Feminism and Psychology*, Vol. 18, No. 4, pp. 505–14.

Marching, S. T. (2007) 'The Representation of the Female Body in Two Contemporary Indonesian Novels: Ayu Utami's Saman and Fira Basuki's Jendela-Jendela', *Indonesia and the Malay World*, Vol. 36, No. 102, pp. 213–45.

Muhawi, I. and S. Kanaana (2001) *Speak Bird, Speak Again: Palestinian Arab Folktales*, Institute for Palestinian Studies, Beirut.

Popular Memory Group (1998) 'Popular Memory: Theory, Politics, Method', in R. Perks and A. Thomson (eds.), *The Oral History Reader*, Routledge, London and New York.

Raafat, S. (2003) *Horyyat*, Women and Memory Forum, Cairo.
Said the Female Storyteller (1999) 'Pamphlet of Said the Female Storyteller', Women and Memory Forum, Cairo.
Vandecasteele-Shweitzer, S. and D. Voldman (1984) 'The Oral Sources for Women's History', in M. Perrot (ed.), *Writing Women's History*, Blackwell, Oxford and Cambridge.

2

Islam in Urban Bangladesh

Changing Worldviews and Reconfigured Sexuality

Samia Huq

In recent years, the socio-political climate in Bangladesh has signalled increased religiosity. This has manifested through increased veiling by women (Rozario 2006), the proliferation of madrasas amongst the poor (Asadullah and Chaudhury 2009) and faith-based schools for the middle classes, as well as the advent of Islamic media.[1] Islam has always been a part of the consciousness of Bengali Muslims. However, it is through events of the past four decades, beginning with the end of Sheikh Mujib's era (1972–5) that Islam has gained a special political significance, thereby representing and accompanying altered socio-cultural conditions (Gardener 1998). It is especially in the light of the post-1990 political context that Islam has gained maximum attention nationally and internationally as regressive and even cruel towards women.

Prior to the democratic era that began in 1990, the manner in which state policies were formulated and Islamist critiques were managed led to promotion of the image of women as marching towards progress. Women came to be seen as emblems of a modernizing nation. For example, during the regime of General Zia (1977–81), the government manipulated Islamist positions vis-à-vis women to support the expansion of nongovernmental organizations (NGOs) in engaging poor landless women. The government also created greater opportunities for women to join the cadres of government service. In the regime of

General Ershad (1982–90), the government's export-led strategy allowed for scores of women to join the booming ready-made garments (RMG) industry as workers. Through their labour force participation, women, who were never before as visible, created a stir in the popular as well as the conservative imaginary. While these women's access to income and mobility was left unhampered, Ershad attempted to curtail the mobility of another group of women – middle-class housewives – through their bodies. He ordered police to tar the midriffs of sari-clad women frequenting a popular shopping area – symbolically gesturing that women's sexuality and its visibility in the public space needed to be curtailed. After heavy condemnation by women's groups, these actions were stopped. As Feldman writes:

> The example highlights the apparent challenge embodied in the shift in women's visibility and behaviour and suggests why women's public behaviour can be seen to embody all that is distinctive about that which is modern. It is also likely that the conservative reactions to women working in the factories and utilizing the shops and cinema halls are a means to criticize, if indirectly, the emerging urban upper middle class that has benefited from the new wealth that once were (sic) controlled by selected rural elites. (Feldman 1998: 46)

Thus, the requisites of a modernizing state were predicated upon the female body and its activities, where tensions and conflicting interests ended up preserving the image of a working, mobile, cinema-frequenting woman. The story of modernity and progress was written on a particular kind of female body. The tensions around that body were 'managed', and religious and conservative critiques were kept at bay.

The 'democratic phase' began in 1990 when Islamists, notably the Jama'at-e-Islami, emerged as kingmakers, aiding the Bangladesh Nationalist Party (BNP) to form a government. During this period, the tensions around women's bodies came to a head. An example of this was the fatwas that were declared against women for offences ranging from speaking to a man to being raped, and from having an affair to continuing to live with a husband in the midst of pressure asserting that the marriage had been nullified in the eyes of religion. Women's opinions were rarely accorded any significance and were seldom taken into account before arriving at a final judgment.

Islamists largely wanted to unravel the intertwining of women's sexuality and the modernity of the state. Through the tyranny of fatwas, women's images as representing the modern state came under assault, and Islam, which had thus far been kept at bay, gained a political legitimacy by which it asserted a kind of influence unseen in the past. Islamists, to a great extent, (co) directed the political scene, constructing hegemonic parameters by which women interacted with men. At the same time, they imposed serious limits on women's bodies and activities. The players in this new game were the Islamists and the ruling political parties. Women were the targets, and secular liberal civil society – which also included women – constituted the critics.

There are also accounts of Islam that are not brutal, where women engage with it actively and consciously. Shanti Rozario's (2006) account of women veiling asserts that the burqa gives women a positive sense of self. However, Rozario is reluctant to accord that positive sense the status of agency. She asserts that before we label such acts as demonstrating agency, giving rise to empowerment, we need to be clear that these acts lead to gender parity. Underlying her position is the assumption that gender parity occurs in particular ways, and yields certain fixed ends. In Rozario's argument there is also suspicion around the transformative potential of an engagement with religion. Thus, even when the relationship between Islam and women is not a violent one, religious engagement is slow to be incorporated into a model of agency and empowerment.

In this chapter, I seek to understand the place of religion outside the political sphere by looking at Muslim women's talk about heterosexuality via their bodies in the ever-changing world they inhabit. I do this by exploring how factory workers, students and taleem participants conceptualize religion, with a view to illuminating how their sexualities are configured within their religious worldviews. My view of sexuality stretches our understanding beyond the purview of sex acts. I draw from the ideas of Cornwall and Molyneux (2008: 56) who, from a framework of sexuality, human rights and development, make the following statement:

> sexuality is about a lot more than having sex. It is about the social rules, economic structures, political battles and religious ideologies that surround physical expressions of intimacy and the relationships within which such intimacy takes place. It has as much to do with being allowed to move freely outside the home and walk the streets without fear of sexual harassment or abuse as it has to do with whom people have sex with. It is as much concerned with how the body is clothed, from women feeling forced to cover their bodies to avoid unwanted sexual attention ... And where society and the state collude in policing gender and sex orders, it can be about the very right to exist, let alone to enjoy sexual relations.

I explore how women talk about their sexuality in the context of their espoused religious worldview, by analysing the narrative conventions they use to discuss relations between men and women. Three categories of such relations are examined: premarital relations, marriage and divorce, and polygyny. For each category, I highlight the religious/cultural values and norms that women invoke when talking about the manner in which they interact with men. For an understanding of norms, I draw on the ideas of Judith Butler (1993) who argues that norms are not necessarily an external imposition on the self/subject, but give shape to her interiority.

Taking the understanding further than Butler, and drawing from Saba Mahmood (2005), I argue that the invoked norms are important not just because they reveal the ways in which norms are consolidated or subverted, but because they enable us to understand the various ways in which norms are inhabited. In order to understand how norms are inhabited, I analyse how women articulate the relationship between religious/cultural norms and interiorities such as feelings, emotions, values or inner states. The coordination between the internal (states, dispositions), and the external (norms, expectations) allows us to understand the different ways in which the self engages with norms, resulting in different ways of acting. These, in turn, reflect the different kinds of authority that steer the self.

By examining the manner in which corporeal and non-corporeal capacities are deployed in the configuration of the sexualized or non-sexualized self, I demonstrate that every group is influenced by different kinds of authority. This makes it difficult to conceptualize women's sense of their sexuality as being purely constrained by a religious discourse or liberated by virtue of a non-religious discourse. The power that is exerted on the self is thus a diffused/splintered power, devoid of a singular structure, location or intentionality by which it is executed on the individual or community. Foucault argues that power is a force that should be conceptualized as webs touching upon lives in both enabling as well as coercive ways (Foucault 1990, 1980). In this conceptualization, power is enmeshed in the self.

When the self resists power through her agency, that agency is not external to the power that oppresses but rather emerges from within it – an argument Foucault (1978, 1980) sums up in his construct of the 'paradox of subjectivation'. Lila Abu-Lughod (1990) draws on Foucault's construct to critique the manner in which agency has been equated with resistance, whereby resistance is viewed as representing opposition and ideally yielding transformation, and thereby overriding the constraints posed by the workings of power. Abu-Lughod argues that seeking transformation through power whose source is different from the power which oppresses has resulted in agency being reduced to everyday forms of subversion that do not quite meet the criteria of change that is 'good enough' (Abu-Lughod 1990). Saba Mahmood takes Abu-Lughod's argument further, writing that 'the very processes and conditions that secure a subject's subordination are also the means by which she becomes a self conscious identity and agent' (2005: 17).

Once it is established that power and authority are splintered, and that they frame the field within which one lives, it follows that all actions of conformity as well as of subversion have particular grammars. These grammars and the workings of power that undergird them have led to a shift from the question of liberation versus oppression based on some static markers, to the manner in which norms are engaged, and what that engagement reveals about a person's ability to articulate and experience herself in the particular context in which she lives. Highlighting this engagement not only reveals the construction and mutation over time of various norms, but also sheds light on what it means for different actors to accept, negate and override normative expectations. Thus, we are able to appreciate not only the self's struggles in transcending expectations, but also the strife with which one engages more deeply with particular expectations to the point that such engagement feels liberating. This latter kind of relationship between the norm and the self is described by Saba Mahmood's pious Cairene interlocutors. Their struggles in training the self to better inhabit the norms of piety are compared by Mahmood (2005: 29) with the discipline and training of a virtuoso pianist whose 'agency is predicated upon her ability to be taught, a condition classically referred to as "docility"'. Although we have come to associate docility with the abandonment of agency, the term literally implies the malleability required of someone in order for her to be instructed in a particular skill or knowledge – a meaning that carries a sense less of passivity than of struggle, effort, exertion and achievement (Mahmood 2005).

The very different focus that underlies this notion of agency is the question of desire. Mahmood calls upon the social scientist to (re)conceptualize agency as foregrounding different forms of desire, which lead to different kinds of engagement with ideals. In the process, corporeal and non-corporeal capacities are exerted towards different ends in the expression of women's religious worldviews. In the sections that follow, I take clues from the approaches outlined above to demonstrate the place of particular norms that speak to women's sexuality and the manner in which women talk about their engagement with these norms towards ideal outcomes. This analysis intends to highlight the role women accord religion in shaping their lives, what their understanding of religion grants them, and how the different modes of engagement with norms point to changing narratives of sexuality. Before embarking on a more detailed discussion of these points, I must first describe the women who provide the substantive core of this chapter.

The women

Three groups of women were selected for the newness they add to the social landscape. They were university students, factory workers, and taleem participants.[2] The rationale for including university students is that they represent the educated masses of the country and are expected to leave an important mark on the direction in which society travels. The factory women were selected for the sheer numbers and the significant contribution to the economy that they represent. Factory work emerged in the early 1980s, and now employs tens of thousands of women who, prior to joining the labour force, were not as visible as is the case now; whilst neither did their labour contribute as much to the economy as it does now.

Taleem participants are women who attend a particular type of religious class. Women getting together around religion is not a particularly new phenomenon. However, today's congregations, commonly referred to as taleem or *tafsir* classes, are different. First, they are composed of members who are not necessarily family or ever known to one another, and, second, their focus of discussion is textual learning rather than prayer. They advocate a particular kind of Islam, which they assert to be the only authentic and therefore the most credible kind of Islam, and women who participate regularly engage very actively and consciously with that standardized Islam. However, very little is known about these classes (Shehabuddin 2008; Nahar 2010) and the changes in the women who attend them. By addressing women who attend taleem, this research sheds light on a new space that may offer avenues of change and transformation for many women who attend.

Religious worldviews

The research revealed that there was a real desire amongst women from all three groups to textualize and authenticate Islam. It is this 'educated and knowledge-based' Islam that separates and shapes itself differently from the religion of the past. Previously, Islam was passed down within the family and learnt from home-based religious tutors of the Quran, referred to in the vernacular as *hujur.* The majority of the factory workers also reported the increasing prevalence of taleem – classes organized around discussion of the Quran and the Hadith (examples and events from Prophet Muhammad's life).

Other scholarly accounts on changes in religious practice towards textualization and authenticity have focused on altered power relations within the community and new social/cultural restrictions that include the imposition on women to veil, and restrictions on music and singing (Gardener 1998). In this chapter, I shift the focus from the societal to the individual and briefly discuss how the rhetoric of textualization informs the worldview of the individual subject. In other words, as women express their desire to understand their religion better through recourse to texts, how are their own religious worldviews being shaped? For insight into this question, I pursue an analysis of women's understanding of religion by looking at how women relate external acts of religiosity, such as praying, fasting and veiling, to inner states and dispositions that are considered to be the requisites of a good Muslim.

Amongst the factory workers, religion was primarily about Imaan or faith. While rituals such as prayer were articulated as *very* important, a majority of the women said that the pressures of home and work, and the time constraints resulting from these, were barriers to the performance of rituals. As one woman said, 'God will understand that I need to feed my family – in fact He would want me to feed my family. Prayers don't turn a human being into a good Muslim. Being a good Muslim is about having qualities that do not affect others negatively.' Thus the sins incurred from the failure of ritual performance were to be assuaged by fulfilling one's social duties – duties that are expected of women by kin and the larger society. These duties include being obedient to the husband, being good and dutiful towards the in-laws, and avoiding conflicts at home and outside. These qualities constitute the good person as well as an important part of a good Muslim.

Like factory workers, students also maintained a separation between religious rituals and emotions, internal values and dispositions. Students also referred to time constraints as a barrier to the performance of religious rituals. For them, a person becomes moral not simply through prayers, but also through fulfilling familial obligations. While in their opinion both are not given equal importance in the construction of the moral self, many students argued that one's morality can be strengthened through prayer, provided the latter is performed sincerely and correctly. Thus, while the moral self is constructed through a separation between religious and social obligations, there is greater effort on the part of the students than the factory workers to envision morality in a way in which the gap between religion and social duties is bridged, endowing religious rituals with a certain force that is absent from the narratives of factory workers.

The invoking of religious rituals in the articulation of the moral self may be read in several different ways. It may be the case that such a narrative convention points to a general regard for religion in society where the individual does not want to come across as disrespectful. After all, the centrality of claims to morality lies in morality being constructed not only through religious registers, but also through an active engagement with other domains emanating from other discourses. I argue that the individual, notably the student, wants to lay claims to all important domains and discourses without abandoning any. Thus students want to be educated, want to appear and frame themselves as progressive and modern, without necessarily jettisoning Islam. The moral self forms at the intersection of various discourses about being young, about being modern and about the future of Bangladesh.

The research, however, did reveal some interesting insights that signal a special place granted to religion via the individual's interiorities. A student stated that she had once donned the hijab headcover but subsequently abandoned the practice. Further exploration into what looked like a flexible engagement with religious norms revealed that her apparent flexibility was related to ideas that informed her sense of self at a deeper level. The student said, 'When I was covering I was still doing a lot of bad things. I just couldn't be a covering woman with those habits thriving. It was disrespectful to the hijab. So I gave it up. I still think of taking the hijab one day, but this time I will ensure that I have got rid of the bad things and so be able to give the hijab the respect it deserves.' This statement reveals the salience of religion in the lives of Bangladeshi youth, even as they lead apparently 'secular' lives. It corroborates the students' ideas of religion, and their understanding that religious obligations, while often coterminous with cultural acts, can also be conceived separately to speak to one's inner self.

The taleem participants made the sharpest distinction between culture and religion. They placed the utmost importance on religious rituals. They believed that since the Quran does not mention any other religious obligation as many times as it does the daily prayers, it was extremely important that they should not neglect this duty. In fulfilling their obligation to pray, the taleem participants urged one another (and anyone who was interested in listening) to overcome their shyness of praying in public. One woman said, 'Society has made religion so marginal that we allow it to intimidate us ... we feel shy of praying. Are we then being shy of our true identity, of the person our creator expects us to be?' These women believed that ritual performance did not end there but that it was a means to an end – to a better-guided interiority and therefore to becoming a better Muslim. In other words, they believed that an interiority that was not guided and conditioned by the religious rituals as representing the word of God was not a valid interiority.

The distinction between the inner and the outer was collapsed in such a way that the outer – the external acts and performances

– was endowed with the power to mould the inner into that of a good Muslim. Without this ritualized guidance and moulding, the inner values, feelings and desires that the self espoused – those that were prioritized by the factory workers and the students – could pose the risk of leading one astray, far from the good person that religion expected one to be. For example, one woman narrated as follows:

> When I started attending taleem, my family didn't think much of it. Once I started praying regularly, they still didn't object although they thought I may have been going overboard. Then when I took the hijab, they really came down hard on me. They said 'Why, aren't we religious? Aren't we good Muslims? Why do you need to go so far?' I'm not going far at all. I'm just doing what is expected of me, and taking the help of God's words as constant reminders of the way I should behave, the way I should feel, care and react.

Thus, there exists a clear primacy of the religious register, where certain prevalent cultural norms and expectations may even be refuted so that the religious may thrive.

The narratives

In what follows, I analyse women's narratives by examining their articulated coordination between norms and inner states. I highlight the ways in which women talk about how they live their gendered and sexual existence, showing how different ways of engaging with norms – through appropriation as well as negotiation – yield different results. I analyse how different modalities of doing and living influence women's subjectivities and how, through their variegated engagement with norms, women are able to foreground change and agency. In the process, I highlight how women invoke religion to legitimize or denounce certain practices pertaining to their sexuality.

Premarital relations

All the factory workers interviewed agreed that romantic relationships between unmarried men and women were on the rise. A good number of them spoke of such relationships favourably, as a part of mass literacy and the generally closer ties and openness that education had fostered between the generations. One woman said, 'Nowadays parents are friendlier with and have more respect for their children, who are more educated. Children also have the confidence and courage to tell their parents that they have chosen a particular person to marry.'

This view is consonant with other findings that premarital romance is more permissible, and that young men and women have greater opportunity to exercise their right to choose their own partners (Jesmin and Salway 2000). Jesmin and Salway argue that the increased prevalence of love marriages is indicative of the decreased parental authority and control over children brought on by new income opportunities for young people in the rural areas. In urban settings, the migration away from familiar surroundings as well as from familial networks has also led to young men and women choosing their own partners in marriage.

The research findings suggest that while having a boyfriend and entering into a love match are viewed as a positive extension of the modernity that education is thought to bring about, religious and cultural authority works simultaneously on the subject by invoking the question of parental obedience in choosing one's own partner. One woman said, 'It is OK for a girl to go ahead and choose a partner, but it should be someone her parents would approve of. Parents raise their children with a lot of hope. The children should remember that and not disappoint their parents.'

Thus, the ideals of education and obedience sit uncomfortably together in these women's lives as they engage in romantic ties and seek out marriage partners. Obedience is considered to be a virtue that is sanctioned both by religion and society. In other words, pleasing one's parents in choosing one's partner is considered to be both a social and a religious obligation. The failure in obedience occurs first when a woman chooses a man not after her parents' hearts, and also when she has 'crossed the limit', and has had a sexual relationship with him. Not a single informant spoke favourably of premarital sex. Women worried that if the relationship failed to lead to marriage, then a woman would be subject to criticism and condemnation by the man whom she did eventually marry.

Here I ask: what are we to make of women invoking religio-cultural sanctions in enforcing parental obedience, especially in relation to premarital sex, an issue that foregrounds much tension and vulnerability over the female body? First, there is the possibility that women take recourse to such answers because they constitute culturally appropriate responses, leading to a conclusion that there is a gap between how they talk about such issues and what they actually do. Or, when women invoke sanctions – religious or otherwise – and relegate sex before marriage to the realm of sin, it may be common to assume a connection between a sense of sin and the real stigma and logistical problems associated with dealing with an unwanted pregnancy.

It is clear that the relationship between what women say and what they do needs to be more intensively investigated. However, before assigning the sense of sin a space defined by convenience – born out of insufficient facilities and support systems for women – we need to assess women's own sense of self in relation to the manner in which their bodies are deployed in sexual acts. We then need to ask how religion reinforces or erodes that sense of self. While the factory workers refused to talk further about the relationship between premarital sex and a woman's interiority, the students' responses were more telling.

Students were highly tolerant of romance before marriage. Many of the interviewees claimed to be in romantic relationships, while all agreed that it was an extremely common phenomenon. Most of the students who were romantically involved were in a relationship with a classmate. For these women, many of whom resided in university hostels away from home, it was the 'openness and friendship', rather than romance, that was new. Regarding parental and familial authority, one woman said, 'My parents always warn me against being too friendly with male friends. They would not approve of my riding a rickshaw with a boy, and so I don't really discuss the extent to which I hang out with my male friends.' While most expressed little guilt and fear of family finding out, they were also confident that if the relationship progressed further, which it was expected to, the woman would break the news to her family in anticipation of marriage. Thus, obedience to parents was negotiated in a way that sanctioned the act of mixing with men, while keeping the physical aspect of the relationship at bay. In this way, students navigated obedience to parents as well as policing by parents and society.

Along with premarital romance, physical relations were also on the rise. One woman reported, 'Now if anyone with a boyfriend says that she has not kissed him, she is lying!' However, all the students interviewed claimed to disapprove of premarital sex. Like the factory workers, they too feared pregnancy to be an undesirable outcome of such liaisons. However, unlike the factory workers, what plagued the students was more the fear of being left pregnant without adequate support (to keep or terminate the pregnancy). For example, one woman said, 'In case of pregnancies the girl could just marry the father of the child or take other kinds of recourse.'

While the anxiety amongst factory workers was centred around social policing, the students had taken the policing to a level where they were less concerned about the societal gaze than about their own sense of self. Women's fear of societal repercussions at unwanted pregnancies was superseded by a disdain for what they saw as the effects of premarital sex on one's interiority, namely, the steady erosion of emotional capacity. One woman said:

> Imagine if a girl has had sex with her boyfriend and the relationship does not end up in marriage! It is then very likely that she will have another boyfriend, and in most probability will have sex with this person too. If she just keeps having sex, eventually will she even be able to feel the same kind of love, same kind of emotions every time? Probably not, and so it is best to refrain from sex before marriage.

All the women agreed that religious teachings informed the dislike they harboured towards premarital sex. While many did not think through the mechanisms by which religious teachings had left a mark on their consciousness, when probed further, women gestured at the aims of religious and cultural sanctions as logical and often in the best interests of an ideal, desirable femininity. Consequently, female students were prepared to negotiate their religious sensibilities in relation to romance rather than sex. Despite their attitude to patience, all the women claimed that premarital sex was becoming increasingly prevalent. Many of the women reported knowing girls who had already engaged in sex. One woman said, 'Who knows? It may become very common not too far in the future!'

Taleem participants had thought through the practical consequences of premarital relations, and used that knowledge to avert such consequences for themselves. For the taleem women, a romantic relationship prior to marriage was not acceptable. These women were intolerant of such relationships, first and foremost because they went against the dictates of God as presented in the Quran and the sayings of the Prophet. The women made sense of these injunctions by going into the depths of the Quranic interpretations of these rulings. They believed that proximity of most sorts, especially that which was laden with emotion and affection, could lead to the arousal of sexual desires. These were desires that could lead to acts that should be confined within marriage. Thus romance before marriage was to be avoided at all costs.

One woman said that the hardest thing for her when she 'came into' Islam anew was to cut off ties with her boyfriend. She had been involved with him for a long time and considered him an integral part of her life. She said, 'Before I came to religion, I was very different. I was fashionable and would hang out at cyber cafés.' Her repeated mention of frequenting cyber cafés was telling, as these cafés are commonly known to be places where couples can find a space to have sex. She continued:

> When I discovered what was expected of me, I realized that I was erring. However, I didn't want to give him up. I was in love with

> him, and so I remained in the relationship for a while longer, all the while plagued by the thought that I was sinning and transgressing the limits set by Allah. As I kept praying and engaging more and more deeply with religion, breaking up became easier. Then one day I decided to end the relationship. I was depressed for the longest time. But my prayers helped me through the break-up, and to appreciating the truth and being content with it.

When I asked her what 'truth' she had come to appreciate, she said that premarital relations were ripe with possibilities for premarital sex. Several taleem women's comments reverberate in the following statement:

> There are reasons why Allah forbids it. Women are sexual as well as emotional creatures. Opening the self up to a man so much, without commitments for a future together, may leave her vulnerable, exploited and hurt. Even if there is genuine commitment, the relationship may not end in marriage. And so it's better to stay away from it altogether.

Thus, the students' argument that premarital sex, which leaves the ground open for multiple experiments and multiple partners, would lead to a 'hardening' of femininity was taken further to assert that sex before marriage could be hurtful and exploitative and therefore detrimental to the self. This sort of argument suggests that in the taleem women's worldview, women's sexuality is simultaneously potent and fragile, and therefore needs to be contained. This is necessary as a service to women and what they believe is their dignity. While the policing appears cultural, it is more overtly steered by religious authority.

The privileging of religious authority over a culturally influenced familial authority comes to the surface especially when the taleem women talk about their role in choosing spouses. While women claimed that they would never again have a 'boyfriend', they would still like a role in choosing their partner. One woman said that she would definitely want to meet him and talk to him, to assess whether the couple would be compatible in marriage. The women interviewed asserted that while they would want their husband to get along with their family, the criteria by which they would choose their spouse might not be the same as those set by their family. A very common complaint amongst taleem participants in the middle to lower-middle income group was that the men their families singled out as prospective grooms were not religious enough. What several women reported can be summed up through the following comment made by one taleem participant:

> Our families pick men that they deem to be from good families, with a good education and respectable job. But that's not enough. These men have to understand how important and primal being a Muslim is for us. We would be willing to compromise on the worldly aspects, but not on religion. Our husbands have to see eye to eye with us on religious obligations.

Marriage and divorce

Marriage, for factory workers, was an extremely defining and life-altering event. However, most women expressed regrets about the instability that characterizes this very important institution. One woman said, 'These days, couples take marriages so lightly that everyone mocks at married people, especially those that work in garment factories.' The women claimed that marriages were becoming unstable for a number of reasons. First, they asserted that the media's portrayal of men's and women's fashion, along with its portrayal of romantic liaisons between men and women, worked as a temptation that disrupted the marital unit. The temptation arose from the nature of employment and the increased mobility and physical proximity which it facilitated.

However, deeper in the architecture of the fragility characterizing marriage lay the values deemed its ideal markers and the roles played by husband and wife. Factory workers agreed that the relationship between a husband and wife was free of certain impositions and interferences that were previously integral to marriage. For example one woman said, 'Before, being married meant that we had to take a lot of nonsense from our husbands, mothers-in-law. But nowadays, our work outside the home has taken many of those pressures off.'

In spite of the lessening of stringencies, however, women continue to bear the brunt of domestic responsibilities, and failure in performing household duties to desired levels justifies male discord and even aggression. One woman said, 'I learnt at taleem that we must obey our husband, we must do everything we can to please him and his family. That is a duty Allah demands of us.' Another woman said, 'If at the end of a long day, my husband comes home to find the food not ready and the home is a mess, of course he will beat me.' While on the one hand women talk of men 'deserving' a certain amount of reverence, they also point out excesses of male behaviour that they deem unjust. One example of this was men beating their wives 'too much' and leaving their wives and children for another woman. The women unanimously agreed that the break-up of the family, especially as a result of extramarital relations, was disapproved of by religion. It was despised and even feared by the women interviewed. The sense of helplessness and vulnerability that women experience by abandonment is intense enough for them to claim that a marriage should be maintained at any cost possible.

While only 'bad' men cheated on, beat excessively and abandoned their wives, the ultimate responsibility of keeping a marriage alive was to be shouldered by the wife. 'There's nothing a woman can't do. If her husband is "bad", she should know that it is very much within her power to turn him into a better man.' Thus, a woman was powerful, and her potency was to be utilized in making her relationship with her husband successful. However, underlying the power that could preserve a marriage was the value of patience (*dhorjo*), which was considered to be both societal and religious. The women claimed that it was the failure to engage with this virtue that was leading to the increasing fractures in marriages. Such fractures could be cemented by women exerting their inner power and combining this with being patient. Thus society and religion were invoked in tandem in the ensuring that women made use of their strengths to cultivate a patience that would allow them to overcome injustices and problems in their marriages.

For students, the value that defined the ideal, modern-day marriage was not patience but understanding or *shomjhota*. For most of the students interviewed, a good precursor to having understanding in the marriage was choosing one's own partner, that is, love marriages. Most students pointed out that this was the best way to get married. Love marriages were considered to keep evils such as dowry at bay. One woman said, 'Dowry has nothing to do with Islam. In a love marriage, the boy and the girl are so keen anyway that people don't really bring up the issue of dowry, which plagues the arranged marriage.' Through this the women indicated that society diminished the worth of women by giving in to dowry demands. Religion, however, was seen as preserving women's honour and value. Interestingly, the women's preferred route to shaping the type of woman that Islam upholds was through a particular form of the institution of marriage – the love marriage. As we will see later, this is a form of marriage that very religious women shun.

The students considered the roles of husband and wife to be fast changing, such that women had much more of a role in the public arena than was previously the case. Most students did not focus on domestic roles, which the factory workers and taleem participants stressed. In fact, students said that pressure over the performance of housework, especially pressure by in-laws, was to be resisted. One woman said, 'If my mother-in-law wants to stop me from working, my husband has to support me.' Thus, the *shomjhota* or understanding which was considered to be the most defining feature of a marriage was expected to lead to the creation of a marital unit where the husband and wife stand as one, taking on the rest of the world together and on behalf of themselves and each other. With *shomjhota* as a key feature, domestic duties became peripheral to the functioning of a marriage.

Students also critiqued the validity of the 'religious/social' notion that a wife is beneath the husband, questioning the authenticity of its religious roots. Thus, in questioning the absence of gender parity that characterizes conventional notions of conjugal relations, women set aside what was viewed as religion, ascribing the injustice to the workings of a patriarchal social order.

The students further argued that a lack of understanding bred incompatibility which might lead to extramarital relations. In their opinion, this was a chief instigator of divorce. Extramarital affairs were not favourably looked upon. While women's opinions resonated with an understanding of how and why extramarital affairs can happen, all the women said that it was better to get divorced and then move on to the next person. There was much awareness among students that as Muslim women they have a right to divorce. In fact, unlike the factory workers, students felt that divorce was a valid option if the marriage was bad.

Thus, in the maintenance of marital ties, *dhorjo* was not invoked as a religious ideal, and was not always engaged with, in order to have or to preserve what the women deemed a good marriage. One woman narrated the story of her murdered professor who exercised patience in staying with a philandering husband. Her patience left her lying dead in her apartment. It is suspected that her husband had her killed. Despite their attitude to patience, the women were also acutely aware of the fact that many obstacles faced a woman who wanted a divorce. These included the lack of familial support, the lack of social acceptance, and economic vulnerability. However, the women thought that such stigma was yet another manifestation of a patriarchal social system. Religion, on the other hand, offered every right to divorce.

Amongst the students, we see a perceived separation of the religious from the cultural. Students see marital relationships, their beginnings and endings as an outcome of women's greater public participation through education and work. They appreciate the fact that their marriages are now characterized by certain freedoms enabled by women's income and nuclear households. These, according to the students, have eased the stringency of norms that have long been oppressive for women. As these norms lose their salience, students also talk about oppressive norms through the registers of the cultural as opposed to conflating the cultural with the religious as do the factory workers. In this separation, they speak of religion as giving women greater rights than culture, especially by setting some standards for, and certain limits to, virtues such as tolerance, and by allowing for divorce. Students argue that failure to execute Islam's position on the limits of marriage and divorce is attributable to persistent patriarchy. A religious discourse can be teased apart from this, enabling religion to be read as more egalitarian and therefore offering more to our understanding of gender norms and roles than is currently possible.

Such a perspective on Islam on the part of the students can be, and usually is, taken as a sign of a 'superficial' deference to a religious ethos, where other aspects of one's life move in a 'secular' manner. While there is no denying that many aspects of the students' lives are steered towards progress by a liberal and secular ethos and actions, I would also like to point out that using religion in a 'modern' way is symptomatic of a globalized world where modern education, technology, and greater income, movement and exposure have given women and men greater choices and avenues of self-expression. In this world, it is also possible for religion to compete with other components of modern life, and on equal terms. This means that religion becomes a choice, amongst other choices, where older more 'traditional' pressures of religious compliance take on a new garb and religion presents itself as a way of being and living that can be drawn on sometimes for some issues. The research shows that students draw on a 'liberal' discourse as they envision relationships with men. In this, they invoke religion in a way that tallies with their 'liberal' aspirations. Consequently, striving towards new 'liberations' does not mean jettisoning Islam. Rather, it leads students to think about and articulate (often on the basis of particular textual interpretations) the place of religion, as distinct from the cultural, in delivering for women a more emancipatory trajectory towards self-expression, especially in relation to men.

For the taleem-goers, who are from a lower-middle income category, many amongst whom are also younger women and students, we see a perceived separation of the religious from the cultural, privileging the former. However, as I elaborate below, this separation engages norms very differently, yielding different outcomes for women's sense of self via their bodies and relationships with others.

Marriage, for the taleem women, was not only defining and life-altering, but also a special relationship that needed to be invested with a lot of wisdom derived from religion. All the taleem women claimed to share a closer relationship with their husbands once they understood the 'correct' roles and duties of husbands and wives. They argued very fervently that women's domestic duties were sacred, and that in performing them they served the society by raising children that were obedient to 'the will of Allah'. The women argued that these duties were or should be a source of pride, not simply because the women were carrying out God's will, but because performing these duties meant that they were resolving the 'battle of the sexes'. The gender division of labour was about responsibility of equal value, rather than engaging with power in a way that was laden with conflict and competition. Many of the women claimed to be in close communication with their husbands, especially when decisions needed to be made about home, children and finances.

The taleem women considered divorce to be one of God's least favourite things. However, they recognized that Islam allows divorce. They said that if a woman had tried her best and failed to change her husband for the better, she had the option to leave him. Here we see a parallel with the factory workers, who viewed the woman as having certain powers which she could use to turn around a problematic marriage. Before assuming an essentialized similarity between the two instances, however, we need to bear in mind a number of dimensions. These include the different features to which taleem women and factory workers attributed their prowess, the different issues they deemed worthy of tolerating, the different physical and emotional limits on forbearance, and finally the privileging of different authorities in defining all of the above. Taleem women knew that their right to divorce was God-given, although that right needed to be exercised with caution and counsel. Thus, patience was interceded by religious knowledge which women believed gave them the right not to bear the unbearable. As a result, the norm that marriage had to be permanent did not hold, even as women recognized the practical obstacles that stood in the way.

Polygyny

While women were held culpable for fragile marriages, polygyny was clearly the man's fault. The women claimed to be aware that Islam sanctioned the act. However, women also engaged with religious discourse and argued that a man could take a second wife only if he could treat both with equal attention and affection. Thus, while the onus of patience was on the woman and therefore needed to be cultivated for a marriage to work, the women did not talk of patience if a man sought out a second wife. Women detached themselves from the situation and used religious reasoning to deter husbands from engaging in polygyny.

The taleem women did not look upon polygyny favourably, although all of them were aware of the fact that Islam allows it under certain conditions. They were very forthright in asserting that polygyny was not something they would accept in their own lives. The taleem women further critiqued the reasons behind men having multiple wives. One woman said, 'Men these days do not take a second wife out of duty, but out of lust. Lust is not allowed by Islam, and this prohibition is for both men and women. So, I don't think I would like to be married to a lustful man.' Here, like the factory workers, women distanced themselves and endowed men with responsibilities. However, the responsibilities that ought to deter a man needed to be more internal, marked by the absence of lust, rather than practical, such as the equal financial maintenance of two wives.

Implications for women's agency and empowerment

The stereotypical notion of Islam is that it frames sexuality by burdening women with sexual potency which then needs to be policed, controlled and contained. However, it is now accepted – at least within academia as well as elsewhere – that such generalized notions dissipate in the face of contextual variation. Contextual differences arise through different economic and political factors, and can be gauged through an understanding of different kinds of discourses that frame the links among Islamic ideas, ideals, acts, women and their sexualities. Thus, an understanding of the relationship between Islam and sexuality is produced through the intersection of multiple discourses and also through the play of multiple identities, formed culturally and historically, on the self. Consequently it becomes very difficult to pinpoint what is intrinsic to Islam, and what is derived from other cultural registers. While that may be true, it is also important to engage with people's own constructions – how they identify what is religious and set it apart from the mundane (Asad 1986). This allows for insights into how others think of religion and into the justifications that frame particular engagements with discourses on religion, along with the outcomes they are likely to yield.

In this chapter I have highlighted women's narratives relating to the construction of the religious as part of, or distinct from, other spheres in culture, and the effects on women's relations with men and the ensuing sense of self. I have argued that there exists a spectrum of normative engagement with religious discourse on femininity, gendered relations, the body and sexuality. Of all the women studied, it is the poorer women who see the religious and the cultural as the most coterminous. By conflating the religious with the cultural, the factory workers are able to deploy the cultural to negotiate with religious obligations, and then again collapse the two in articulating their freedom from religious norms and the consequent liberating sense of self. Given that women speak of the ability to bypass religious and ritualistic obligations, and since factory workers' lives are marked by greater income and autonomy than before, it is very easy to ignore the normative claims that a religious discourse may make on their lives. It becomes all too simple, in other words, to see these normative claims as a remnant of a particular cultural consciousness, as appropriate responses, especially when women do not necessarily bear overt markers of religiosity such as the head cover (Deeb 2009).

It is important to point out, however, that amongst the factory workers, women's lingering sense of sin and guilt, especially around their sexuality and bodies, was the strongest of all the groups of women investigated. What do we make of this sense of sin and guilt? Women who work have been the ground upon which development activities have been tried and tested, and many of these activities have been deemed successful enough to help chart Bangladesh's modern trajectory. Yet what has entered narratives of change and modernity are the changes that are tangible. These include incomes, access to credit, consumer power and the like. But where are we to leave the lingering sense of guilt that is marginalized by, and excluded from, the paradigm of progress, empowerment and modernity? Would our neglect of such non-tangible realities yield a holistic understanding of empowerment? What is at stake in not addressing women's sense of guilt and shame which roots itself sometimes in the religious, sometimes in the cultural, and often, as in the case of the factory workers, in both? I return to these points shortly.

The other two categories of women – the students and the taleem-goers – were much clearer about what falls within the purview of religious norms and what lies outside. In their greater clarity, what we find is the granting of religion a higher standing than cultural constructions that work against women. In such a framing, students and taleem-goers delineate different trajectories and different ways of engaging with similar norms such as modesty, patience, and the like. We also find that even while women confront certain norms and practices that are widely considered to be religious, such as polygyny, they do so by 'sparing religion' and ascribing patriarchal cultural strictures to the distresses caused to women by polygyny, albeit with differing pleas and arguments against the custom.

The narratives on sexuality thus undergird different concepts of religion and different ways of engaging with religious discourses. The tendency to separate the cultural from the religious indicates much reflection about what constitutes both. This may lead to several outcomes, especially for an understanding of women's sexuality and their lives. One possibility may be the deployment of a more liberal discourse and ethos in thinking about religion, where Islam is incorporated into a liberal pathway to empowerment. The students show some indications of this – their lives are modern, they are being educated and are aspiring to independent incomes and residential patterns, and marriages are envisioned on the basis of inner emotions such as respect and understanding rather than on the basis of duties and obligations. Another vision is espoused by the taleem-goers, for whom respect and duties go hand in hand. In fact, for them the duties – as ordained by God – are essential to bringing about respect, understanding and love in a marriage. And while the taleem-goers and factory workers express apparently similar views about domestic duties, they invoke religion differently in their understanding of respect and complementarity. The outcomes of the links between obligations and emotions for taleem-goers and factory workers are bound to show many differences, in spite of the shared focus on duties.

Taleem-goers' views of Islam are strict and textual, representing the extreme end of the textual interpretation that a majority of our respondents (including students and factory workers) reported favouring. Ayesha Imam (2000) writes that Muslim religious right movements tend to share certain underlying assumptions about women. First, they are made repositories of culture as opposed to participants and co-creators. Next, their place in heteronormative relations leads to the 'increased domesticity of women, their identities and sexualities, tamed into a restriction to women's "primary roles as wife and mother"' (Imam 2000: 129). This was very much the case here too.

The research shows that attending taleem and striving to live more pious lives gives women a new sense of direction, a newfound certainty and even new objectives and modes of achieving them. Taleem women's efforts at training and conditioning the self – making the external speak to the internal – entail responsibility, and accountability to religious authority. The accountability may even lead to the questioning and subverting of societal norms and expectations. Malleability and a feeling of achievement endow the self with a sense of agency. External acts, such as giving up a romantic relationship, refraining, drawing on feminine prowess to turn around a bad marriage – all these become do-able and bearable because of the sense of agency women experience. For the majority of women who choose such a life, they are less concerned with the reinforcement of certain patriarchal norms and strictures than with the pleasures in finding a sense of certainty, and unintentionally reconfiguring power relations within a patriarchal context, especially in matters related to women's bodies and their relationships with men. All the taleem women we spoke to were quite enamoured by the call and struggle towards piety.

It is in this deep sense of certainty and newfound resolutions to the vexed question of women's bodies and their sexuality that a strictly textual religious discourse anchors its projects of change. The taleem thus lays out a particular kind of trajectory of inner empowerment emanating from a containment of sexuality that may be seen by many religious aspirants as another road for women. This is especially so for those who struggle with notions of sin and external and internal uncertainty in relation to their understandings of sexuality.

In Bangladesh, we see multiple deployments of religious discourses that yield very different outcomes and speak of different possibilities with regard to ideas around sexuality and self-expression. Whilst the last few decades have brought about many empowering changes to women's lives in Bangladesh through development initiatives, conceptions of women's sexuality and their sense of self, especially in relation to men, have been surrounded by a certain nervousness. Discourses on Islam have either been absent in these discussions or have been seen as playing an atavistic role (Shehabuddin 2008; Nahar 2010). The research highlights the different levels at which discourses on Islam are engaged and the consequent different ways in which women relate to norms around their bodies and their relationships with men.

In this, I argue that sexuality is not experienced and lived out in a uniform manner. We have seen that there is greater acceptance of a women's right to choose a husband, and an acknowledgement of heightened premarital sexual relationships along with the scope for divorce. At the same time, there is also a particular use of religious rhetoric that is much more conservative about the female body and its sexual expression outside marriage. Given this scenario, it is difficult to pinpoint a conceptualization of sexuality as wholly liberating or wholly oppressive as a result of current engagements with Islam. This complex picture needs to be borne in mind, further researched and clarified as women citizens – unbelievers, superficial believers and the devout – seek to empower themselves, honour their bodies and arrive at greater equity while dealing with men.

Notes

1 General observations as well as findings from this research.

2 Maimuna Huq (2009) has worked on Jama'at-e-Islami discussion circles, which are overtly political in their function as a mass mobilization base for a political party and the political cause of gaining state power. In contrast, the three sites that we looked at are non-political. Two circles were organized by the Tabligh Jama'at which takes a strongly non-political stance, focusing exclusively instead on personal and group piety. The third circle was neither Jama'ati nor Tabligh but consisted of a group of women who had decided to congregate in a mosque to study the Quran. The preacher was strict about keeping political talk and slander out of the discussions.

References

Abu-Lughod, L. (1990) 'The Romance of Resistance: Tracing Transformations of Power through Bedouin Women', *American Ethnologist*, Vol. 17, No. 1, pp. 41–55.

Asad, T. (1986) *The Idea of an Anthropology of Islam*, Occasional Papers Series, Center for Contemporary Arab Studies, Georgetown University, Washington DC.

Asadullah, N. M. and N. Chaudhury (2009) 'Reverse Gender Gap in Schooling in Bangladesh: Insights from Rural and Urban Households', *Journal of Development Studies*, Vol. 45, No. 8, pp. 1,360–80.

Butler, J. (1993) *Bodies that Matter: On the Discursive Limits of 'Sex'*, Routledge, New York.

Cornwall, A. and M. Molyneux (eds.) (2008) *The Politics of Rights: Dilemmas for Feminist Praxis*, Routledge, New York and London.

Deeb, L. (2009) 'Emulating and/or Embodying the Ideal: The Gendering of Temporal Frameworks and Islamic Role Models', *American Ethnologist*, Vol. 36, No. 21, pp. 242–57.

Feldman, S. (1998) '(Re)Presenting Islam', in A. Basu and P. Jeffery (eds.), *Appropriating Gender*, Routledge, New York and London.

Foucault, M. (1978) *The History of Sexuality*, Allen Lane, Harmondsworth.

—— (1980) 'Truth and Power', in Foucault, *Power/Knowledge: Selected Interviews and Other Writings 1972–1977*, ed. and trans. C. Gordon, Pantheon Books, New York.

—— (1990) *The History of Sexuality*, Vol. 2, *The Use of Pleasure*, trans. R. Hurley, Vintage Books, New York.

Gardener, K. (1998) 'Women and Islamic Revivalism in a Bangladeshi Community', in A. Basu and P. Jeffery (eds.), *Appropriating Gender*, Routledge, New York and London.

Huq, M. (2009) 'Talking Jihad and Piety: Reformist Exertions among Islamist Women in Bangladesh', *Journal of Anthropological Institute*, N.S., S163–S182.

Imam, A. M. (2000) 'The Muslim Religious Right ("Fundamentalists") and Sexuality', in P. Ilkkaracan (ed.), *Women and Sexuality in Muslim Societies*, Women for Women's Human Rights (WWHR)/Kadmin Insan Haklari Projesi, Istanbul.

Jesmin, S. and S. Salway (2000) 'Marriage among the Urban Poor of Dhaka: Instability and Uncertainty', *Journal of International Development*, Vol. 12, pp. 689–705.

Mahmood, S. (2005) *The Politics of Piety: The Islamic Revival and the Feminist Subject*, Princeton University Press, Princeton, NJ.

Nahar, A. (2010) 'Defending Islam and Women's Honour against NGOs in

Bangladesh', *Women's Studies International Forum*, Vol. 33, pp. 316–24.

Rozario, S. (2006) 'The New Burqa in Bangladesh; Empowerment or Violation of Women's Rights', *Women's Studies International Forum*, Vol. 29, pp. 368–80.

Shehabuddin, E. (2008) *Reshaping the Holy: Democracy, Development and Muslim Women in Bangladesh*, Columbia University Press, New York.

3

Loving and Fearing

Township Girls' Agency amidst Sexual Risk

Deevia Bhana

> Researcher: … what makes a guy great?
> Phume:[1] Good-looking, wearing brands, wearing jewellery, like jokes a lot, just a good guy actually. Every girl should want that kind of a guy …
> Nobuhle: My boyfriend is loving, he's patient, he's kind, he's got all the things a girl should want in a boy … a great heart, he's loving.
> Nomsa: … we're scared of boys, cos boys force you, even say 'shut up' and make you scared … you get scared of telling … someone that he raped you … (Focus group interviews with African schoolgirls aged 16–17, in Inanda township, Durban, South Africa)[2]

What kind of guy should every girl want? Most of the girls in this study of 16- to 17-year-old African girls situate their responses within the conundrum of love, money, fear and violence. Taking a cue from work on love in Africa (Cole and Thomas 2009; Hunter 2010; Thomas 2009; Wood *et al.* 1998), this chapter argues that girls' claims to love are localized, and intersect in complex ways with money, gender, sexualities and violence. The ubiquitous intertwining of materiality, love and sexual violence is highlighted in girls' expressions of sexuality, asserting sexual agency but entwined within gender and economic structures which sustain gender asymmetries. In understanding girls' relationship formations, as this chapter will show, it is necessary to attend both to the local permutations of love and to the social structures and inequalities that shape girls' claims to love. Such claims are not simply reproduced by material inequalities: girls' strategies are claims to power and resources in ways that are conflicted in their relationship to patriarchal structures.

Phume, Nobuhle and Nomsa live in township contexts shackled by the history of apartheid, poverty and HIV, and are largely visible in growing accounts of sexual violence and coercion. They, like other participants in this study, are located in informal settlements in the Inanda township of Durban, KwaZulu-Natal. Inanda, like many other townships in South Africa, manifests unequal social forces, as historical inequalities, poverty, poor housing, high unemployment and violence interact with young people's vulnerability to HIV. Under such circumstances, the sexualities of young Africans in townships are the site of intense surveillance, particularly in this context where HIV rates are reported to be higher than they are in urban or rural areas (Human Science Research Council 2005). Within the AIDS epidemic, sexuality has become contaminated and sex has become the vector of death (Susser 2009). Girls' vulnerability to disease exists in circumstances not of their own making. It is this tragedy that embodies South Africa's young women with its legacy of apartheid, structural inequalities, unemployment and sexual violence.

Of the 5 million people estimated to be infected with HIV in South Africa, over 50 per cent became infected before the age of 25, and of the 15–24-year-old age group, 8.6 per cent are infected. There are striking gender disparities, as estimates in a population-based household survey suggest that HIV prevalence remains disproportionately high for women in comparison to men, peaking in the 25–29-year-old age group. One in three in this age group (32.7 per cent) was found to be HIV-positive in 2008 (Human Science Research Council 2009). The township offers the context through which girls' sexualities are understood. Scholars have argued that pervasive poverty, gender inequalities and other forms of structural inequalities shape sexual practices which heighten the risk of disease infection (Arnfred 2004). Love is dangerous, as Wood *et al.*

(1998) elucidate, and in intimate partner relationships, ideologies of gender and everyday practices of subordination interact with social and economic forces to generate violent gender relations and inequalities.

Amidst the elaboration of danger around HIV and AIDS, young love has become more audible in research in South Africa (Hunter 2010). Whilst important contributions have been made to the understanding of the structural forces that shape sexualities and vulnerabilities to disease (Jewkes *et al.* 2010a), girls' relationship negotiations are not simply determined by social and material inequalities. Girls' ideals of love include its association with a stylized form of masculinity, branded clothes and money. As Salo (2002, 2003) notes, the consumption of fashionable dress styles and presence in popular spaces are key signifiers of changing youth identities in South Africa. Beyond money, however, there are complex patterns underlying the negotiation of relationships. These range from the constitution of love being based on boys having a 'great heart' to the omnipresence of sexual violence and masculine domination within relationship formations.

This study draws from a larger interview project entitled '16 Turning 17: Youth, Gender and Sexuality in the Context of HIV and AIDS'. Based on an interview study carried out in schools, the project sought to explore the ways in which young people in diverse social and racial circumstances in Durban, KwaZulu-Natal, give meaning to gender and sexuality in the context of AIDS. In this chapter the focus is only on Inanda High, an all-African township school. Schools were selected across the South African social landscape, the main aim in this project being to understand the ways in which social location had effects for the specific meanings given to gender and sexuality.

Teachers assisted in the selection of students for the interviews. Students were mainly in grade 11, as their ages in this grade are generally between sixteen and seventeen. When arranging the interviews at Inanda, teachers were asked to consider the following factors: learners who, in their view, reflected a range of levels of academic ability; students' willingness to participate; obtaining informed consent from guardians/parents; and, in the case of Inanda High, availability during non-school hours. Six girls and six boys participated in this study. The participants live in a variety of informal settlements in Inanda. Some live in one-room 'shacks', most live in dwellings made from scrap materials which include metal, wood and sheets of plastic. Water supply and toilet facilities are shared in the community. Participants' personal circumstances vary, with most living in female-headed households either with their mothers or grandmothers. They rely on the child support grant of R260 per month and their grandmother's government pension. Their mothers usually sold fruit and vegetables or worked as domestic workers in middle-class areas of Durban.

I conducted interviews in English using mixed-sex and single-sex groups. Data from both these interviews, with a particular focus on girls, form the basis of this chapter. In total, three focus group interviews were conducted. All interviews were tape-recorded and transcribed. The mixed-sex focus group interviews foreground girls' claims to love. Here, love was linked intimately with money and materiality, such that the major theme discussed was girls' desires in relation to provider masculinity. Girls were particularly vocal in their discussions about boys and boyfriends, and did not feel inhibited talking about their choices. However, in single-sex girls' interviews, the narrative of fear was foregrounded. In all interviews, young people set the agenda, and in the girls-only interview, violence was raised by the girls as a matter of concern.

This chapter elucidates two important areas in young girls' narratives of sexuality: provider love and fear. A central argument here is that girls approach relationships not as passive victims but instead uphold provider masculinity in order to access power and resources in ways that can both resist and reproduce patriarchal structures. Second, sexuality is constructed not only as a domain of love and desire but also as a domain of fear, violence and restriction, thus curtailing girls' agency.

Before discussing each of these dimensions of girls' narratives of sexuality – provider love and fear – I begin by contextualizing sexualities in South Africa.

Contextualizing sexualities

In 1984, Carole Vance argued that sexuality is simultaneously a domain of curtailment and of agency. Vance cautioned that focusing only on agency would ignore the ways in which patriarchal structures continue to restrict agency. Recognizing only sexual violence and fear, on the other hand, would erase women's experience of agency and choice. This tension between love and fear remains a powerful one. Such a tension articulates not only the possibilities of sexuality that include a claim to love but also restrictions in experience, and the everyday reality and terror of sexual violence.

In South Africa, a dominant narrative around sexuality is that of violence (Jewkes *et al.* 2002, 2005, 2010a, 2010b). Bourgois (2004) notes that the context of political, emotional, economic and institutional forces affects the narratives of sexuality that unfold. Political struggles, the history of apartheid and colonialism as well as persistent economic crises have been established as important co-factors in understanding sexual violence (Wood *et al.* 2007). Connecting sexual violence with the construction of masculinities, research has illustrated how entrenched notions of masculine power, unemployment, and the history of apartheid have produced emasculation, particularly for African men on the edges of poverty (Hunter 2007).

The preponderance of male violence within particular racialized places in South Africa must be understood within the context of socio-cultural notions about male power as well as the social impact of apartheid, political enfeeblement and unemployment on generations of African men (Dunkle *et al.* 2007, Wood *et al.* 2007). Sexual violence is thus understood as located within specific social and material contexts where expressions of male power are embodied in male vulnerabilities and weaknesses.

Statistics on gender and sexual violence in South Africa show that one in three South African women has been raped, and one in four has been beaten by her domestic partner (Moffett 2006). More than 55,000 cases of rape are reported annually (South African Police Services 2010). Being raped is a major cause of concern in South Africa but so too is being infected with HIV during rape (Jewkes *et al.* 2010a). In KwaZulu-Natal province, where the girls in this study come from, HIV prevalence among mothers who attend antenatal clinics is estimated to be a staggering 39 per cent (Wand and Ramjee 2010).

HIV and AIDS have exacerbated girls' vulnerability to death, disease and danger. The risk of contracting HIV intersects with material inequalities and gender and cultural norms. This configuration has been identified as significant in the sexual and violent subordination of young women. The enormity of HIV increases the already significant role of sexual violence in the subordination of young women. Risk of exposure to HIV infection is strongly associated with gender and sexual violence; gendered power inequalities lead many scholars to argue that ending violence against women and girls is critical for both health and human rights (UNAIDS Joint Action for Results 2010; Susser 2009; Greig *et al.* 2008).

Understanding sexuality as a domain of pain and suffering, as Reddy (2004) does, is therefore not unjustifiable in the face of sexual risk and violence. Whilst this does not assume a lack of desire in Africa, the materiality of sexuality is such that for most people it is aligned with restrictions, sexual violence and disease. Within intimate partner relationships, research highlighting violence against women is increasing (Greig *et al.* 2008). Male sexual conduct and coercive sexual practices dominate sexual relationships. When and how sex is initiated, it is argued, is defined by male partners (Wood *et al.* 1998). Gender power inequalities at both the social and the intimate level serve to reproduce male domination within sexual relationships. Violence limits the extent to which women can control the circumstances around sex, resulting in more frequent sex and less condom use (Jewkes 2010).

In intimate partner relationships, certain practices of love are legitimized through which female submission is achieved. Wood *et al.* (2007), in their study of sexual violence within relationships in local youth sexual cultures in South Africa, argue that force may not always mean violence. The authors argue that force can include several culturally sanctioned practices that can be viewed both positively and negatively. For example being persuaded to have sex can be seen as force, but for young men persuasive practices are culturally sanctioned and acceptable where young women accede to sexual relationships if a 'guy persuades you in a nice way' (Wood *et al.* 2007: 296). Other forms of persuasive practices include flattery, expressions of love, sweet-talking and pleading that sex was important for the relationship (Wood *et al.* 2007: 288). Locally grounded meanings of male persuasion in sexual relationships point to the need for a more nuanced understanding of sexual propositioning and sexual violence. Social and cultural constraints thus have an impact on the extent to which women can express free will and autonomy.

Scholars have missed expressions of love and desire, given the onslaught of danger described above. As Hirsch and Wardlow (2007) argue, love is not often present in understandings of sexuality except when the gendered optic is turned to inequality and domination. Sexuality is a domain of exploration, agency, sensations and connections, not just a domain of danger (Vance 1984). In transmuting sexuality into danger alone, the daily experiences of sexual excitement, thrills, love, romance, desires and action are made invisible. Criticizing the one-sided focus on sexuality as danger, repression and disease, scholars are now arguing for a more prominent place for considerations of love and desire in the sexual economies in Africa (Hunter 2010; Cole and Thomas 2009; McFadden 2003; Pereira 2003). It is argued that the absence of love reduces African sexuality to sex, serving an instrumental logic which tends towards depictions of cultural practices as causal factors in the spread of HIV. This in turn overlaps with racist suppositions which frame Africans as hypersexual, with men constructed as sexual predators pitted against a repressed and fearful African female sexuality. The aggregate effect of such interpretations is to produce a version of sexuality which is located in the domain of fear and repression.

The affect and ideals of love that are also dimensions of sexualities take on different coordinates in different contexts, intersecting with cultural and material conditions. In the context of girls in this study, they converge with deep historical inequalities. Thomas and Cole (2009) argue that sexuality is embedded in historical processes, cultural practices and material conditions that enable particular kinds of relationships. Whilst it is important to maintain the focus on sexual violence and fear, it is equally important to understand how love is enmeshed within sexual behaviour. It is through such configurations that we might understand girls' vulnerability and the economic formations which shape and reshape love.

Expressions of love are linked to social class and economic circumstances. Masvawure's (2010) study of young women in Zimbabwe notes how the desire for commodities allows young women to re-enact themselves by forming relationships in ways that confirm the intimate connection between love and money. In South Africa, Hunter (2010) has begun to argue that material provision and emotions are mutually constitutive. In the context of ever-sharp social and economic inequalities, Hunter (2002) notes how young women's claims to resources and power both challenge and perpetuate patriarchal structures.

Today in South Africa, Hunter (2010) argues that high unemployment and rising expenses have made it difficult for men to forge families and build homes – processes that are key to the construction of hegemonic masculinity. Multiple partnerships must be situated within the economic and cultural turbulence in which provision of material support, particularly for women, is evidence of emotional commitment. However, as research has shown, sex and material exchange have implications for the spread of AIDS (Jewkes and Morrell 2010). Prevention programmes for young people must attend not only to social structures of power, gender norms and material inequalities, but also to young people's ideologies of love. These are expressive of agency and constraint as well as of enduring gender inequalities. The following section explores the first of the young girls' narratives of sexuality – provider love.

Provider love

In this section, I argue that when girls talk about love and make claims to it, they uphold a version of love based on the provision of material goods. Hunter (2010) refers to this as 'provider love', arising from economic and social circumstances. In a social and cultural context marked by daily privations, the capacity of young men to provide is experienced emotionally by girls as love. In this process, men with money are idealized and desired. Notwithstanding the racialization of unemployment and poverty in South Africa, which sees African men marginalized from economic livelihoods, the gendered material realities are such that men, including African men, with their ability to provide, are still more privileged economically than African women.

Provider masculinity, as Hunter elucidates, draws from such gendered and cultural privilege. Tracing the historical development of provider masculinity in KwaZulu-Natal, Hunter argues that in the early twentieth century men provided a homestead, headed the household, and invested in the payment of bride wealth and in marriage. In this way, male power was circulated and entrenched. In contemporary townships, provider masculinity is linked to disposable income and consumption, and to the widespread use of gifts and/or money in exchange for love and sex.

Girls' ideals of love are not separate from the love–money–masculinity complex. Love, as others have shown, is sewn to the privileged economic position of men (Hunter 2010). Young girls' ideals of love are congruent with the desire for money and consumption. Such ideals uphold a counter–feminist masculinity that models itself around fashionable clothes and access to middle-class leisure activities, goods and money. These ideals of love are also important, as Hunter (2010) notes, in understanding the high HIV prevalence amongst young women in KwaZulu-Natal.

Even though the girls in this study did not claim to be sexually active, their imagined and fantasized consumerist-rooted middle-class futures aspired towards 'hot stuff', including fancy cars and big mansions. Some women who do engage in transactional sex (see Masvawure's 2010 study conducted in Zimbabwe) do so to attain an elusive middle-class lifestyle, which includes consumption items such as 'flashy' fashions and hairdos. Being 'flashy', as Masvawure also notes, is an assertion of power and prestige and a claim to status. Carving out a life very different from the drudgery of poverty, the girls link love and 'hot' consumerist stuff in less than straightforward ways:

> Phume: If he got money I could think that he could do anything that I like ... like buying me hot stuff ... like clothes.
> Researcher: Clothes ...
> Phume: Maybe he could take me out.
> Researcher: Where to?
> Phume: Maybe Gateway [name of a shopping mall] … take me to some expensive restaurants, spoil me, do these kind of things that I like so much because he has money.
> Nu: I think if he got money he will buy things that I like, like Phume said, and I think that he's the one only for me and he will, he will marry me. I think of that cos I see him at this age that he got money if he gets older he will get a lot more money.

Provider masculinity is being upheld here, as girls imagine and aspire towards middle-class futures. There were contestations. Some of the girls mentioned compassion, having a great heart and being 'loving', as ideals of love. Phili, for example, expressed love in romantic terms, contesting the claim to love and money and stating that 'love is about feelings'. As the interview proceeded, however, she stated that 'she would date person who has money' because he will do more for her.

> Researcher: Right, money, you like boys with money?
>
> Phili: Of course yes, I like them because when you love a person who has money you feel that this person can do more for you, ya, maybe you going to get married with this person. Like my sister dated a foreigner … who was driving a Ford Focus, and he had money. Every time he wanted to see her, she will say to us, come let's go with this man and let's take money out of him, and what I learnt from this you must not love a person just because you want his or her money, you must love a person just because you love and not for their money … but I would date a person who has money because I think it will do more for me.

Phili contests the ways in which her sister 'milks' money out of her boyfriend, arguing first that love overrides money as she did earlier, yet falling back on the love–money entanglement. This results in her stating, 'I would date a person who has money because ... it will do more for me'. Love could also be fostered, as Phume notes earlier, in spaces like shopping malls and restaurants as well as through clothing. These attractions and desires are a direct contrast to the grinding poverty which makes dating a 'person who has money' attractive and contextually relevant. Girls' ideals of love thus exist in tension with inequalities that play out in contested ways. In the process, provider love is exalted:

> Phili: It's important to look nice … let's just say … you are walking with your friend and maybe your friend is wearing nicer clothes than you, and then you'll find out that boys won't come to you because you are wearing bad things.

Here it is important to note Skeggs's (2004) view, derived from her study of working-class girls in the UK, that a negative association is attributed to working-class embodiment and adornment. What you look like, Skeggs adds, becomes shorthand for class. 'Looking nice' is a means through which sexual energies are sustained, and through which poverty is contested and status is attained. Appearance thus operates as a signifier for class, and 'looking nice' offers better prospects for girls in the love market than working-class poverty and despair.

Not only did girls in this study position themselves positively within the fashion–money discourse, but for them nice-looking boys added shape to the meaning of class, love and romance:

> Researcher: What makes a guy great?
> Nu: Hairstyle … waves, trimming and waves.
> Phume: And if a guy has a gold tooth or a silver …
> Letse: Daniel Hechter, Giorgio Armani … Levis …

The girls here uphold masculinity performed around good looks, hairstyles, gold teeth and brand-name clothing – all of which are linked to economic power. In poverty-stricken township contexts, fashion is hotly pursued by many young people identifying with the allure of the middle class, differentiating themselves as they do from the poverty of the township but also from poorer rural-based counterparts. In the context of a lack of material comfort, the attraction of fashion and brand names is their statement of power, interlocking with making a 'guy great'. Hunter's (2010) study of men in KwaZulu-Natal notes that it is men who are seen in the company of attractive women who are envied as being sexually successful. A great guy is also a source of other girls' envy and a demonstration, for the young girls in this study, of their success in attaining middle-class status and prestige.

Brands like Daniel Hechter, Armani and Levis are not commodities that Letse or any of the girls could ever afford. Tensions exist here in the desire for commodities and overwhelming poverty. In managing these tensions the girls imagine and enact sexual subject positions which entangle love and money.

> Phume: Because … when he's wearing brand names I think that he got money.

In the context of abject poverty, the investment in clothing and fashion is linked to and shaped by broader social structures. Hunter (2010) argues that the provision of gifts by men to girlfriends is a symptom of gender inequality. In such scenarios, women can demand cash, cell phones and clothes: 'if in the past man provided love through supporting a wife, today he provides love by giving gifts to a girlfriend' (Hunter 2010: 148). Wearing brand names indicates girls' status in the broader social context whilst signifying provider masculinity. Fashion and the desire for consumption sustain ideologies of sexuality which reinscribe patterns of inequality. Girls subscribe to such ideologies through their own agency, against the backdrop of poverty, while sewing themselves into the very fabric of provider masculinity.

In the process, girls reject farm-boy *inyoni* rural-based masculinity, which is constructed as backward, without money, and with offensive dress style.

> Letse: Bonelo from Inyathi [rural area] … he accompanied me to the city and he was wearing like formal shoes with socks, with white socks and he wore shorts and he wore a tight, a tight shirt and I was like, I was so offended by him … people were staring at me, laughing at me, saying where, where did you get this, this farm boy, this *inyoni*?
>
> Researcher: What's *inyoni*?
>
> Letse: Behind the syllabus … If you don't have a girlfriend, you are behind syllabus … so that means he's not clever, he's behind the syllabus of having sex.

In contrast to the idealized expressions connected to provider masculinity, *inyoni* masculinity was rejected as inferior, farm-based, without a stylized performance and economic resources. Significantly, *inyoni* boys were regarded as 'behind the syllabus' not only in relation to fashion and adornment but also in relation to sex. Talbot and Quayle (2010) note that women are actively involved in constructing and maintaining counter-feminist masculine ideals. The rejection of *inyoni* masculinity is based on the strong appeal of hegemonic masculine ideals, which in romantic contexts complexly connect style, looks and consumption with provider masculinity.

In a context where girls rely on child support grants of R260 per month and live in insecure economic households, resistance against *inyoni* masculinity and the positive expressions and ideals around provider masculinity must be situated within a context of sharp social inequalities. It is within particular sets of circumstances and social relations that young people's claims to love are embedded. Their ideologies of love and expressions of desire have consequences for the ways in which love is imagined and negotiated. *Inyoni* masculinity cannot serve the elusive lifestyle that the girls have described earlier. Rejecting this form of masculinity is a material manifestation of gendered environments.

The stylization of provider masculinity around brands was important in the construction of love but was not necessarily connected to sex.

> Nu: Wearing brands … if you got a boyfriend you have to see his style what he's wearing … I don't want sex. I don't want to sleep with him cos I'm not ready for such a big commitment …

The girls in this study, like Nu above, claimed not to be in sexual relationships although they knew of others their age who were in such relationships. In relation to sex, Nu contests the instrumental logic that links love–money to sex. Here she argues that sex is a big commitment, expressing her agency as she does. Significantly she recognizes a sexually coercive environment yet states, 'I will tell him … that I'm not ready'. In the following section, I explore the second narrative of young girls' sexualities – fearing love.

Fearing love

South African literature is replete with evidence of sexual violence in intimate partner relationships, with 'love being described as dangerous' (Wood *et al.* 1998, 2007; Jewkes *et al.* 2010a). The 1998 study of young South Africans conducted by Wood, Maforah and Jewkes shows young men and women performing masculinity and femininity in ways which engender unequal relations of power and increase sexual risk for young women.

Girls in this study expressed the same concern about the dangers of love in relation to their boyfriends:

> Nu: ... we are scared of boys because you can have some fun with ... your boyfriend but as the time goes on he will ... act, act differently towards you and force you to do things that you are not ready to do so I can say we are scared of boys ...
>
> Nomsa: ... they use girls ... they want to have sex with them, that's all. They don't love them.
>
> Nu: You love the guy but ... you become scared of that guy ... when he start giving you different ideas, confusing ideas that makes you scared of him ...

In the 2007 study by Wood, Lambert and Jewkes, many young girls relate their fear of forced sex in their relationships. Here, Nu talks of love entwined with fear. She relates force and coercion to established relationships and goes on to talk of implicit threats. Nomsa suggests that boys use girls, contaminating the space of love with callous sexuality and toxic masculine conduct. Rejecting the violence of boys, Nomsa expresses her anger at the masculine conduct invested in sex, not love. The masculinity under discussion here instils fear and is coercive and condemned. It is also important, however, to take account of the local context of love, force and rape, as Wood *et al*. (2007) do. Locating sexual coercion within a wider context of propositioning, they argue that forcing was scripted and expected by both boys and girls. It was thus specific to the cultural context. This however does not negate the fear that girls experience, as Nu and Nomsa relate above.

Many young South African girls in township contexts face not only the fear of forced sex but experience sexual violence as a recurring feature of their relationships (Wood *et al*. 2008). In the Inanda High study, girls experience sexual coercion:

> Nobuhle: ... we argue about something and he told me that he's going to hit me. We were in the road, in a stop. When he hit me, he clout me, that's why I don't date boys who hit girls because I, I don't like those kind of boys so then I dumped him. I got another boyfriend and I, I said to him, if you love me you will wait for me and you will not pressure me to have sex with you because I'm not ready ... Whenever, whenever I said no he will, he'll, he will sulk.

Researcher: He will sulk? And what did you do about him sulking?
Nobuhle: I didn't care, I just told him, if you love me you won't pressure me to do certain things and if you will be patient with me, maybe next time I will, if you show me that you love me by being patient.

Love is not separate from sexual coercion and the pain of violence. The important point here is that intimate partner relationships in some settings are based on gender inequity and gender violence. This is related to increased risk of contracting HIV for young women, particularly in townships. Young women are vulnerable to sexual coercion in relationships, and the girls know this. However, the tragedy of this situation is that whilst girls abhor this conduct and express their criticism of it, research illustrates that girls largely acquiesce to this conduct, particularly in developing contexts (Jewkes 2010).

Young women do show agency despite their vulnerability. Girls are not simply victims of male sexual power, and even within constraints, Nobuhle is able to assert her agency, saying that she is 'not ready' for sex. Resistance against male power is also evident in how Nobuhle talked about boyfriends. Rejecting the violence of boys and resisting sexual pressure, Nobuhle expresses her contempt for boys who hit girls, and situates love within violence and sexual coercion.

The local framing of sex is relevant here. Nobuhle states that patience is proof of love, 'showing patience is showing love'. This meaning of love sits in tension with Vance's (1984) conceptualization of sexuality as desire. Here, patience and waiting to be ready to have sex are quite the opposite of desire. Being persuaded to have sex, as Wood *et al.* (2007) show, is often understood as positive talk and expressive of love. Persuasive practices as well as practices of patience and waiting to have sex are thus local examples of how love is understood. Nomsa, though, is clear that she doesn't want sex and is not ready for such a 'big commitment'. She understands too that boys can 'force sex' but she says 'I will tell him that I'm not ready':

> Nomsa: … I don't want sex. I don't want to sleep with him cos I'm not ready for such a big commitment, and if he would tell me to sex, I will not agree with him … cos I'm not ready for such a big commitment and I will say, if he force, if he force me to do sex, I will tell him that I'm not ready.

Nomsa's determination not to have sex stands in contrast to the limits of girls' choices and agency. Given the overwhelming constraints around gender power and impoverished girls within patriarchal contexts, it may be hard for Nomsa to realize and exercise her choice. Nonetheless, Nomsa resists male power and asserts her sexual rights. Instead of acquiescing and fearing, her exercise of agency is upheld.

Girls are highly aware of their vulnerability to the risk of sexual violence. Importantly, the chapter shows how girls are sensitive and alert to early signals and coded messages from boys which could lead to abusive situations. This chapter shows how, in fearing boys and boyfriends, girls derive their understandings of their vulnerability to sexual violence from material, symbolic and discursive forces which effectively limit their opportunities and freedoms, thus diminishing their agency. More broadly, this calls into question the social conditions which allow sexual and gender violence to flourish in South Africa (see Posel 2005). Invocations of violence in the masculine construction of sexuality, as Hearn (2009) notes, are overwhelmingly negative in form and content. Applied to the study of African girls, sexual violence remains a pervasive form of domination and inequality but it is not situated outside of desire, attraction and love.

Conclusion

In this chapter I have argued that African girls in Inanda, Durban, invoke sexuality in ways that tie together love, money, fear and violence. Located on the edges of poverty, the girls aspire towards middle-class futures, connecting love and money and upholding provider love. There is a growing perception among girls that love is associated with a stylized masculinity, branded clothes, and middle-class leisure activities, such as visiting shopping malls and restaurants.

The girls reject *inyoni* masculinity, and their claims to love relate to changing gender ideologies through which they are able to imagine and realize a different life from the drudgery of township living and poverty. They do so with passion and desire, excited by love and the prospects of love. In articulating their claims, the girls derive their understandings of sexuality from the surrounding social and economic context. Sexuality is thus experienced through material structures of power but also through affect. All over the world, young people talk about the importance of affective relationships (see Allen 2005). Significantly, the specificities of young people's love have important manifestations in the ways in which gender ideologies and structural inequalities are challenged and reproduced. In the context of Inanda, Durban, they take on different coordinates and have different effects.

Men's inabilities to forge hegemonic masculinity in ways that uphold provider masculinity have led to some young women seeking relationships with multiple partners, where material support is evidence of emotional commitment (Hunter 2010). Whilst the girls in this study are just sixteen turning seventeen, their vulnerability in idealizing men with money has grave implications for the spread of AIDS. Girls' ideologies of love in relation to their gendered and material conditions uphold a version of masculinity which provides access to resources and power. At the same time, girls' vulnerability to multiple partnerships and AIDS is increased as gender asymmetries are reproduced. As Hirsch and Wardlow (2007) and Thomas (2009) note, love is an ideology which ties people into power imbalances. For African girls in Inanda, such ties in the context of their overwhelming vulnerability to AIDS could be deadly.

The narrative of fear underpinned by sexual violence within relationships provides rich testimony to the wider social tensions in South Africa, through which girls' claims to love are constricted. Sexual violence and rape are deeply connected to gender insubordination and cultural/local meanings that uphold masculine power and violence. Describing boys and boyfriends, the girls show the grip of sexual violence, rape and fear which lock them into familiar roles, reducing the expansive freedoms and agency offered by South Africa's celebrated democracy. Arguing against the positioning of African girls as pathetic victims, this chapter centralizes their concerns – about rape, violence and the fear of boys. Statistically, they should be afraid, and their fear has been vocalized here as they search for whatever resources they can find to block, fight and resist the status of victims.

Nobuhle and Nomsa reject being undermined by sulking boyfriends if they refuse sex and assert their power as they attempt to define the conditions and timing of sex. The opportunities to develop and exercise their agency, however, are restricted by the tragedy of their social circumstances which offer very little resources and protection against sexual violence. Jewkes and Morrell (2010) note that South African masculinity demands that men exercise power over women and this expectation provides fertile ground for men to use violence against women, both to achieve power and to show power. In relation to sex, male violence and risky sexual practices have effects for women and girls. The level of powerlessness that girls experience in relation to men and boys is of huge concern, particularly in the context of HIV and gendered vulnerabilities to AIDS. Indeed, research has shown how the link between masculine violence, risky sexualities, and intimate partner violence increases the risk of disease for young women.

What can girls do in these contexts? We need to understand the combination of gender inequalities, social and economic depression, violence, HIV, rape and cultural norms in order to understand what it will take to intervene effectively in enhancing girls' ability to navigate the social worlds constricting their lives. This will mean addressing all forms of structural violence. It will also mean ensuring that social and economic inequalities are addressed, preventing vulnerabilities around love and money. This might appear to be an overwhelming task, but the South African government has begun the shift in creating more jobs, providing housing and basic essentials within a democracy that supports gender equality. These interventions at the structural level are necessary and ongoing.

There is also a need to address gender norms and constructions of masculinities (Jewkes *et al.* 2010b). Investing in education and working with young people to enhance gender-equitable relationships remains an ongoing possibility. Barker *et al.* (2010) raise the possibility of gender-transformative interventions through which men work towards radically changing gender relations, and address themselves within such relations. Such interventions must necessarily reflect on how HIV is enmeshed within gender relations and how vulnerabilities are created and reduced.

All of this requires giving attention to the actual lives and identities of young girls, as this chapter has done, creating spaces for them to talk freely about love, life and danger. Young people in the most precarious townships have few opportunities to engage in discussions around love and gender. It is time that intervention programmes began to take love seriously, as young people themselves do. Working with teachers and peers might be one way in which interventions begin to address gender norms and notions of love which reduce choice and create vulnerabilities. In particular the assertions of Nobuhle and Nomsa that they will state that they are not ready for sex – articulating the narrative 'showing patience is showing love' – are examples of girls' agency.

Both teachers and peers could work to enhance such expressions of girls' agency. Against the familiar representation of a pitiful African female sexuality, the girls offer a lens through which alternate narratives of sexuality can be created. Teachers could draw upon love and patience and tie this to sexual well-being and reduced vulnerability. Delaying sex is certainly a key area of intervention to prevent sexual disease. However, as mentioned earlier, it is important to locate such narratives within the cultural context in which sex is negotiated. Wood *et al.* (2007) argue that sexual practices, including propositioning, are part of cultural notions of love and sex. Boys are expected to proposition and girls are expected to resist. 'Showing patience is showing love' should also be situated within these practices, which teachers should aim to do while deploying the narrative in ways that serve girls' safety. Working to address ideologies of love within gendered social environments requires continuous efforts. Any prevention and intervention programme aimed at changing behaviour must be designed with careful attention to the specific realities of girls and the pivotal ways in which love works.

Acknowledgements

This material is based upon work supported financially by South Africa's National Research Foundation. Any opinions, findings and conclusions or recommendations expressed in this material are those of the author and therefore the NRF does not accept any liability in regard thereto.

Notes

1 The names of all respondents have been changed to protect their identities.
2 Under apartheid, the population of South Africa was divided into 'African' (black people), white, 'Indian' (with family origins in the Indian subcontinent) and 'coloured' ('mixed' race, mainly between black and white). While there is no longer racial classification, the use of these categories has continued because of the ways in which they mark the South African landscape, particularly as race and class are intimately connected and make significant differences to people's life chances and lived experiences.

References

Allen, L. (2005) *Sexual Subjects: Young People, Sexuality and Education*, Palgrave Macmillan, Basingstoke.

Arnfred, S. (2004) *Re-thinking Sexualities in Africa*, Almqvist and Wiksell, Uppsala.

Barker, G., M. Ricardo, A. Nascimento, A. Olukoya and C. Santos (2010) 'Questioning Gender Norms with Men to Improve Health Outcomes: Evidence of Impact', *Global Public Health*, Vol. 5, No. 5, pp. 539–53.

Bourgois, P. (2004) 'The Everyday Violence of Gang Rape', in N. Scheper-Hughes and P. Bourgois (eds.), *Violence in War and Peace*, Blackwell, Oxford.

Cole, J. and L. M. Thomas (2009) *Love in Africa*, University of Chicago Press, Chicago.

Dunkle, K. L., R. Jewkes, M. Nduna, N. Jama, J. Levin, Y. Sikweyiya and M. Kosse (2007) 'Transactional Sex with Casual and Main Partners among Young South African Men in the Rural Eastern Cape: Prevalence, Predictors, and Associations with Gender-based Violence', *Social Science and Medicine*, No. 65, pp. 1,235–48.

Greig, A., D. Peacock, R. Jewkes and S. Msimang (2008) 'Gender and AIDS: Time to Act', *AIDS*, Vol. 22, No. 2, pp. 35–43.

Hearn, J. (2009) 'Patriarchies, Transpatriarchies and Intersectionalities', in E. Oleksy (ed.), *Intimate Citizenships: Gender, Sexualities, Politics*, Routledge, London.

Hirsch, J. and H. Wardlow (2007) *Modern Loves: The Anthropology of Courtship and Companionate Marriage,* University of Michigan Press, Ann Arbor.

Human Science Research Council (HSRC) (2005) *South African National HIV Prevalence, HIV Incidence, Behaviour and Communication Survey, 2005*, HSRC Press, Cape Town.

—— (2009) *South African National HIV Prevalence, HIV Incidence, Behaviour and Communication Survey, 2008: A Turning Tide among Teenagers?*, HSRC Press, Cape Town.

Hunter, M. (2002) 'The Materiality of Everyday Sex: Thinking Beyond Prostitution', *African Studies*, Vol. 61, No. 1, pp. 100–20.

—— (2007) 'The Changing Political Economy of Sex in South Africa: The Significance of Unemployment and Inequalities to the Scale of the AIDS Pandemic', *Social Science and Medicine,* Vol. 64, No. 3, pp. 689–700.

—— (2010) *Love in the Time of AIDS: Inequality, Gender and Rights in South Africa,* University of KwaZulu-Natal Press, Pietermaritzburg.

Jewkes, R. (2010) 'Gender Inequities Must be Addressed in HIV Prevention', *Science*, No. 329, pp. 145–7.

Jewkes, R. and R. Morrell (2010) 'Gender and Sexuality: Emerging Perspectives from the Heterosexual Epidemic in South Africa and Implications for HIV Risk and Prevention', *Journal of the International AIDS Society*, Vol. 13, No. 6, pp. 1–11.

Jewkes, R., J. Levin, N. Mbananga and D. Bradshaw (2002) 'Rape of Girls in South Africa', *Lancet*, No. 359, pp. 319–20.

Jewkes, R., L. Penn-Kekana and H. Rose-Junius (2005) '"If They Rape Me, I Can't Blame Them": Reflections on Gender in the Social Context of Child Rape in South Africa and Namibia', *Social Science and Medicine*, No. 61, pp. 1,809–20.

Jewkes, R., K. Dunkle, M. Nduna and N. Shai (2010a) 'Intimate Partner Violence, Relationship Power Inequity, and Incidence of HIV Infection in Young Women in South Africa: A Cohort Study', *Lancet*, No. 376, pp. 41–8.

Jewkes, R., K. Wood and N. Duvvury (2010b) '"I Woke Up After I Joined Stepping Stones": Meanings of an HIV Behavioural Intervention in Rural South African Young People's Lives', *Health Education Research*, Vol. 25, No. 6, pp. 1,074–84.

Masvawure, T. (2010) '"I Just Need to Be Flashy on Campus": Female Students and Transactional Sex at a University in Zimbabwe', *Culture, Health and Sexuality*, Vol. 12, No. 8, pp. 857–71.

McFadden, P. (2003) 'Sexual Pleasure as Feminist Choice', *Feminist Africa*, Vol. 2, pp. 50–60.

Moffett, H. (2006) 'These Women, They Force us to Rape Them: Rape as Narrative of Social Control in Post-Apartheid South Africa', *Journal of Southern African Studies*, Vol. 32, No. 1, pp. 131–44.

Pereira, C. (2003) '"Where Angels Fear to Tread?" Some Thoughts on Patricia McFadden's "Sexual Pleasure as Feminist Choice"', *Feminist Africa*, Vol. 2, pp. 61–5.

Posel, D. (2005) 'The Scandal of Manhood: "Baby Rape" and the Politicization of Sexual Violence in Post-Apartheid South Africa', *Culture, Health and Sexuality*, Vol. 7, No. 3, pp. 239–52.

Reddy, V. (2004) 'Sexuality in Africa: Some Trends, Transgressions and Tirades', *Agenda*, Vol. 62, pp. 3–11.

Salo, E. (2002) 'Condoms Are for Spares, Not the Besties: Negotiating Adolescent Sexuality in Post-Apartheid Manenberg', *Society in Transition*, Vol. 33, No. 3, pp. 403–19.

—— (2003) 'Negotiating Gender and Personhood in the New South Africa', *Cultural Studies*, Vol. 6, No. 3, pp. 345–65.

Skeggs, B. (2004) *Class, Self, Culture*, Routledge, London.

South African Police Services (2010) 'Crime Statistics 2010', www.saps.gov.za/statistics/reports/crimestats/2010/crime_stats.htm (accessed 25 July 2011).

Susser, I. (2009) *AIDS, Sex and Culture. Global Politics and Survival in Southern Africa*, Wiley-Blackwell, Malden, MA.

Talbot, K. and M. Quayle (2010) 'The Perils of Being a Nice Guy: Contextual Variation in Five Young Women's Constructions of Acceptable Hegemonic and Alternative Masculinities', *Men and Masculinities*, Vol. 13, No. 2, pp. 255–78.

Thomas, L. (2009) 'Love, Sex and the Modern Girl in 1930s Southern Africa', in J. Cole and L. Thomas (eds.), *Love in Africa*, University of Chicago Press, Chicago.

Thomas, L. and J. Cole (2009) 'Thinking through Love in Africa', in J. Cole and L. Thomas (eds.), *Love in Africa*, University of Chicago Press, Chicago.

UNAIDS Joint Action for Results (2010) http://data.unaids.org/pub/Report/2010/jc1713_joint_action_en.pdf (accessed 10 December 2010).

Vance, C. (1984) *Pleasure and Danger: Exploring Female Sexuality*, Routledge and Kegan Paul, London.

Wand, H. and G. Ramjee (2010) 'Targeting the Hotspots: Investigating Spatial and Demographic Variations in HIV Infection in Small Communities in South Africa', *Journal of the International AIDS Society*, Vol. 13, pp. 41–50.

Wood, K., F. Maforah and R. Jewkes (1998) '"He Forced Me to Love Him": Putting Violence on Adolescent Sexual Health Agendas', *Social Science and Medicine*, Vol. 47, No. 2, pp. 233–42.

Wood, K., H. Lambert and R. Jewkes (2007) '"Showing Roughness in a Beautiful Way": Talk about Love, Coercion, and Rape in South African Youth Sexual Culture', *Medical Anthropology Quarterly*, Vol. 21, No. 3, pp. 277–300.

—— (2008) '"Injuries are Beyond Love": Physical Violence in Young South Africans' Sexual Relationships', *Medical Anthropology*, Vol. 27, pp. 143–69.

PART II
Body Politics and Sexualities

4

Reporting Anita

Nudity in Nigerian Newspapers

Charmaine Pereira and Bibi Bakare-Yusuf

In August 2006, the publication in the print media of nude pictures of a well-known Nigerian actress, Anita Hogan, marked a moment of shock and transgression. A decade earlier, such an event would have been inconceivable. The publication of the photographs was not only illegal but transgressed normative social prescriptions of what constitutes legitimate exposure of the female body in the public arena, in this instance the media. Newspaper versions of this sex scandal did not conform to the actress's own narrative, as it unfolded in successive editions of the story. It is this scenario that forms the focus of this chapter.

Newspapers and other textual materials, as Moran (2000) points out, have provided a rich source of evidence for the analysis of gender and sexuality in contemporary Africa. The scapegoating of urban women in African newspapers as 'sexually uncontrolled, spiritually dangerous and, most importantly, unpatriotic parasites' (Moran 2000: 114) has been emphasized in a number of earlier studies. Tseayo (1996: 53) points to an invidious tendency to 'use the image of women as schemers and manipulators of "innocent" men for material gains'. Research by Bastian (1993, cited in Moran 2000) on the popular press in Nigeria addresses the ambivalence surrounding modernity and urban life in an account of its representation in highly gendered narratives about the bodies of women and men.

Underlying the derogatory representations of women in

much of the media is a conflicted orientation towards women's sexuality. At one level, women are present in newspapers when their sexuality is the prime purpose of their inclusion, as is the case for 'Page Three' girls. In the 1990s, a number of newspapers (*Punch*, *Sunday Tribune* and *Vanguard)* ran pages featuring photos of 'radiant and beautiful ladies to brighten your day or weekend, as the case may be' (Ibie Owens 1992: 50). At the other end of the spectrum, there are the 'women's pages' which include all manner of items concerning women. 'Modern treatment lumps together news on women doctors, discriminatory laws, recipes for *Gbegiri* and *Ogbono* soups, the length of skirts and the latest make-up tricks' (Tseayo 1996: 56–7). To the extent that it is represented on the women's pages, women's sexuality is generally more sanitized there than it is on page three.

Some insight into the gendered and sexualized dynamics of journalistic practice may be gleaned from an early study by Schuster (1979, cited in Moran 2000). Schuster highlights the situation in which many male journalists find themselves competing professionally and personally with similarly educated women. In a number of instances, some of the women seem to have an advantage in gaining access to jobs and the patronage of powerful men by deploying their sexuality. Whilst desirable to their male colleagues, many of these women are not interested in romantic relationships with relatively poor journalists. In Schuster's view, the hostile newspaper campaigns against urban women – particularly educated, modern women – found in so many African countries stem from the ambivalence felt towards such women by male journalists (Moran 2000).

The conflicted orientation towards women's sexuality evident in newspapers is a particular manifestation of a more general dynamic operating in social life. Contemporary expressions of this in Nigeria include the furore in different quarters over 'indecent dressing' and the corresponding emphasis put on policing women's bodies and sexualities through the imposition of dress codes and a proposed Bill on Public Nudity, Sexual Intimidation and Other Related Offences (see Alliances for Africa

2008, Bakare-Yusuf 2009). In Lagos, the police virtually took the law into their own hands by arresting several young women for 'indecent dressing'. Although the state government acted by reprimanding the police, it avoided the opportunity afforded by the incident to discuss issues of bodily exposure and its possible limits (Oloruntoba-Oju 2007).

Some sections of the media carry out their own policing, for example the Sunday 'Oops and Kudos' column of *The Nation* newspaper. This column highlights different ways of dressing, which are referred to using the terms 'oops' or 'kudos', depending on the perceived degree of indecency or decency respectively. Oloruntoba-Oju (2007) notes, however, that this practice is sometimes understood in terms contrary to those intended. The author gives the example of a reader whose letter to the editor stated, 'If your aim is to encourage decent dressing, I advise you only show decently dressed women in your fashion page' (*The Nation*, 30 September 2007: 12).

Several theorists point out that the media not only construct, reflect and provide changing definitions about the world, including representations of women and social values; they also interpret and reinterpret these constructions from a variety of perspectives (Van Zoonen 1991; Hall 1980, 1997). The importance of media texts thus lies in the way they become sites of struggle over what constitutes normativity, including the social meanings attached to women, gender, sexuality and power. Jill Johannessen (2002: 264) has suggested that as a conduit for change, the media 'can challenge dominant discourse by providing [...] alternative representations of women, new gender ideas and identities, values and ways of living that crosscut earlier traditions and beliefs'.

At the same time, the media can and do 'reinforce traditional definitions and cultural patterns and thereby legitimate, justify and preserve dominant ideologies of gender' (Johannessen 2002: 264). Ayesha Imam (1991) showed how the media play a substantial role in contributing to the acceptance of the status quo. Her analysis of three radio programmes broadcast in Hausa by the Federal Radio Corporation of Nigeria showed that all three programmes put forward predominantly negative images of women, involving themes that condoned the control and subordination of women.

Although the media send out powerful messages about acceptable configurations of gender, sexuality, modes of behaviour and lifestyle, these are always mediated and reinterpreted through a set of diverse responses within a discursively pluralized community. As Van Zoonen notes, the reality produced by the media is always one of negotiation between 'media-institutions, texts and audiences' (1991: 43). No matter how powerful media messages are, they can never completely determine or influence audience response in advance of their dissemination.

This is because the interpretative responses to media texts are always 'polysemic', that is, multiple and overlapping (Fiske 1987), providing contradictory and contested notions of femininity, masculinity and reality (Van Zoonen 1991, 1995). The relationship between the media and the media consumer is therefore one of an engaged struggle over meaning, which ensures that neither one exercises more power over the other. This is not to say that there is no clear or preferred reading of reality that is advanced by media producers, because there is always a privileging of a particular perspective that is being pushed over others. Rather, the polysemic nature of the media disrupts any notion of a stable, coherent audience or unitary interpretation of any media text, as we saw earlier in the reader's interpretation of *The Nation*'s 'Oops and Kudos' column. The media therefore constitutes a vital space for cultural debate that is integral to the enactment of public culture.

In this chapter, we draw on textual analyses of Anita Hogan's story as it was represented in newspapers at the time, in order to outline the contours of the narrative produced by Anita about her experiences as well as how Anita was represented by actors in the media. Our analysis of these processes is intended to provide a basis for opening up the space for further exploration and debate around issues of sexuality, power and gender in the politics of representation. The gender and sexual politics of representational contestation is explored, with a view to understanding the terrain and scope of possibilities for women's empowerment.

Anita's story

This section traces the unfolding of the story sequentially from Anita Hogan's point of view. In attempting to outline Anita's story, it is not our contention that there is a singular, linear or rational account that either has been or should be produced. Instead, there seem to be many narratives overlaid against one another. Tensions and inconsistencies among them are neither an indication that Hogan is 'not telling the truth' nor a sign that anything goes. Our analysis proceeds on the basis that the particular configuration of the consistency and inconsistency of narrative threads may be interpreted as conveying the dynamics of conflicted understandings and relations of gender, of sexuality and of power.

On 11 August 2006, the same day that Hogan's nude photos appeared in *P.M. News*, she also had an interview printed in the same publication (Olasebikan and Adetu, *P.M. News,* 11 August 2006: 1–2). Questions about her acting career, interest in music and so on preceded the interviewer asking Hogan if she agreed that a person (read 'woman') could become 'an instant sex symbol' if they posed nude. Anita replied:

> I don't believe you because ... I read a lot of magazines from abroad. Even if the person is not fine [that is, good-looking] ... they will use computer graphics to bring out a particular perception because that's nice for you ... the computer will help you fix it and your boobs will be 20 inches big. (*P.M. News*, 11 August 2006: 2)

Although Anita first responded by appearing to disagree, she subsequently went on to stress the role of computer graphics in changing and improving a 'person's' bodily appearance. By referring to the possibility of media images being manipulated, Anita is also questioning what it means to be 'nude'. When the interviewer asks, 'So you won't pose nude for any amount?'

Hogan affirms, 'I won't pose nude for any amount' (*P.M. News*, 11 August 2006: 2). It is towards the end of the interview in response to a question about her age that Hogan says, 'I am sure you guys are aware of some pictures of myself going around.' The interviewers say they are not aware of this, and Anita responds as follows:

> I know you guys are lying. Well, some people got some funny pictures of me in nudity and they wanted to get money from me. I said sorry, I don't have anything to offer, you know. So, maybe they did it to know the extent of the truthfulness of the pictures. Maybe if I had yielded, then an iota of truth would be in it. But I said look, there's no truth in whatever they are saying. So, when they saw that I did not yield, they started spreading the pictures round media houses. (*P.M. News*, 11 August 2006: 2)

When asked what the pictures look like, Anita states, 'They look like me (laughs). They look like me in a very incriminating manner' (*P.M. News*, 11 August 2006: 2).

Hogan is sure that the reporters have already seen the photos and, at the same time, seems keen to give her explanation of how they came to be circulating in the public. She does this even before being questioned about the photos. This suggests that Hogan is hoping to set the agenda in terms of 'what actually happened'. We may identify a number of elements here of the narrative that Hogan attempts to construct: there are incriminating photos (ostensibly of her) circulating in the public; the photos look like her; the photos are not 'truthful' – perhaps not what they appear to be; she does not know the source; and she would not pose nude for any amount of money. Having earlier alluded to the manipulation of media images, it is possible for Hogan to state both that the photos look like her *and* that they are not truthful.

Eight days later, in an interview with the *Saturday Sun* (19 August 2006: 28), the narrative had shifted. When the interviewer asks Hogan if the nude photos in the newspaper were 'really yours, because I read the story where you said they could not be yours', she answers, 'Yes, they are mine.' The interviewer wanted to know how the photos got to the public; Hogan stated that she did not know. Some of the photos featured a white man, and Hogan was asked who he was. She responded as follows:

> He is my fiancé. We were just having fun and toying with the camera. He snapped me and I snapped him. The photographs were downloaded onto my laptop. The laptop crashed and was taken for repairs. I think that's how the pictures got into the wrong hand [sic]. And they have been used to blackmail me. (*Saturday Sun*, 19 August 2006: 29)

What is significant about this extract is that it is the only instance we have found where Hogan alludes to the context in which the photos were produced. This context is a private space, in which the photos are said to be the result of playful interaction between Anita and her lover. Hogan reacts angrily to the interviewer's suggestion that she had 'posed nude for the whiteman [sic] for money'. She cuts in: 'How can I descend so low? I can never pose nude for all the money in this world' (*Saturday Sun*, 19 August 2006: 29).

At this stage, the previously questioned status of the identity of the woman in the photos appeared to be resolved, given Hogan's agreement that the photographs were 'really' of her. Although the issue of how the photos reached the public is not clear, we have some clue as to how this could have happened in terms of the intervention of a third party at the time the computer crashed. Regarding why the photos were taken in the first place, Hogan is clear that it was *not* done for money, and that to do so would be to stoop too low. 'Posing nude' seems to be understood as 'posing for money', a position that she rejects.

The day before this interview appeared, an article in *P.M. News* stated that Anita Hogan had 'finally admitted through her lawyer that the pictures were hers' (*P.M. News*, 18 August 2006: 1). In a petition written by Hogan's lawyer, Tony Dania of Dania and Associates, to the Deputy Commissioner of Police in Lagos, Dania confirmed that the nude pictures in circulation were Anita's private pictures with her fiancé. The article quotes

Dania as saying, 'Our client (Anita) actually had her pictures in the system. Shortly after the computers were repaired and returned, one Emeka Nwankwo returned and informed our client that he has some pornographic pictures of our client and a white man' (*P.M. News*, 18 August 2006: 6). The article further stated that *P.M. News* had carried out its own investigations which showed that three suspects had been arrested by the police in connection with the photos, which had been removed from Anita Hogan's computer and sent to a number of media houses.

About a week later, in an article in the *Daily Sun* (25 August 2006: 4), Anita Hogan stated that her lawyers were taking the case to court. The article goes on to say that Hogan had alleged that her private photos, stored in her computer, were stolen, manipulated and published after she refused to pay the two million naira sum demanded by Emeka Nwankwo, the leader of the group involved in the attempted extortion. According to Hogan, the group's target was 'the white man'.

> They could not locate the white man, so they turned to me and desperately tried to extort money from me. I was unyielding, so they falsely attacked and debased the collective morality of the Nigerian female stars, particularly actresses, by obnoxiously publishing the obscene pictures. (*Daily Sun*, 25 August 2006: 4)

The assumption that a white person has plenty of foreign exchange, and is therefore wealthy, is widespread; this informs the targeting of a white person for extortion efforts. In the absence of her fiancé, Hogan becomes the target. Extortion, along with attempted extortion, highlights the process by which women's bodies become commodified. Payment enables the exposed body to remain private; not paying results in exposure. These are the two extremes of what might transpire; what actually happens may be far less clear. Hogan condemns the actions of the gang, highlighting their exploitation of her vulnerability to extortion as a collective assault on 'Nigerian female stars, particularly actresses' (*Daily Sun*, 25 August 2006: 4).

Hogan expands further on the character of this collective assault:

> It was a callous and unwarranted sadistic affront on Nigerian womanhood. It was a most wicked falsehood. It was, for whatever reason(s), calculated to negatively stigmatize my person and portray me to be a prostitute who commercializes her body and poses nude for white men. The publications were outrageously irresponsible, immoral, unfounded, libellous and malicious. It was an unnecessary invasion of my privacy, done with such careless impunity. I did not pose nude for any person or any photographer. I have never been known or reported or even suspected to have been involved in any scandalous immorality. (*Daily Sun*, 25 August 2006: 4)

Once again, the commodification of women's naked bodies is emphasized and condemned. Hogan alludes to the many-faceted character of such commodification. One aspect is the assumption that the photos could only have been produced by her 'posing for white men', and that for one reason only, namely money. Hence the fact that the photos were now in the public domain 'must mean that Anita was a prostitute' who sells her body. Yet it is not she who is at fault here, says Hogan, but the media publications that accepted the photos in the first place, thereby becoming directly responsible for creating an impression of Hogan as 'involved in scandalous immorality'. This could only come about as the result of the breaching of boundaries between public and private, namely, by invading her privacy. What is not mentioned here is that the circulation of images deemed pornographic is against the law in Nigeria.

In an interview published the following day in the *Saturday Independent* (26 August 2006: C10), Hogan was asked whether the photos were 'actually hers', that is, of her. At this point, Hogan states that the photos have been manipulated.

> AH: The pictures were doctored to suit the purpose of blackmail ... The inconsistency in the pictures alone is even enough to discredit them. Some have flab, some were straight and some were fat ...

> Interviewer: You said the pictures were not yours, but in the petition by your lawyer he said they were yours.
>
> AH: That is what I'm saying, read properly. People just want to read what they want to see. Those pictures were Anita's, but doctored to suit the purpose of blackmail. What else should I say? ... If you look at them, the story says it was in a yacht and are they saying on the yacht I cut my hair, I braided my hair and did dreadlocks on one trip. What I'm saying is that those things were manipulated. (*Saturday Independent*, 26 August 2006: C10)

Here Hogan seems to be arguing that although the pictures were 'Anita's', they are not the original versions. She points out that the fact of 'doctoring' is evident from the lack of consistency in the images as well as the unlikelihood that all the images produced could have come from the single outing from which they were supposed to have emanated.

A day later, *ThisDay* (27 August 2006: 78–80) carried an interview in which the reporter asked Hogan whether she had nude pictures of herself on her computer. Hogan replied, 'No, not at all. The truth of the matter is that I can't remember storing any nude pictures of myself ... I didn't take any nude pictures that I could store in my computer'. Hogan also stated in this interview that the man in the pictures was not her lover. 'That's not the man ... These people had worked for a while on this job before they decided to go to town with it.'

The reporter stresses the inconsistency between Hogan's statement that she did not store nude pictures of herself on her computer and the statement by her lawyer, Tony Dania, on a live FM programme broadcast on 15 August 2006. The lawyer had confirmed that the nude pictures were Anita's, stating that they were her personal copies and that they were stored on her computer. Also highlighted in the *ThisDay* article was, in the reporter's view, the inconsistency between the lawyer's statement and Hogan's statement during a press conference held on 24 August 2006, that she had never posed nude. It is worth noting that this is a position that Hogan has consistently maintained, namely that she had never posed nude for anyone, and this was emphasized in the *Daily Sun* article (25 August 2006) quoted earlier.

On 18 October 2006, Anita Hogan got married to Ted Mark (the white man in the photos) at the Federal Marriage Registry, Ikoyi, Lagos. The event lasted for four hours. Nollywood actors and actresses, comedians and journalists were present (*Daily Sun*, 19 October 2006). When a reporter from the *Saturday Punch*, asked Anita 'how she felt being a bride after the scandal', she pointed out that, unlike the reporter, she had not viewed her life in terms of 'scandal and problems'. Instead, she had gone on with living her life and 'nothing has changed that. I feel wonderful. I feel great. This is the happiest day of my life' (*Saturday Punch*, 21 October 2006: A7). Effectively, Hogan refused to be defined by the scandal. Instead, she seemed to be celebrating marriage as the epitome of womanhood. This is reiterated by her response to the question of what the future held for her. It was, according to Anita, 'going to be bright. I am going to have 10 children and together, we will live happily ever after' (*Saturday Punch*, 21 October 2006: A7). Marriage is not only the proverbial sunset on the horizon that marks the end of troubled times but also the happy ending that marks the successful accomplishment of respectable womanhood.

When asked what Hogan could have found attractive in the 'old-looking expatriate' and whether it was a love for money, Hogan quickly replied, 'My husband is a real man ... He stood by me when many others left. He did what many other men would not have done. That is one of the numerous things I like about him' (*Saturday Punch*, 21 October 2006: A7). Contrary to received expectations, the attraction here was not money but the character of Ted Mark's masculinity. Being a 'real man' in this context meant standing by Anita, in circumstances where images of his prospective wife's naked body were splashed across daily newspapers. The subtext here is that this was something that a white European man might do, and in this case which Ted Mark actually did, but which a Nigerian man would have been most unlikely to do.

Nearly two months later, Hogan was interviewed about 'how she faced the nudity scandal' by the *Daily Sun*. She observed as follows:

> ... a lot of people are confused about my personality. But many people love me and my bravery ... I mean if you ask a lot of girls out there, they will tell you they would have run away ... But it is my country, I have been violated, why should I run away? ... I should stay back in my country and fight for my right [sic] ... By your staying back, you are source of courage to other people that have been violated out there ... They will say you stood to face the adversity, you teach a lot of people out there so many things ... Most importantly, a lot of people are happy about my bravery. My ability to look people in the face, despite the bad picture that has been painted about me, I smile, laugh and still thank God. It only could have happened to someone as special as I am. (*Daily Sun*, 12 December 2006: 26)

Hogan speaks of her bravery in facing the press and not leaving the country (running away). This was a necessary step in order to seek redress, she says, and the process of doing so provides an example to other women who have been violated and encourages them to do likewise. The other side of her bravery is that she has maintained her good spirits and this, according to Hogan, can only have come about because she is 'special'. Hogan ascribes what is 'special' about this scenario to characteristics in her person, rather than to her response to extraordinary circumstances.

The role of God in Hogan's life following the publication of the photos is a dimension she refers to explicitly, saying that she is now much more spiritual. In her view, that is the only choice one has in a society like Nigeria, since there is 'no other person to run to but God. And He has been very wonderful' (*Daily Sun*, 12 December 2006: 26). She poses the question of what else she could ask for 'in a society that is so hypocritical like this?' (*Daily Sun*, 12 December 2006: 26). The hypocrisy of the society is apparent from the stories that circulate about the goings-on, sexual and otherwise, of 'big' people. Their immunity from public outcry is ensured by the fact that their privacy, unlike Anita's, is not violated.

The interviewer asks about the nude pictures. Hogan speaks about several other matters, but not the nude pictures. The interviewer then asks her if she would ever do a nude scene in a movie. Hogan replies:

> AH: No, I won't do it because it's not my style. I have never done it before. This issue that is out there is very complicated, it is not an issue that is clear. It's not my style, I cannot be forced to become what I am not ...
>
> Interviewer: So why take the pictures?
>
> AH: That's why I am saying it's very complicated. I don't wanna talk about it anymore. I have made enough statements about it ... I am saying that the pictures were manipulated ... I am not going to pretend that this chapter of my life did not happen because wherever I am going to go, it would be referred to. That's one's life ... The reason I would never act nude in any movie is because I never act nude in any movie, and I have never for any commercial reason done any nudity. So, I won't start irrespective of whatever [sic]. (*Daily Sun*, 12 December 2006: 26)

Hogan's reason for not taking part in a nude scene in a film is because that is not her way of doing things, it is not something she does generally – 'it's not my style'. Interestingly, Hogan does not give morality – she does not think it is right – as her reason for not going nude in a film. She reiterates the point that she has never done any nude scenes for the purpose of making money. The question of why nude photos of Anita would exist at all, if she would never go nude in a film, is one that is posed because it is assumed that there is little, if no, difference between the two situations. This in itself is interesting because it suggests that the reporter does not think that Hogan might have *private* reasons for taking nude photos, which could be quite different from any reasons Hogan might have for *not* taking nude photos in public. What Anita does not tell us in the narrative she constructs is what that private reason might be and this is not surprising, particularly if the unspoken motive here is sexual pleasure and/or desire. This is both the most central dimension of Anita Hogan's story and the most silenced.

Asked about the court case, Hogan affirmed that she was going ahead with it. 'Yes, obviously I have to go ahead with the court case. I am representing a whole lot of women out there, I am. And if I have been violated, it's only fair that I get justice ... The suit is against every paper that published those pictures' (*Daily Sun*, 12 December 2006: 44). The case was in the High Court and all the media houses who published the story had been served. Hogan speaks of herself as representing other women; this is not representation in an official sense but in an imagined, symbolic sense. The experience of violation requires justice and that was what she sought in the court case.

Ten months later, Hogan was interviewed yet again, this time by the *Saturday Champion* (27 October 2007) about the nude photos. The reporter asks Hogan for her story about the incident. Hogan replies that talking about the incident is like asking for sympathy. 'I don't need anybody to know what the truth was, the most important thing is that God has rewritten the script of my life and the conclusion is very satisfactory to me' (*Saturday Champion*, 27 October 2007: 19). Overcoming the incident had been very difficult, 'particularly when you are alone and you are faced with recounting the story of your life ... If it made me or marred me, I don't know yet, but how I feel about it is also of mixed feelings' (*Saturday Champion*, 27 October 2007: 19). Hogan also noted that she had often been misunderstood. 'Many people have mistaken my strength for feminism because I am quite a strong character' (*Saturday Champion*, 27 October 2007: 30).

Hogan states categorically here that conveying the 'truth' to the public is not her goal. What was important to her was getting over the incident, and since God had emerged as a major player in her life and the script had been rewritten in her favour, this was what mattered most. The meaning of the incident for her life is poignantly alluded to here, in terms of having had to tell her story so many times and weigh up its implications. Not surprisingly, Anita refers to having mixed feelings about this episode, a reference to her efforts to remain positive in the face of unanticipated exposure, vitriolic abuse and rejection.

Anita makes sure she informs us that the fact that she survived the ordeal – her strength – should not, in the last instance, be confused with feminism! This begs the question of popular understandings of feminism and how women's strength might otherwise be constituted.

Reporting Anita

In this section, we analyse Anita Hogan's story as represented in the Nigerian print media. The stories produced by the media focus on Hogan as a transgressive figure, through two interwoven narrative conventions about the representation of the female body. First, Hogan is depicted as a morally marked figure who, by consenting to having nude photographs of herself taken and then made available for public consumption, represents the morally and sexually transgressive figure *par excellence*. Second, the question of why Hogan would allow her nude body to be photographed in the first place is addressed by pitting the increased commodification of African flesh in the global market space against the private expression of Hogan's romantic union with her lover. We examine each narrative convention in turn to show how Anita Hogan's own narrative both departs from and re-inscribes media accounts in their efforts to control the production and interpretation of her images.

Constructing morality, enacting transgression

In her nude photos, we see Anita looking straight into the camera, effectively into the eye of her lover (and the unintended viewers), as though self-consciously aware of being looked at. As she looks at the viewer, she teases the latter to look at her, thus directing the look. John Berger once famously declared that 'men look at women and women watch themselves being looked at. This turns her into an object – an object of vision or a sight' (Berger 1972: 47). Hogan turns this declaration on its head. Instead of a man (or men) being the bearer of the look, Anita Hogan lets the viewer(s) know that she is looking at them looking at her. Thus, she unwittingly disrupts the notion of masculine scopic mastery and turns herself from object of the gaze to a subject who not only directs but actively invites the gaze.

Hogan's controlled pose expresses a field of desire that is repressed by the patriarchal order: a desiring woman who also offers herself to be desired and gazed at, even if not intended for public consumption. Still, Anita's nude images suggest the appearance of erotic agency and sexual enjoyment, in which she presents herself to the voyeuristic gaze of her lover (and the unintended viewers). In so doing, Hogan transgresses the conventional narrative of chastity and care-giver reserved for and expected of women in this context. Her apparent satisfaction at being photographed refuses any conventional association of female sexuality with passivity and reproduction – the very connection that hegemonic media narratives try to secure. It is precisely because Anita's nude images appear to reject the normative scripts of female sexuality aligned with marriage and maternity that her action is seen as so destabilizing.

The disjuncture brought about by the refusal of Anita Hogan's images to be conscripted into the conventional narrative of appropriate femininity creates a space that is potentially empowering for women witnessing the unfolding media narrative. Against the patriarchal nostalgic fiction/fantasy of an originary (perhaps precolonial) culture of chaste women obeying male directives, Hogan's images propose an alternative reality. This is one in which Nigerian women can be, and often are, both subjects of desire and desiring subjects. Just as Eve is the repressed sexually active 'Other' to Mary in Christian discourse (Eve's presence is a form of absence in Mary), so too does the Anita Hogan story disturb the surface of apparent normative calm. This it does by revealing the secret that the sexually desiring woman is often a *precursor* to the mother figure. Desire must always be repressed in order to sustain and privilege the archetype of the virtuous mother.

By making Hogan's nude photos available for public consumption, the media unintentionally opened up the multiple fields of sexual play, outside of conventional 'straight' sexual scripts, that are available to Nigerian women. Hogan's nude images point to a pluralized zone of desire which may include women who derive pleasure as sexual exhibitionists or voyeurs, or who indulge in other forms of sexual fantasies with their partners. In their expansion of the horizon of the female sexual universe, media circulation of Anita's nude photos unwittingly points to the silences and repression around active African female sexuality.

There is an apparent moral dilemma in Anita's public appearance as a woman fully in control of, and even enjoying, the display of her own eroticism. Not only is Anita considered a morally transgressive figure but she dares to 'talk back' to the media in order to construct her own narrative about the event. Hogan thus disrupts normative conventions about female virtue and voice which are expected of *all* African women. Anita's apparent self-possessedness is what the media find so troubling. This dynamic is central to the production of meaning and the 'moral panic' – the state of generalized anxiety and public attention focused on a perceived social emergency – surrounding the media's narration of Anita's nude body.

Anita Hogan's nude figure is presented as an example of the increasing moral laxity of Nigerian women who act as a corrupting influence on the body politic. This media narrative is captured in existing cultural anxieties about female impropriety and cultural pollution, which are generally framed around young women's sartorial expression (Bakare-Yusuf 2009; Pereira and Ibrahim 2010). The discomfort with Hogan's nude image suggests that women's bodies are *over*invested with moral meaning and are expected to be the transmitters and preservers of cultural and ideological archetypes concerning ethnicity, nationhood, religion and propriety (Yuval-Davis and Anthias 1987; Pereira and Ibrahim 2010; Entwistle 2000; Cover 2003).

In the media narrative, women are expected not only to be submissive but also to uphold tradition and transfer cultural values to the next generation. As one writer commented, 'The beauty of the world is in womanhood. Imagine a world without women.

Such a world would be awful, devoid of beauty, attraction, tenderness, procreation and fulfilment. Gradually the world will cease to exist. That shows the central [role] of womanhood in the scheme of things' (Onyekakeyah, *The Guardian*, 12 September 2006: 65). With womanhood constructed in this pristine vein, women's bodies and behaviour become an important site of contestation and socio-cultural policing. Anita Hogan's nude images are therefore an affront to the media machinery that sees itself as cultural and moral arbiter. The editor-in-chief, Bayo Onanuga, of the two papers that broke the story, *The News* and *P.M. News,* argues that the role of media practitioners is 'to wage a war against a dangerous and immoral trend among our ladies [... and] to expose a pervasive and dangerous trend among ladies about which most parents and indeed Nigerians are ignorant' (cited in Alex Orji, *Saturday Independent*, 2 September 2006: D2).

Hogan is presented in media narratives as not only 'derob[ing] herself of her virtue, glory, excellence and honour' (Onyekakeyah, *The Guardian*, 12 September 2006: 65) and bringing shame on herself, but as violating a whole continent which is forever chaste: 'her entire behaviour is indecent and totally against the African culture' (Onyekakeyah, *The Guardian*, 12 September 2006: 65). Underlying such statements is the assumption of an untouched and unblemished African society where the figure of woman-as-mother is supreme. This stands in marked contrast to the polluting influence of Occidental moral degeneracy, hedonism and the derogation of womanhood. For Ajike Asiegbu, the president of the Actors' Guild of Nigeria, Nigerian 'culture and society do not permit that a guy or girl should pose nude no matter how we may want to look at it' (cited in Emeka Enyinnaya's 'Actors and Actresses', *Sunday Sun*, 29 April 2007: 18). Since African culture rejects public nudity, Anita Hogan's decision to have herself photographed nude is seen as an attempt to imitate 'the stars she has read about in California, India, Britain or Nollywood' in order to enjoy 'all the glitz, the contour and all the media attention' that supposedly comes with stardom (Tunji Sodeinde, *The Sun*, 11 September 2006: 30).

Anita Hogan's eroticized body finds itself tangled up in a wider set of social changes where a retreat into the cultural insularity of African exceptionalism has become normative. This is also a world in which particular interpretations of religion and extreme religiosity act as the framing device for understanding social experiences and responding with the 'appropriate' moral judgement and outrage (Pereira 2009). The recourse to Christianity in the media's narration of Anita Hogan's story is evident from the various texts which repeatedly cite the Bible as the sole form of moral adjudication: 'The ancient Hebrew King Solomon said that the price of a virtuous woman is far above rubies (Proverbs 31:10). That is what makes a model woman and not a whore' (Onyekakeyah, *The Guardian*, 12 September 2006: 65). The biblical comparisons serve to highlight expectations of appropriate femininity and female sexuality. Any woman who transgresses the conventional notion of womanhood outlined above is likened to '[a] rotten bone [...] and [...] danger to her children' (Onyekakeyah, *The Guardian*, 12 September 2006: 65). The fact that the somatophobia exhibited by nearly all the commentators is itself foreign to African cultures, prior to the advent of colonialism, remains unacknowledged.

The threat that Hogan poses to the patriarchal order is not that of one individual posed against the order of things in a David versus Goliath style. Rather, Hogan's nude images threaten the entire symbolic field and myth about African femininity, precisely because they speak for, and of, Nigerian women as sexually desiring beings. Media representations of her story therefore deploy patriarchal disciplinary machinery to punish Hogan through recourse to tradition, religion, the nation and the cult of motherhood as a warning to other women who dare to assert, publicly or privately, their autonomous desires. The media frenzy and public outcry in the wake of the pictures are expressions of a web of entrenched patriarchal control over female sexuality and its representations. This is the collective nexus that creates and develops structures, processes and interpretative frameworks which both enable and reproduce masculinist power.

A central function of the media is therefore to produce a representative device that can either 'reveal or distort what is assumed to be true about the category of women' (Butler 1999: 3). The circulation of such distortions and assumptions supports the myth of the desexualized African woman. This is a myth that can be read as a response to another myth – that of the hypersexualized black/African woman which has been in circulation since the European colonial encounter. Yet the very existence of these nude images reveals the fact that there is no uncontested truth or directly accessible reality behind any representation. Rather, each narrative representation about femininity and sexuality must be understood as a construction amid multiple sites of truth claims.

The media-orchestrated moral panic may have partially succeeded in vilifying Anita Hogan and policing active female sexuality. However, it also exposes the masculinist impulse at the core of the media industry which works to control and circumscribe women's sexual agency. The moral panic also reflects a patriarchal anxiety about the possibility of active female sexuality going awry and of male loss of power and control. The ultimate threat posed by media narration of these images therefore has to do with the fear surrounding unbridled female sexuality and agency at a time when more and more women are refusing to be symbolically used as the carriers of cultural traditions.

Commodified sexuality or romantic love?

How to interpret Hogan's nude images became a source of tension and indecision in the media. The press were divided over whether to treat Hogan's images as an example of commodification of female flesh and sexuality available for public consumption or whether they represented a private moment of romantic engagement between two consenting adults: 'Was Anita in love? Did she do it for money?' (Funke Egbemode, *Saturday Independent*, 19 August 2006: back page). This uncertainty produced one of the most interesting and protracted debates in media accounts of her story, especially as it relates to the question of privacy.

For one columnist, Tayo Agunbiade, by publishing her nude pictures *P.M. News* and other papers violated Hogan's right to privacy. He writes, 'people have the freedom to do what they want in their private lives as long as it does not infringe upon the rights of another individual. Anita took those pictures in private. She is entitled to do whatever she pleases with her friends [...]' (*ThisDay*, 15 September 2006: back page). Another writer, Dr Chukwuweta Onuorah, argued, '*P.M. News* violated media laws by publishing the pictures'. He further argued that since the 'distribution of pornographic images is an offence in Nigeria', the very act of publishing the images itself is not only illegal, 'it is [...] unethical to publish a person's nude picture without permission' (*Daily Independent*, 25 September 2006: 24). For both Agunbiade and Onuorah, the issue at stake has less to do with whether Hogan consented to having her nude pictures taken than with the initial theft of the images and their eventual publication. According to Agunbiade, 'the very printing of the photographs was an affront to womanhood and should be denounced as such' (*ThisDay*, 15 September 2006: back page). Onuorah asked that, 'The man who sold this picture to the papers and the papers that published them ought to be punished' (*Daily Independent*, 25 September 2006: 24). These commentators supported Hogan's right to privacy from the roving public eye, whilst admonishing profit-motivated newspapers for providing the means for objectified commodification.

Countering the issue of the publication's illegality and Hogan's right to privacy, another commentator argued that insofar as her image is deemed pornographic and insofar as pornography is against the law, Hogan cannot expect protection of her privacy under the same law which already deemed her action illegal. According to the writer, since 'nudism and pornography are illegal practices' (Onyekakeyah, *The Guardian*, 12 September 2006: 65), a nudist has no legal recourse to protection. The fact that the image was produced for private consumption is beside the point. Onyekakeyah argues that, 'A woman who strips herself naked in picture [sic] has unwittingly published herself free of charge to the public. There is nothing private in pictures that have been seen by more than one person' (Onyekakeyah, *The Guardian*, 12 September 2006: 65). For this reason, there can be 'no question of invasion of one's privacy in nudity' (Onyekakeyah, *The Guardian*, 12 September 2006: 65) since she made herself available for pornographic consumption.

What such an argument does not address is why the illegality of pornography should be so selectively applicable to the actions of Anita Hogan, as opposed to the actions of media houses. Although divided on the merit of publishing Hogan's pictures, most commentators are united in condemning the actress for posing nude in the first place, an act regarded as a debasement of African femininity. Media ambivalence as to how to rationalize the production of the images seeks first to blame and chastise Hogan for the initial act of posing as well as for being insufficiently careful subsequently with the handling of the photographs.

The circulation of Hogan's image is linked to the apparent growing incidence of young women posting still and moving images of their naked bodies on the internet for transactional purposes. Hogan's nude pictures are therefore read as part of this transactional exchange in the context of an increasing interest in the use of black/African nude pictures for pornographic imaginings. This transactionality is facilitated by new technologies which allow for the digitalization of erotic life in order to forge new (commodified) relationships. Access to new forms of technologies such as personal computers, mobile phones and the internet have transformed our understanding and experience of privacy, such that what might have previously remained an intimate moment or private experience becomes easily available for wider public dissemination and consumption. In many instances, the circulation of intimate experience is often made publicly accessible by the subjects of the images themselves.

With the increasing democratization of technology, coupled with the rise in celebrity culture, it is not surprising that there is a corresponding interest and theft in compromising images of celebrities by both media and consumers. All this has created a situation in which our desire to know every aspect of celebrities' lives has fuelled the interest in big news stories that explore sexual intimacy. This has turned the public sphere into what Ken Plummer (1995: 4) has called a 'veritable *erotopian* landscape', a landscape in which private activities such as sex are being acted out and produced as though for public consumption. Media accounts of the scene of Hogan's private moments thus end up generating a complex and contradictory debate about how sex and sexual imagery produced in private places are consumed and reinterpreted in public spheres.

The transactional reductionism surrounding Hogan's images is compounded by the fact that Hogan is an actress. The body of the actress across cultures signifies the commodification of desires and is therefore considered 'fair game' for the spotlight of late modern commodity fetishism. This association of actors and actresses with commodified sexuality is corroborated by Ajike Asiegbu when he states that, 'As far as the Nigerian movie industry is concerned, Anita's action does not speak well for the industry against the backdrop of the perception that actors and actresses are prostitutes and never do wells in the society' (cited in Emeka Enyinnaya, *Sunday Sun*, 29 April 2007: 18). As a desiring machine, to borrow the Deleuzian phrase, the production and consumption of Hogan's images must be understood as an example of the digitalization of intimacy which contemporary technology allows couples to capture. However, by linking the production and consumption of Anita Hogan's images with commodification and degenerate morality, media accounts reject any mutuality and erotic agency in the production of the images and reaffirm the notion that 'actresses are prostitutes [and] are rejected by the society' (Ajike Asiegbu, cited in Emeka Enyinnaya, *Sunday Sun*, 29 April 2007: 18). Precisely because Hogan's sexual agency is threatening to the patriarchal sexual order, as we saw earlier, it is necessary for her to be reduced to flesh for sale, a narrative that draws on strands of transactionality as well as victimhood. The tendency to project commodification on to the Anita Hogan story is part of the failure to view women as sexual agents in their own right: sexuality and sexual pleasure can only be expressed in terms of masculine cohesion and commodification.

The transgressive transactionality of Hogan's action is finally evidenced in the fact that the image is produced for, and with, her white European lover: 'The fact that she posed with a white was enough to condemn her' (Olusegun Adeniyi, *ThisDay*, 26 October 2006: 64). Here, the repressed memory of colonialism rises to the surface in the form of the latent narrative of the white figure of power in Africa who selects his women at will. This repressed memory is maintained by reading and reducing Hogan's relationship with her white European lover to a purely monetary exchange. The question repeatedly asked was: 'What could have attracted this young girl to this old-looking expatriate?' (Nonye Iwuagwu, *Punch*, 21 October 2006: A7). The man's age and race erase any possibility of a romantic union between the two, thus only leaving room for a commodified reading of the relationship. The fact that sexual relationships between young Nigerian women and older Nigerian men are widespread is ignored here. The older white man who engages in sexual relations with a younger Nigerian woman is a convenient exculpatory mechanism for maintaining the fiction of an indigenous masculine piety. Sexual union between a black woman and a white man can only be read as a commodified relationship.

The question of whether Anita Hogan's sexual display for the camera is an act of sexual commodification or an act of romantic union is one that the media expects only to be resolved through marriage. One commentator writes, 'I hereby dare this Oyinbo [foreign] lover boy to come and save Anita and what is remaining of her reputation [...] in addition to that, I won't mind publishing the photographs [of] the traditional wedding[...]' (Funke Egbemode, *Saturday Independent*, 19 August 2006: back page). The eventual marriage to her white male lover allowed the media and patriarchal regimes to resolve the ambivalence and anxiety surrounding the debate over whether Hogan's action entailed commodification or indeed a romantic union. The corrective power accorded to matrimony is the only instrument capable of taming and legitimizing a defiled femininity. Marriage thus allows for the media to return Hogan triumphantly to the system of male control, ownership and protection to which all women must submit. Such a return to the patriarchal sacrament allows for the reaffirmation of women's emotional, socio-economic and sexual dependency on men and accessibility by men. 'Now that her Dutch fiancé has made a wife of her, she would now be in a position to put the unfortunate story behind her even though the scars may remain for life' (Olusegun Adeniyi, *ThisDay*, 26 October 2006: 64).

The status-conferring power of marriage is evidenced in the glee expressed by the President of the Actors' Guild of Nigeria, Ajike Asiegbu: 'we've been able to record a remarkable achievement in the industry this year. For instance this year alone some [of] our girls got married. We have people like Chioma Chukwuka, Monalisa Chinad and so many others. It is not what it used to be in the beginning that our people are not responsible' (cited in Emeka Enyinnaya, *Sunday Sun*, 29 April 2007: 17). Marriage therefore reduces women's (especially actresses') vulnerability and their being perceived as simply flesh for sale.

Despite the marriage, the postcolonial–racial nexus comes into play yet again. The consensus was that while Hogan should be thought of positively for returning to the legitimizing sanctity of marriage, only a white man could have walked her down the aisle. One commentator writes, 'let's face the fact, if Anita's fiancé were to be a Nigerian, we would not be talking of any wedding today' (Olusegun Adeniyi, *ThisDay*, 26 October 2006: 64). The view is that no self-respecting, culturally grounded African man would ever concede to marrying a woman whose sacred body had been so defiled not only by a white man, but by the collective gaze of the media and the public. The transgression therefore remains as a scar within the narrative, in the twofold sense that the eventual marriage is viewed as a form of rescue from sin, *and* that this could only have occurred with a non-Nigerian, white male. The fact that a white man filmed Hogan enables Nigerian commentators to reinstall the notion of the ideal Nigerian man in control of his submissive wife/sexual partner. This ideal man is unlike the white man who cannot control his woman and would even offer her body for public display. Again, the suggestion that a Nigerian man would not marry her, given the circumstances, functions as a warning sign to other Nigerian women who might dare to step outside the boundaries of 'acceptable' forms of sexual agency.

On narratives of sexuality and women's empowerment

This chapter has explored contestations in newspapers between Anita Hogan and journalists, and among journalists, over the meaning of Anita's nude body and her sexuality. Media accounts of Anita's story were predominantly apprehended through discursive constructions of gender roles within heterosexuality – women's active exercise of sexual agency is deemed to be particularly transgressive (far more than men's); women's sexual relations consequently fall either into the (legitimate) realm of 'romantic love' or else, beyond the pale, the realm of sexual commodification; all sexual wrongs by women can therefore only be made right by marriage. Narratives produced by readers and journalists alike often rested on the assumptions inherent in these sexual discourses.

Our interest lies not only in the diverse narratives of sexuality that form the bases for these contestations but also on the implications for women's empowerment. By this, we do not mean to argue that Anita's actions and inaction were in some sense empowering or disempowering. What *is* disempowering for women, however, is the determinism surrounding issues of sexuality – the sense in which the status quo is presented as 'being *meant* to be the way it is'. This determinism applies particularly to the masculinist exercise of power and agency in heterosexual relations, and the conflation of women's sexuality with the potential for immorality in general. It is this dynamic that underlies the telling of particular kinds of stories about women's sexuality – narratives that erase the possibility of women exercising sexual agency outside the boundaries of male control and narratives of the transgressive character of women who present themselves publicly or privately as active, sexually desiring subjects.

By examining, through the case of Anita Hogan, a particular moment in the process of contestation and negotiation over the meaning of women's bodies in the print media, our intention has been to lay bare the workings of patriarchal power relations, in particular narrative constructions of Nigerian women's sexuality and gendered heterosexual relations. The complexity of this terrain necessitates greater understanding in order to pave the way for more open exploration and debate around issues of bodies, sexuality, power and gender in the politics of representation. Debate makes possible the voicing of conflicting perspectives; it is in the spaces within and against the contradictions of gendered power relations in matters of sexuality that we may advance the struggle for women's empowerment.

References

Alliances for Africa (2008) 'Unconstitutional and Indecent: A Legal Opinion on the Indecent Dressing Bill', in collaboration with the Women's Unity Forum and the Open Society Justice Initiative.

Bakare-Yusuf, B. (2009) 'Nudity and Morality: Legislating Women's Bodies and Dress in Nigeria', *East African Journal of Peace and Human Rights*, Vol. 15, No. 1, pp. 53–68.

Berger, J. (1972) *Ways of Seeing*, British Broadcasting Corporation and Penguin Books, London.

Butler, J. (1999) *Gender Trouble: Feminism and the Subversion of Identity*, Routledge, London and New York.

Cover, R. (2003) 'The Naked Subject: Nudity, Context and Sexualisation in Contemporary Culture', *Body and Society*, Vol. 9, No. 3, pp. 53–72.

Entwistle, J. (2000) *The Fashioned Body: Fashion, Dress and Modern Social Theory*, Polity Press, Cambridge.

Fiske, J. (1987) *Television Culture*, Methuen, London.

Hall, S. (1980) 'Encoding/Decoding', in S. Hall, D. Hobson, A. Lowe and P. Willis (eds.), *Culture, Media, Language*, Hutchinson, London.

—— (1997) *Representation: Cultural Representations and Signifying Practices*, Sage, London.

Ibie Owens, N. (1992) 'Media, Cultural Imperialism and Nigerian Women: Whose Culture, Which Imperialism?', *Journal of Social Development in Africa*, Vol. 7, No. 2, pp. 39–52.

Imam, A. (1991) 'Ideology, the Mass Media and Women: A Study from Radio Kaduna, Nigeria', in C. Coles and B. Mack (eds.), *Hausa Women in the Twentieth Century*, University of Wisconsin Press, Madison.

Johannessen, J. (2002) 'Alternative Representations of Women in the News: NGOs as a Source for Gender Transformation', *Nordicom Review*, Nos 1–2, special issue on the 15th Nordic Conference on Media and Communication Research, pp. 263–76.

Moran, M. (2000) 'Uneasy Images: Contested Representations of Gender, Modernity and Nationalism in Pre-war Liberia', in T. Mayer (ed.), *Gender Ironies of Nationalism: Sexing the Nation*, Routledge, London.

Oloruntoba-Oju, T. (2007) 'Body Images, Beauty, Culture and Language in the Nigeria African Context', *Understanding Human Sexuality Seminar Series*, African Regional Sexuality Resource Centre (ARSRC), Lagos.

Pereira, C. (2009) 'Interrogating Norms: Feminists Theorizing Sexuality, Gender and Heterosexuality', *Development*, Vol. 52, No. 1, pp. 18–24.

Pereira, C. and J. Ibrahim (2010) 'On the Bodies of Women: The Common Ground between Islam and Christianity in Nigeria', *Third World Quarterly*, Vol. 31, No. 6, pp. 921–37.

Plummer, K. (1995) *Telling Sexual Stories: Power, Change and Social Worlds*, Routledge, London.

Tseayo, L. (1996) 'Culture, Mass Media and the Image of Women in Nigeria', in B. Odejide (ed.), *Women and the Media in Nigeria*, Women's Research and Documentation Centre (WORDOC), Ibadan.

Van Zoonen, L. (1991) 'Feminist Perspectives on the Media', in J. Curran and M. Gurevitch (eds.), *Mass Media and Society*, Edward Arnold, London.

—— (1995) 'Gender, Representation and the Media', in J. Downing, A. Mohammadi and A. Sreberny-Mohammadi (eds.), *Questioning the Media*, Sage, London.

Yuval-Davis, N. and F. Anthias (1987) *Women-Nation-State*, Macmillan, London.

5

Ageing Women and the Culture of Eternal Youth

Personal and Theoretical Reflections from a Feminist over Sixty in Brazil

Cecilia M. B. Sardenberg

In this chapter, I propose to reflect upon some of the dilemmas faced by women over sixty living in the 'culture of eternal youth' which, nowadays, rules Brazilian society.[1] This might be considered quite an ambiguous theme, one might even say 'suspicious', for a woman like me, in her mid sixties, to undertake. So, you may ask yourselves, and rightly so: would it be feasible for someone no longer young and fresh, nor within the dominant standards of feminine aesthetics, to address the theme at hand without resentments? Could someone whose youth is already long gone provide an objective critique of the culture of youth?

Let me confess from the start that I have asked these questions myself. Like other women of my generation who enjoy a good portion of self-respect, I am also facing the difficult task of getting older – without resentment and with due dignity – in a society where old age and even 'middle age' are treated ruthlessly insofar as women are concerned (Britto da Motta 1995).

This challenge is even greater for us feminists in our sixties and older, given that it involves issues dear to us which extrapolate the personal sphere. We are part of the so-called 'second wave of feminism', that generation of women who broke the chains of patriarchal oppression and went out on to the streets to conquer new spaces for participation in society. We vehemently opposed the ideals of femininity that made women passive objects of consumption, modelled on the dominant standards of feminine aesthetics that have been imposed on women by society for centuries. We chose, instead, to be subjects of our own histories and to claim ownership of our destinies and bodies. And we recognize in the cult of eternal youth that characterizes the present times a disconcerting discourse around ageing that especially questions women.

However, despite our public courage and past struggles, in our own private lives it has not been easy to resist the constant pressures imposed on us to look 'beautiful', to look 'young', to hide the signs of ageing in our bodies as we face, every morning, our own images reflected in the mirror. Indeed, we must resist the marketing appeal of an infinite array of products, services and new body technologies offered to women of all ages to produce ourselves as 'women' within the dominant standards for femininity. On top of this, we must also resist all the products geared towards women of a 'certain age' which vow to help us fight or disguise the unwanted marks of ageing on our bodies and skin, and, magically, bring us back that youthful body that time has taken away from us. Indeed, we are caught between, on the one hand, dominant narratives of ageing that depict it as decline and, on the other, 'positive ageism' discourses, such as those publicized by the cosmetics industry, which thrive on 'a false optimism and cosmetic, youthful activity' that tries to 'deny decline altogether' (Chivers 2003: xv).

Yet, I ask: how can we resist all these appeals to fight ageing when we live in a society that not only makes a cult of young and well-built bodies, but also 'feeds off a culture that is highly narcissist and visually oriented, where the main preoccupation with appearance has become central, especially for women?' (Bordo 1997: 20). And this is particularly so in Brazil, as women over sixty, especially heterosexual women, and those who 'look their age' have little social capital (Bourdieu 1977) in the mating arena. This is true particularly for women of the middle and upper classes, white women especially, although black women are also known to face a similar problem (Pacheco 2008; Berquó 1987). In either case, it is difficult not to make this connection for, as we age and gain wrinkles and weight, the opportunities of finding possible mating partners dwindle considerably. This is a fact I have experienced myself and have seen other women of my age – friends and colleagues, both black and white – experience as well.[2] Only famous older women and those who are well off seem to escape this fate – of being alone – as they age.

Perhaps there lies the reason why I have contributed generously to the cosmetic industry of this country, submitting myself to daily rituals of applying anti-ageing creams and gels. I confess to also relying on body disciplining such as dieting and exercising (without great success, unfortunately), in an attempt to exorcise that strange image that is reflected back to me when I look in the mirror. So there I am, despairing over the unwanted wrinkles, the stains of age, the love handles (we call them 'spare tyres' in Brazil), the dragging skin and the invasive cellulite that the current discourses around ageing have made me discover in my body. I even think about other more drastic rituals that could possibly reverse the effect of time. Plastic surgery? Liposuction? Botox? Are they worth it? How much do they cost? Could I, should I, or not?

I believe that I have resisted such temptations thus far because, as a feminist, I defend the thesis that 'the personal is political'. By this I mean that I firmly believe that the problems, dilemmas and frustrations that I have experienced in relation to my ageing body, the doubts that bring me down, and the rituals that I submit myself to, are not just my personal hang-ups. Not at all. I maintain that these are feelings that overwhelm other women of my age as well, exposed as we all are to the same discourses, which means that all of this has a social basis. Furthermore, I maintain that the individual solutions we seek against the marks of time – plastic surgery, facial creams and so on – are only provisional measures. Running against time, investing in a fight against ageing, is a fight that cannot be won, it is a struggle that will only end with the end – death – itself.

Therefore I propose instead a new discourse – a feminist discourse on the female body in the process of ageing. In what follows I intend to share with you some thoughts I have had recently around the control over the body that the culture of eternal youth imposes on us. Perhaps together we can discuss these issues more in depth and come to the root of the problem, formulating a more effective strategy of collective resistance to fight it. More specifically, in this chapter I propose to look at these issues from a feminist perspective, reflecting upon how gender, age and generation, along with race and class, structure the construction of body and self. Since I am basing my reflections on my own personal experience, I focus here primarily on how narratives of decline and the positive ageism of the cosmetics industry at large speak to ageing white, middle-class women.

A question of gender

First of all I am sure that my problem, or our problem, is first and foremost a question of gender. More precisely it is a problem of gender, age and generation, which affect primarily (but not exclusively) white, middle-class women. With gender, I am referring to the analytical category that tries to take into account the various cultural elaborations that different societies in different eras construct in terms of perceived differences between males and females, from which they then construct their social practice (Scott 1988). To clarify: I am not referring here to the dualistic concept where biology is opposed to culture, that is, in the notion that distinguishes on the one hand 'sex', which is associated with the body and seen as something 'natural', 'universal' and thus ahistorical, and on the other hand 'gender', seen as something psychological, cultural and subjective.

What stands out in this dualistic concept is that sex and gender appear as different phenomena, leading thus to two different forms of identity: on the one hand the sexual and physical, and on the other hand a gender identity, associated with the social roles that we play, with the socially constructed. In this perspective, the body is thus contrasted with the plasticity of the constructed gender identity, while gender is seen as something immaterial, not part of the body, just as discourse or representation.

I recognize that the conceptualization of sex and gender in these terms was a fundamental force in the fight against biological determinism as it enabled us to think of both 'masculine' and 'feminine' and 'man' and 'woman' as socially constructed. This opened up the path to denaturalize both sexual identities in terms of the sexual division of labour and social asymmetries and hierarchies based on sex, showing their historicity and, therefore, the possibility of transforming and transcending inequalities. Beyond the possible theoretical and methodological advances, it also had important political connotations, as an instrument of legitimization for feminist struggles (Scott 1988).

Nevertheless, without denying the theoretical and political relevance of the previous conceptualizations of gender, issues raised by the current deconstructionists are engendering new reflections in terms of the relationship between sex and gender. In particular, 'the perception of the limits of Western scientific thought that isolated the "biological factors" and which based itself on the universal premise of the distinction between the natural and the cultural' (Giffin 1991: 94) has raised the question of whether sex and gender could, in fact, be considered distinct phenomena or capable of being treated separately. Such separation is now regarded as based upon an essentialist notion in which sex – identified as the body – is understood as part of nature, existing outside of history (Bleier 1984; Butler 1990).

In this context, Collier and Yanagisako (1987) observed that the dualistic construction of sex/gender presupposes 'male' and 'female' as 'natural' categories of human beings, whose relationships are universally constructed by their physical difference. For these authors, this cannot be taken as a fact; there needs to be investigation of whether 'this is really the case in the societies we study, and in this case, which specific social and cultural processes make men and women become different from one another' (Collier and Yanagisako 1987: 15). It is a case not of ignoring or denying biological differences but of questioning the notion that the 'trans-cultural variations of gender categories and inequalities are merely a result of elaborations and various extensions of the same natural occurrence' (Collier and Yanagisako 1987: 15).

Following this line of argument, Judith Butler notes that 'if the immovable character of the sex is put into question, maybe this construct known as "sex" will be culturally constructed as gender; maybe sex was always gender and consequently the distinction between sex and gender does not express any difference' (Butler 1990: 6–7). For Butler, therefore, it does not make sense to define gender as a cultural interpretation of sex; the very construct of 'sex' is shaped as a construct of gender. Hence the proposal that gender is to culture as sex is to nature does not fit: such a proposition is already a gender construct.

It is thus a question of deconstructing the dichotomy of sex/gender, as gender embodies this and it is materialized in sex: in the very recognition of the differences between male and female. In this way, we do not have sex (understood as body or the biological) on the one hand and gender (the psychological and the cultural) on the other. We have, instead, gendered bodies. At the same time, gendered identities and subjectivities are not immaterial; they are not separate from their bodies. Just as the body has to be understood not only in terms of anatomy but also as the product of representations, so too identities and subjectivities cannot be understood only as consciousness, separated from the body. We have to speak instead of embodied identities and subjectivities (Rothfield 1995).

I intend to show here that this deconstruction of the dichotomy between sex and gender is fundamental to understanding the difficulties which women face in the process of ageing. I begin by characterizing what is understood by 'gendered bodies'.

Gendered bodies

In order to speak of 'gendered bodies' we need to think of the body not as something naturally given, but as a product of history – as an object that is a product of representations and various social practices related to specific moments in history. Different societies use different codes to fix the boundaries of the body which bind all subjects according to sex, class, race and age/generation and other culturally perceived differences, to specific social positions and relations (Grosz 1994: 141). In this way, historically specific concepts of gender, race, ethnicity, age and other categories differentiate, classify and categorize the bodies, to the point where even the naked body without any adornment or specific cultural inscriptions is never a 'natural' body. On the contrary, this body is always subject to a culturally specific reading and in this way classified according to the existing social boundaries – for example, how journalists describe the body of someone (a 'case') found dead on a highway: 'white male, about 25 years old ...'

In this way, you could say that the body is a surface upon which culture engraves itself (Douglas 1976); in all societies there are always specific ways of engraving the body and/or decorating it, ways that can even mean deformation or mutilation, but which have socially relevant meanings (Rodrigues 1983). Apart from this, different societies also have other procedures of socializing and disciplining the body, be it specific procedures to educate, subjugate, manipulate and control the body, to sharpen it according to the current standards and, in this way, put it in the service of the norms of cultural life (Bordo 1997: 20).[3]

In fact, from a young age we learn in our societies what, how, when, where and with whom to eat, thus sharpening our palate and appetite to the culturally appropriate tastes and timetables. In the same way we are trained to control other physiological necessities, for example, urinating in certain places and, in the case of our society, in certain ways according to sex: men standing up and women sitting down. We are also trained to respond to certain sexual stimulations and not to others, allowing our sexual desires to flow, or not, depending on the person's sex, age, race and heritage, and so on. We are also trained from an early age to discipline the externalization of other emotions and feelings, such as in crying or laughing, according to the context.

This is not to forget the most sophisticated and invasive practices that interfere directly with our physical body, for example reproduction technologies and their products (contraceptives, fertility treatments, hormone treatments and so on), or those which belong to the sphere of production, which discipline and leave their marks on the body according to class, race, sex and occupation (Bolstanski 1989).

All this means that beyond a 'metaphor of culture' the body also becomes a practical place of social control (Bourdieu 1977) and of disciplinary power (Foucault 1995), and thus it is constructed as an effect of social practices, or, even better, 'not an effect of genes but of power relations' (Gatens 1992: 131). All in all, it is fundamental to observe that if, on the one hand, the body is de/marked involuntarily, on the other, it is also engraved through voluntary procedures of modelling or of self-production. These express the internalization of different ways of life, habits, behaviours, social relations (Grosz 1994: 141), and, ultimately, the embodiment of subjectivities (Rothfield 1995: 169). As Elizabeth Grosz (1994: 143) rightly points out:

> The various procedures for inscribing bodies, marking out different bodies, categories, types, norms, are not simply imposed on the individual from outside; they do not function coercively but are sought out. They are commonly undertaken voluntarily and usually require the active compliance of the subject. Body building, to take one rather stark example, is not imposed from without (even if it may be argued that the norms and ideals governing beauty and health do not always serve the interests of those who identify with them) but is actively undertaken; it could not possibly be effective otherwise. It is what Foucault might call a 'technique of self-production' in its most literal sense.

I maintain here that the embodiment of gender identities is thus, to a great extent, self-produced. Here it is well to remember Simone de Beauvoir's saying that 'one is not born, one becomes woman' (or man), for gender identities are not fixed attributes, they are not the result of a supposed essence that emanates from the body. On the contrary, gender identities are social constructs that are fluid and changeable. As noted by Butler (1990: 25), gender identity does not exist behind the expressions of gender; it is always constructed through performance, by the same 'expressions' that are held as results. In other words, gender is not an 'internal state of being', it is neither fixed nor the result of biological attributes; it is rather a performance that all of us create and re-create every day. Gender thus incorporates a whole set of different manipulated codes of embodied costumes that we have adopted.

This of course requires procedures and techniques of self-production and self-representation (De Lauretis 1994). Such procedures and techniques include, amongst others, certain hairstyles and ways of dressing, certain ways of walking and talking, the habit of shaving or not shaving certain parts of your body, or painting your fingernails or not (Brownmiller 1985; Fournier 2002). They may also include having to submit ourselves to certain rituals every day to become a woman (or man) according to society's parameters and, as such, to define our gender identity to ourselves as well as in the eyes of those with whom we interact. All of this, of course, follows the current standards of aesthetics that are imposed on each gender, which will vary with time and space, both geographical and social (Balsamo 1996).

In *Femininity*, Susan Brownmiller (1985) reflects on the process of 'becoming a woman' in North American society, a process which finds parallels in Brazil as well. For example, Brownmiller describes how girls are trained how to walk, run, sit and even how to discipline their own voice and way of talking – a disciplining of gender that is internalized in the process of socialization and which eventually ends up becoming self-imposed. She also looks at the self-production of femininity, calling attention to the various practices of adorning and shaping the body as well as to the different procedures for removing unwanted hairs; manicuring fingernails and toenails by cutting and painting them in fashionable colours; dyeing, cutting, perming or straightening your hair according to the styles in vogue; applying eye shadow and liner to the eyes and lipstick on the lips, and other similar practices that contribute to the production of a 'woman' in North American society.

We should add that in Brazil, as well as in North America, the self-production of femininity has varied through the generations and in terms of race and class. It is important to emphasize here that, despite the specific variations, as we are disciplined in gendered practices since our tender infancy, we embody these procedures as natural or as being part of femininity. However, when you consider that transvestites follow these very procedures in their process of transformation, it becomes evident that 'being a woman' implies to a great extent quite a sophisticated production in order to engender the body.[4] It is thus not by chance that Judith Butler (1990) uses the metaphor of the drag queen to emphasize the extent to which gender is a performance.

Note, however, that women are not necessarily more subordinated than men to the systems of production of gendered bodies, even when we consider only patriarchal societies (Grosz 1994: 144). On the contrary, these body technologies apply as much to men as to women, although in different ways. However, it is true that the construction of women as objects of desire, as is characteristic of contemporary Western societies, results in women investing much more in trying to follow or model ourselves to the given standards of beauty (Davis 1995).

It is not unexpected then that the cosmetic industry, especially that which is geared towards women, is amongst the most rapidly growing in Brazil. This was observed by the magazine *Isto É* a few years ago:

> It is true that improving your appearance is good business here. Brazil is the eighth biggest market in the world. In 1999, this sector had an annual turnover of US$3.5 billion and in 2000 this could reach US$4 billion. (*Isto É* 2000: 101)

More recently, the Brazilian Association of the Cosmetic, Toiletry and Fragrance Industry (ABIHPEC) revealed that this sector has experienced steady growth within the last 13 years, going from approximately 2.3 billion dollars in sales in 1996 to nearly 11 billion dollars in 2008.[5]

Nevertheless, I think we all look in wonder and amazement at the sometimes radical practices that women submit themselves to in order to conform to the current standards of fashion. Such practices sometimes even threaten their lives (Viktor 2001).[6] The news that a Miss Brazil, a young woman of rare beauty, had admitted to having had 19 surgical interventions (read plastic surgery) to reach her ideal of beauty is one example (Neves 2001).[7] A similar sacrifice (19 operations) was undertaken by a young Brazilian woman, married to a plastic surgeon who, in true Pygmalion style, shaped and formed her according to the current standards of fashion: blonde, tall, skinny but with a generous bust, along the lines of the top model Gisele Bündchen, who apparently also has admitted to having silicone implants. Maybe this explains how and why, according to data collected by the Brazilian Society of Plastic Surgeons, 50,000 liposuctions were carried out in Brazil in 1998 (*Isto É* 1999: 24), of which 70 per cent were carried out on women (*Isto É* 2000: 101). Note that in 2008 Brazil came second (to the USA) in the world ranking of numbers of plastic surgeries performed. In that year, 621,000 such procedures were carried out in Brazil, of which 151,000 were breast surgeries and 91,000 liposuctions, and over 70 per cent had a woman as the patient (Collucci 2009).

Let me emphasize, once again, that men are not immune to the body cult. On the contrary, indicators show that men also submit themselves to the current hegemonic standards of aesthetics, battering their bodies, body-building or dieting to lose unwanted flab, taking body-building hormones and even Viagra in their search for the ideal look and performance (Sabino 2002; Courtine 2005; Mamo and Fishman 2001). However, amongst the clientele for gyms, spas and beauty salons, as well as for the plastic surgery and cosmetics industries, women are still the great majority (Davis 2002; Fournier 2002; Negrin 2003; Sassatelli 1999). In fact, it is mostly women (even the skinny ones) who live under the tyranny of fashion, beauty and diets in the effort to control or eliminate the passionate aspects of self in order to gain the approval of the masculine culture (Chernin 1981: 187; Perry 2000; Viktor 2001; Jeffreys 2006). It is of course not by chance that the victims of bulimia and anorexia are, in the great majority, women who live in patriarchal societies where the cult of the slim female body reigns (Bordo 1993; Gremillion 2002; Lintott 2003).[8]

I would like to point out that despite the fact that implants, liposuction and other similar sacrifices might seem a novelty today, what we are talking about is not necessarily a new phenomenon, at least not in terms of the disciplines that are imposed on the female body. 'Female beautifying has a history' (Sant'Anna 2001: 121), and we must not forget that in this history corsets, girdles and other 'tortures' of the sort had similar objectives (Vigarello 2005). The sacrifices imposed on women's bodies in order to comply with the hegemonic standards of aesthetics are varied and appear endless. As my mother used to say in the midst of my screams and protests as a young girl while she tried to comb and plait my hair, 'To look beautiful you need to suffer.' So the question then is, why do we women submit to all this? Why do we accept all this torture 'voluntarily'?

Embodied subjectivities

Certainly the major part of the response lies in the fact that our subjectivities are not merely a question of conscience. Our subjectivities do not walk alone in this world. On the contrary they are embodied. This means that we experience the world through our bodies. As Freud (1984: 364) said, 'the ego is first and foremost a bodily ego; it is not merely a surface entity, it is a projection of a surface'.

It follows that to feel good about ourselves we have to feel good in our bodies (Budgeon 2003). However, to use a colloquial saying, 'that is where the shoe pinches', because feeling good in our bodies is not a matter of personal choice. It depends, to a great extent, on historically specific constructions that play on the notion of the ideal body.

On this point, it is important to remember once again that we are currently living under the aegis of hegemonic ideals of the body cult, propagated not only by the furious marketing strategies of the cosmetics industry and the network of services geared towards technologies of the body, but also – and perhaps most important – by discourses in the medical field. These discourses about the body tend to blend into each other and overlap to the point where what is considered a healthy body is one that is moulded according to the current aesthetic ideals and, most important of all, which uses the young body as its parameter. This is played upon by the mass media in its representations of femininity.

Susan Bordo (1993: 24–5) rightly notes that, despite the possibility of multiple interpretations, 'the everyday deployment of mass cultural representations of masculinity, femininity, beauty, and success' has the effect of homogeniz[ing] and then normaliz[ing] them – 'that is, they function as models against which the self continually measures, judges, disciplines, and corrects itself'. This is particularly so in the case of ageing, and especially in the case of women.

Indeed, even though we know that ageing is a natural, involuntary process, part of the normal cycle of life, nevertheless in Western societies, ours included, ageing is considered something shameful that needs to be disguised and fought against at all costs. Hence the rapid development in efforts to produce new technologies, including the numerous research projects in the field of biomedical sciences (especially in molecular biology) trying to find ways of stopping the process of ageing. As promised by a magazine article:

> In the future, the word youth will be considered something belonging to an imperfect past. Ageing will not be part of the future ... For the first time there exists the possibility for humans to beat time, changing tissues, organs and bones like you would change the tyres of a car. (*Isto É* 1999: 34)

Referring to how the process of ageing is constructed in

American society, Margaret Gullette (1997) observes that middle age is represented as the beginning of the end. Note however that this discourse around the so-called 'decline' comes in gendered versions; a masculine version and a feminine version. For women the line is at menopause when their reproductive capacity ceases; this is vividly expressed, especially for women over fifty, in the following passage:

> Considering the enormous strain that pregnancy puts on women's bodies, nature certainly has its reasons for ending women's reproductive cycle before her fifties. However she committed a great error in making the production of oestrogen of the ovaries also decline during this period, bringing about a rapid atrophy of the genitals, breasts and other physical characteristics of the feminine body. (Soucasoux 1993: 10–11)[9]

Middle-aged women are interpolated by these pervasive and penetrative narratives of 'decline' – which explains to a great extent why hormonal therapy is gathering so many followers amongst middle-aged women, even among those who do not experience any physical discomforts brought about by menopause.

So I will have to recognize that, unfortunately, in spite of all our feminist struggles, our society continues to value women first and foremost for the part they play in the reproduction of the species and as objects of desire who are easily disposable. Because of this, society offers us few reasons why we should feel fulfilled once we get to menopause. Independently of our personal achievements, which could actually be quite substantial, the current ideals of female beauty provide little room for us to escape from the appearance of decline which is bestowed on those who have reached 'a certain age'. The lines that mark our journey through time, our experiences and our wisdom are regarded negatively as 'wrinkles' – that is, as undesirable marks of decline which should be avoided and/or disguised at whatever cost (Brownmiller 1985: 166).

The social pressure to maintain a youthful appearance affects men as well but the weight falls heavier on women for, as observed earlier, women with an ageing appearance have much less social capital on the mating scene than men. As Susan Brownmiller (1985: 167) so adequately puts it, 'the preservation of youthful beauty is one of the few intense preoccupations and competitive stimuli that society expects from women, even though they are then disdained for being so narcissist'.

Even women who have been very successful professionally or who in any other way are in the eye of the public or the press are constantly forced to maintain a youthful appearance, being exposed as they are to criticism when refusing to submit to plastic surgery or any other form of remodelling of the body. At the same time, those who make exaggerated use of plastic surgery are ridiculed. In reality, women who value the 'feminine ideal' and use their appearance as their main strategy for survival in the world do not have many choices when they reach middle age. But what can we say about those of us who choose to fight for other strategies of female fulfilment?

Some conclusions

Of course, we are facing a difficult challenge which demands a lot of courage. We tried to show this before by breaking with the stereotypes of femininity that chained us to certain social roles and to subordination in society. Feminists have deconstructed these stereotypes as much in theory as in practice, formulating a new discourse and a new way of being in the world for all women.

Let us recall that feminists have often argued that the body is a medium through which oppressive cultural norms of femininity are expressed. They have posited, along with Giddens (1991), that experiences of the self and the body are mediated by mass media projections of different lifestyle images and options. Dominant representations of 'feminine beauty' propagated by the media thus render for many women the experience of the body as unsatisfactory and in need of modification. The media also propagate a number of transformative practices and body technologies, making it seem not only easy but actually normal and necessary to pursue radical body modification such as cosmetic surgery. In feminist theory, therefore, cosmetic surgery has usually been regarded as an oppressive body technology, 'colonizing women's bodies' (Negrin 2003).

More recently, however, authors such as Kathy Davis (1995) have argued that the practice of cosmetic surgery may be seen as a means of women exercising agency in actively 'engaging with the dictates of patriarchal ideology'. Moreover, they have argued that these procedures enhance women's sense of self-esteem, and can thus be regarded as an act of empowerment.

Of course, the issue is delicate as it becomes biased in the current debate on body politics. It pays to remember that one of the major issues in feminist struggles for women's reproductive rights was implied in the affirmation that 'our bodies belong to us'. We claimed autonomy over our bodies, but to what extent have we actually exercised this right? Certainly, running after plastic surgery, liposuction and implants and many other technologies that are decidedly dangerous to our health, just to model ourselves according to the current ideals of feminine beauty, cannot be seen as exercising control over our bodies and thus as 'empowerment'. We have to recognize that the old values, and particularly those surrounding older women, remain strong in society to the point of being internalized even by feminists. Many of us still submit ourselves to various rituals of disciplining our body imposed by social pressures.

Clearly, we need to find ways to understand better the interrelationships between gender and the politics of the body. This is especially so because these interrelationships are historically and culturally contextualized, on the one hand, but, on the other, they are always lived and negotiated individually (Lock and Kaufert 1998). It thus becomes fundamental to develop more discussion and analysis around the complexity of women's experiences in relation to new technologies geared towards the reproduction of femininity as well as the fight against ageing.

In this regard, it is important to take into account Susan

Bordo's (1993) considerations regarding feminism as 'systemic critique'. Writing about criticisms she faced when she lost over twenty pounds as a result of joining a weight loss programme – she was even called 'hypocritical' since she has written about anorexia – Bordo (1993: 30) responded thus:

> But in my view, feminist cultural criticism is not a blueprint for the conduct of a personal life (or political action, for that matter) and does not empower (or require) individuals to 'rise above' their culture or to become martyrs to feminist ideals. It does not tell us what to do (although I continually get asked such questions when I speak at colleges) – whether to lose weight or not, wear makeup or not, lift weights or not. Its goal is edification and understanding, enhanced consciousness of the power, complexity, and systemic nature of culture, the interconnected webs of its functioning. It is up to the reader to decide how, when, and where (or whether) to put that understanding to further use, in the particular, complicated, and ever-changing context that is his or her life and no one else's.

Although I do tend to agree with Bordo, I believe that we are still in great need of feminist narratives and 'systemic critiques' that deconstruct the hegemonic representations of femininity and the images of ageing as decline that surround us. Likewise, feminist critiques of the new sacrifices imposed on women's bodies that can reveal how these sophisticated forms of slavery under hegemonic beauty ideals continue to be reproduced and disseminated in Brazilian society will also be important.

Notes

1 This chapter draws on a paper originally prepared for presentation at the Sexuality and Development Workshop, Institute of Development Studies, Brighton, UK, 3–5 April 2008. A previous version of this chapter was published in Portuguese (Sardenberg 2002).

2 See Berquó (1998) and Goldenberg (2006) on the very few choices open to single ageing women in Brazil.

3 According to Rodrigues (1983: 45), 'Culture dictates norms in relationship to the body, norms that the individual will adopt at the cost of certain punishments and compensations until these standards of

behaviour will appear as natural as the development of human beings, the changing of the seasons and the sunrise and sunset.'

4 See Neusa de Oliveira (1994) for a discussion of the procedures employed by transvestites in the neighbourhood of Pelourinho em Salvador, Bahia. Consider, as well, the observations made by Denise Sant'Anna (2005: 122) regarding everyday hygiene and personal care: 'it is in the repetitious rules of elegance and hygiene, in the boring minutia of caring for nails, skin, eyes and hair that we perceive the strengthening of the culture of the intimate space, in which the female body occupies a major role'.

5 See www.abihpec.org.br/conteudo/material/panoramadosetor/panorama_ 2008_2009_pt3.pdf (accessed 7 January 2009).

6 Sheila Jeffreys (2006) reports that many animal diseases can be transmitted through cosmetics and other beauty products, as they usually contain bits of dead animal. She claims that a study in the US has linked hair dye and bladder cancer.

7 Cindy Jackson, a 40-year-old American, went through 29 plastic surgeries to reach her beauty goal: to look like a Barbie Doll (BBC 2004).

8 BBC News stated on 19 March 1999 that close to 5 per cent of British girls suffered from anorexia.

9 For similar narratives see Emily Martin (1989). For analysis of the medical discourses around the female body throughout history, see Del Priore (1993); Shorter (1982); Ehrenreich and English (1973); Smith-Rosemberg (1974).

References

Balsamo, A. (1996) *Technologies of the Gendered Body: Reading Cyborg Women*, Duke University Press, Durham, NC, and London.

BBC (2004) 'Making Cindy into Barbie?', http:://news.bbc.co.uk/1/hi/health/174836.stm (accessed 20 June 2004).

Berquó, E. (1987) *Nupcialidade da População Negra no Brasil* (Marriage in the Black Population in Brazil), Texto No. 11, Núcleo de Estudos de População (NEPO), UNICAMP, São Paulo.

—— (1998) 'Arranjos Familiares no Brasil: Uma Visão Demográfica' (Family Arrangements in Brazil: A Demographic Outlook), in *Historia da Vida Privada no Brasil: Contrastes da Intimidade Contemporânea* (History of Private Life in Brazil: Contrasts with Contemporary Intimacy), Companhia das Letras, São Paulo.

Bleier, R. (1984) *Science and Gender: A Critique of Biology and Its Theories on Women*, Pergamon Press, New York.

Bolstanski, L. (1989) *As Classes Sociais e o Corpo* (The Social Classes and the Body), Ed. Graal, Rio de Janeiro.

Bordo, S. (1993) *Unbearable Weight: Feminism, Western Culture and the Body*, University of California Press, Berkeley.

—— (1997) 'O Corpo e a Reprodução da Feminidade: Uma Apropriação Feminista de Foucault' (The Body and the Reproduction of Femininity: A Feminist Appropriation of Foucault), in A. M. Jaggar and S. R. Bordo (eds.), *Gênero, Corpo, Conhecimento* (Gender, Body, Knowledge), Record, Rosa dos Tempos, Rio de Janeiro.

Bourdieu, P. (1977) *Outline of a Theory of Practice*, Cambridge University Press.

Britto da Motta, A. (1995) 'Os Velhos, os Corpos, as Estações' (Old Age, Bodies, Status), Anais, IV Encontro da Rede Regional Norte e Nordeste de Núcleos de Estudo e Pesquisa sobre a Mulher e Relações de Gênero (4th Meeting of the North and Northeast Regional Network of Women and Gender Relations Study and Research Centres), João Pessoa, UFPb, 3–6 October.

Brownmiller, S. (1985) *Femininity*, Ballantine Books, New York.

Budgeon, S. (2003) 'Identity as Embodied Event', *Body and Society*, Vol. 9, No. 1, pp. 35–55.

Butler, J. (1990) *Gender Trouble: Feminism and the Subversion of Identity*, Routledge, London.

Chernin, K. (1981) *The Obsession: Reflections on the Tyranny of Slenderness*, Harper & Row, New York.

Chivers, S. (2003) *From Old Woman to Older Women: Contemporary Culture and Women's Narratives*, Ohio State University Press, Columbus.

Collier, J. and S. J. Yanagisako (eds.) (1987) *Gender and Kinship: Essays toward a Unified Analysis*, Stanford University Press.

Collucci, C. (2009) 'Plástica de Mama Ultrapassa Lipo' (Breast Implants Exceed Lipo), *Folha de São Paulo*, 13 February, www1.folha.uol.com.br/fsp/saude/sd1302200901.htm (accessed 12 March 2012).

Courtine, J.-J. (2005) 'Os Stakhanovistas do Narcisismo. Body-building e Puritanismo Ostentatório na Cultura Americana do Corpo' (The Stakhanovistas of Narcissism. Body-building and Ostentatious Puritanism in American Body Culture), in D. Sant'Anna (ed.), *Políticas do Corpo* (Body Politics), 2nd edn, Estação Liberdade, São Paulo.

Davis, K. (1995) *Reshaping the Female Body: The Dilemma of Cosmetic Surgery*, Routledge, New York and London.

—— (2002) 'A Dubious Equality: Men, Women, and Cosmetic Surgery', *Body and Society*, Vol. 8, No. 1, pp. 49–65.

De Lauretis, T. (1994) 'A Tecnologia do Gênero' (The Technology of Gender), in H. Buarque de Hollanda (ed.), *Tendências e Impasses: O*

Feminismo como Crítica da Cultura (Trends and Impasses: Feminism as a Cultural Critique), Rocco, Rio de Janeiro.

Del Priore, M. (1993) *Ao Sul do Corpo. Condição Feminina, Maternidades e Mentalidades no Brasil Colônia* (To the South of the Body. Female Condition, Maternities and Mentalities in Colonial Brazil), Edunb, Brasília, José Olympio Editora, Rio de Janeiro.

Douglas, M. (1976) *Pureza e Perigo* (Purity and Danger), Perspectiva, São Paulo.

Ehrenreich, B. and D. English (1973) *Complaints and Disorders: The Sexual Politics of Sickness*, Feminist Press, Old Westbury, NY.

Foucault, M. (1995) *Discipline and Punish: The Birth of the Prison*, Vintage Books, New York.

Fournier, V. (2002) 'Fleshing Out Gender: Crafting Gender Identity on Women's Bodies', *Body and Society*, Vol. 8, No. 2, pp. 55–77.

Freud, S. (1984) *On Metapsychology: The Theory of Psychoanalysis*, trans. J. Strachey, Penguin, London.

Gatens, M. (1992) 'Power, Bodies, and Difference', in M. Barrett and A. Phillips (eds.), *Destabilizing Theory: Contemporary Feminist Debates*, Stanford University Press.

Giddens, A. (1991) *Modernity and Self-identity: Self and Society in the Late Modern Age*, Stanford University Press.

Giffin, K. (1991) 'Nosso Corpo nos Pertence: A Dialética do Biológico e do Social' (Our Body Belongs to Us: The Biological and Social Dialectic), *Cadernos de Saúde Pública*, Vol. 3, No. 2, pp. 10–18.

Goldenberg, M. (2006) *Infiel. Notas de Uma Antropóloga* (Unfaithful: An Anthropologist's Notes), Editora Record, Rio de Janeiro.

Gremillion, H. (2002) 'In Fitness and in Health: Crafting Bodies in the Treatment of Anorexia Nervosa', *Signs: Journal of Women in Culture and Society*, Vol. 27, No. 2, pp. 381–414.

Grosz, E. (1994) *Volatile Bodies: Toward a Corporeal Feminism*, Indiana University Press, Bloomington.

Gullette, M. (1997) *Declining to Decline: Cultural Combat and the Politics of the Midlife*, University Press of Virginia, Charlottesville.

Isto É (1999) 'Datas' (Dates), No. 1,546, 19 May, p. 24.

—— (2000) 'Um Belo Mergulho' (A Beautiful Dive), No. 1,596, 3 May, p. 101.

Jeffreys, S. (2006) *Beauty and Misogyny: Harmful Cultural Practices in the West*, Routledge, London.

Lintott, S. (2003) 'Sublime Hunger: A Consideration of Eating Disorders Beyond Beauty', *Hypatia*, Vol. 18, No. 4, pp. 65–86.

Lock, M. and P. A. Kaufert (eds.) (1998) *Pragmatic Women and Body Politics*, Cambridge University Press.

Mamo, L. and J. R. Fishman (2001) 'Potency in All the Right Places: Viagra as a Technology of the Gendered Body', *Body and Society*, Vol. 7, No. 4, pp. 13–35.

Martin, E. (1989) *The Woman in the Body: A Cultural Analysis of Reproduction*, Beacon Press, Boston.

Negrin, L. (2003) 'Cosmetic Surgery and the Eclipse of Identity', *Body and Society*, Vol. 8, No. 4, pp. 21–42.

Neusa de Oliveira, M. (1994) *Damas de Paus: O Jogo Aberto dos Travestis no Espelho da Mulher* (Fairy Wands: Transsexual Women's Open Play in the Mirror), Centro Editorial e Didático da UFBA, Salvador.

Neves, K. (2001) 'Juliana Borges: a Miss Terceiro Milênio' (Juliana Borges: Miss Third Millennium), www.platicabeleza.terra.com.br/25/gentc/juliana-borges.htms (accessed 15 August 2001).

Pacheco, A. C. L. (2008) 'Gênero, Raça E Solidão Entre Mulheres Negras Em Salvador, Bahia' (Gender, Race and Solidarity Between Black Women in Salvador), paper presented at the 'Fazendo Gênero 8' meetings, Florianópolis, Santa Catarina, 25–28 August.

Perry, K. (2000) 'Most Women Feel Too Fat', *The Guardian: Guardian Unlimited*, 12 October, www.guardian.co.uk/uk_news/story/0,3604,381027,00.html (accessed 3 March 2003).

Rodrigues, J. C. (1983) *Tabu do Corpo* (Body Taboos), 3rd edn, Achiamé, Rio de Janeiro.

Rothfield, P. (1995) 'Bodies and Subjects: Medical Ethics and Feminism', in P. A. Komesaroff (ed.), *Troubled Bodies: Critical Perspectives on Postmodernism, Medical Ethics, and the Body*, Duke University Press, Durham, NC.

Sabino, C. (2002) 'Anabolizantes: Drogas de Apolo' (Anabolics: Apollo Drugs), in M. Goldenberg (ed.), *Nu and Vestido: Dez Antropólogos Revelam a Cultura do Corpo Carioca* (Naked and Dressed: Ten Anthropologists Reveal Carioca Body Culture), Record, Rio de Janeiro.

Sant'Anna, D. B. (2001) 'É possível Realizar uma História do Corpo?' (Is it Possible to Undertake a History of the Body?), in C. L. Soares (ed.), *Corpo e História* (Body and History), Autores Associados, Campinas, SP.

—— (ed.) (2005) *Políticas do Corpo* (Body Politics), 2nd edn, Estação Liberdade, São Paulo.

Sardenberg, C. M. B. (2002) 'A Mulher Frente à Cultura da Eterna Juventude: reflexões teóricas e pessoais de uma feminista cinquentona' ('Women and the Culture of Eternal Youth: theoretical and personal reflections of a feminist over fifty'), in S. L. Ferreira abd E. R. Nascimento (eds.), *Imagens da Mulher na Cultura Contemporânea* (Images of Women in Contemporary Culture), Núcleo de Estudos Interdisciplinares sobre a Mulher-NEIM, FFCH/UFBA , Salvador, pp. 51–68.

Sassatelli, R. (1999) 'Interaction Order and Beyond: A Field Analysis of

Body Culture within Fitness Gyms', *Body and Society*, Vol. 5, Nos. 2–3, pp. 227–48.

Scott, J. W. (1988) *Gender and the Politics of History*, Columbia University Press, New York.

Shorter, E. (1982) *A History of Women's Bodies*, Basic Books, New York.

Smith-Rosemberg, C. (1974) 'Puberty to Menopause: The Cycle of Femininity in Nineteenth Century America', in M. Hartman and L. Banner (eds.), *Clio's Consciousness Raised*, Harper, New York.

Soucasoux, N. (1993) *Os Órgãos Sexuais Femininos: Forma, Função, Símbolo e Arquétipo* (Female Sexual Organs: Shape, Function, Symbol and Archetype), Imago Editora, Rio de Janeiro.

Vigarello, G. (2005) 'Panóplias Corretoras: Balizas para uma História' (Brokerage Operations: Beacons for History), in D. B. Sant' Anna (ed.), *Políticas do Corpo* (Body Politics), 2nd edn, Estação Liberdade, São Paulo.

Viktor, M. (2001) 'Quase Morri para Emagrecer' (I Almost Died to Become Slim), *Revista Corpo a Corpo*, Vol. XIV, No. 147, pp. 98–101.

6

Unmarried in Palestine

Embodiment and (Dis)Empowerment in the Lives of Single Palestinian Women

Penny Johnson

In my work on unmarried women in Palestine, my attention shifted quickly from statistics to stories. I initially became interested in findings from our first national demographic surveys (Palestinian Central Bureau of Statistics 2002, 2006a, 2006b, 2007) which showed an unusually high proportion of unmarried women in the West Bank and Gaza, while men were almost universally married. As I began my project, however, the narratives of two generations of unmarried women engaged me: from the stories of a life in service to the nation, told by older single women, to the tales of moral danger circulating around young unmarried women today.

In two focus groups conducted in the southern West Bank in 2007, we asked young unmarried women aged 19–29 what they would like to accomplish in the next five years.[1] In the Hebron-area village of Sa'ir, the young women answered in a vehement and desperate chorus:

> There is nothing encouraging ahead of us.
>
> We are stuck in the house; that is our life.
>
> Everything is forbidden to us; we can't go to work or leave the house.

And most disturbingly, the young women stated: 'Our life is over.' In Dheisheh refugee camp near Bethlehem, the reactions were dramatically different. Many young women wanted to continue their education to master's level and almost all aimed for a rewarding job and hoped for a sympathetic marriage:

> A bachelor's degree is not enough, I need a master's.
>
> I want to develop my personality and dreams.
>
> I want to be happy in my society, not just cooking and keeping house.
>
> I want an income ... Maybe I want to start a salon, I'm good at hairdressing ...

Both communities are relatively disadvantaged and both subject to Israeli military violence and the profound insecurity of the second Palestinian intifada since 2000. Why then the striking difference in hopes for the future? Why so much hope in Dheisheh and so much despair in Sa'ir? In fact, the aspirations of the two groups of young women are not so diverse. Young women in Sa'ir also clearly expressed a desire for more education and work outside the home – but unlike their counterparts in Dheisheh, they felt these were impossible goals. They also felt they had lost their chances for marriage and movement away from their natal families. The two groups of women in fact were set apart by four different social conditions and public environments. The first difference was access to education: most of the young women in Sa'ir had completed high school, but this level of education proved a dead end for work and for marriage as well. In contrast, at least half of the group in Dheisheh were either engaged in post-secondary education or aspiring to it. Second, the lively and supportive environment of civil society organizations in Dheisheh also played a decisive role in encouraging girls in their dreams and offering opportunities for public involvement – as did the support of their refugee camp families for their daughters' education (see Rosenfeld 2004).

Although both communities had suffered from ongoing Israeli military violence and restrictions on movement, they were located within different regulative and protective environments. Young women from Dheisheh can go to Bethlehem – with its institutions of higher education and wider opportunities for activities and work – without crossing a checkpoint. In contrast, young women in Sa'ir have to cross Israeli checkpoints to reach Hebron, and Palestinian police protection is only infrequently available in their village.[2] Also significantly, Dheisheh's own internal security (both physically and socially) is much stronger due to the camp's very active local or popular committee. This affected the fourth major difference in perceived and actual threats to women's and girl's personal security, defined in explicit bodily terms, in terms of both physical and moral danger. In the case of Sa'ir, families had placed severe restrictions on their unmarried daughters' mobility. This seems to have been the result of intertwined fears of physical and moral danger, whether from Israeli soldiers on the village's outskirts or unruly young men on its streets. It was also related to a specific incident of a so-called 'honour' killing of a young married woman in murky circumstances where a constructed (false) pornographic image of her was circulated on mobile phones. Although murders of women under the rubric of 'honour crimes' were relatively few at 10–20 per year,[3] the effects of this incident were drastic.

The victim was later declared innocent by the imam of the local mosque, but young women were still barred from using the telephone and often from leaving their immediate home environments. The fear – and moral panic – of the village community was in a very literal way 'embodied' in the restrictions placed on these young women's bodies and selves. Their narratives – and the narratives told about them or circulated around them – are 'narratives of sexuality' in their focus on bodily vulnerability and threats to bodily and moral integrity. At the same time, young women tell other stories of bodies in movement, challenging borders and expanding boundaries.

This project relies primarily on the voices of unmarried young women (aged 19–29 years) in ten focus groups conducted in the West Bank in 2007 and 2008, and on nine topical life interviews with unmarried women (aged 45–68 years). Seven of the older women from the West Bank were interviewed by the author and two from Gaza were interviewed by a colleague there.[4] Our first focus group with young women taught us that young women were not eager to be placed under the label 'unmarried', implying a permanent state of singlehood. We thus generally asked for young women below 29 years to gather for a discussion of their problems and aspirations. Most of those who did so were unmarried, with a small minority married (usually accompanying an unmarried friend) and a smaller number separated or divorced. They were sometimes joined by older women, depending on the context. In the first phase of this project, topical life interviews with older women allowed more opportunities to address directly the question of living permanently as a single woman, but always embedded in the woman's larger life story. The response of Wisam,[5] an unmarried woman in her forties living and working in Ramallah, to my request for an interview for this project, is telling:

> The project you are working on sounds very interesting. The problem is that I don't think I have much to contribute to this study. I don't see myself in those terms. I don't think the fact that I am unmarried has any significant advantages or disadvantages over what I chose to do privately or publicly.

Wisam's words serve as a warning to avoid any temptation to consider unmarried women in Palestine or elsewhere as a unitary category – and undermines the assumption that singlehood is at the centre of an unmarried women's identity or perception of herself. It also implied that our interviews should be embedded in a broader life story approach in order to understand the significance or non-significance of being unmarried in the course of life events.

Bodies, borders and biopolitics

In the warlike and insecure times of the second intifada, unmarried young women's bodies seem to constitute a site where the insecurities (and immobilities) of their families and communities – and indeed the body politic – are enacted. In particular, perceived and actual physical and sexual threats to the bodies of young unmarried women point to the liminal status of young unmarried women, not only as 'markers of a normative female sexuality' (Sa'ar 2004) but as representing threats to and violations of the Palestinian body politic.

At the same time, unmarried women can be agents of change as they expand boundaries and borders. This emerges in the ambitions of the young women in the Dheisheh, but it is also evident even in the much more restricted circumstances of Sa'ir. A female secondary school student explains that restrictions cause both despair and stronger resolve among girls:

> The suppression of girls' opinions and our culture of shame means families do not like their girls to study and rent places outside the village. This comes from hearing so much about the problems of girls, particularly honour crimes. This causes girls to be depressed but also causes them to cling to education.

This dynamic of restriction and resolve is a dynamic of bodies and boundaries that, as Butler notes, is central to the relationship of bodies and the world around them: 'Not only did bodies tend to indicate a world beyond themselves but this movement beyond their own boundaries, a movement of boundary itself, appeared to be quite central to what bodies "are" ' (Butler 1993: ix). In the context of contemporary Palestine, bodies and boundaries are critical constituents of an Israeli politics of spatial segregation. An elaborate, shifting and growing matrix of control is formed by the combination of some five hundred checkpoints or barriers that divide Palestinian towns and villages from each other: 'border' terminals between the West Bank and Israel, and the Separation Wall which snakes its way deep inside Palestinian territory. This checkpoint system has 'grown to govern the entire spectrum of Palestinian life under occupation' (Weizman 2007: 147). While Israeli settler bodies move freely through this system, Palestinian bodies are contained and humiliated.

In this extreme form of biopolitics, the three conceptions of the body delineated by Scheper-Hughes and Lock (1987: 7–8) – the embodied individual self, the social body, and the body politic – are intertwined, and the boundaries between embodied selves and the body politic are partially dissolved. Embodiment thus refers also to the inscription of the 'body of the nation' on individual bodies (Weiss 2002) as well as the 'transformation of the body in the contemporary world ... wrought by the incredible proliferation of political violence of all types' (Csordas 1994: 3). The translation of public insecurity, invasive violence and political dissolution and corruption into moral danger in contemporary Palestine is evident in Palestinian daily discourse, particularly in the circulation of rumours and sexualized narratives (see Johnson 2007b), and has been noted in other contexts. According to Scheper-Hughes and Lock, 'When the sense of social order is threatened ... the symbols of self-control become intensified along with those of social control. Boundaries between individual and political bodies become blurred' (Scheper-Hughes and Lock 1987: 24).

The narratives of unmarried women, and the discourses that surround them, offer a lens to this complex present, as well as contrasts and continuities with the past where, as we will see below, unmarried women's bodies at times and in specific social and economic circumstances were conceived of as bodies in service to a national and social project. Older women (45–65 years), interviewed in the initial stage of this project, often expressed this sentiment. A common refrain, articulated here by 52-year-old Mariam from Breij camp in Gaza, was, 'I wanted to be someone, to serve society.' This service was frequently seen as replacing marriage and as advancing the national struggle against occupation. Coming back from her university studies in Cairo in 1971, Zahera Kamal, who later became the first Minister of Women's Affairs in the Palestinian Authority, noted: 'No, I was not thinking of marriage. It was the start of occupation and that was on my mind.' In contemporary Palestine, the notion of the body (and mind) in service to the nation has been radically reconfigured.

The 'crisis' of unmarried women: regional and Palestinian discourses

Wisam's words, in response to being asked to participate in research on 'unmarried' women, also neatly counter contemporary discourses which frame unmarried women as a 'crisis' in society. In media discourse across the Arab world, since 2000 in particular, the growing number of single women in the Arab world is posed solely as a problem, with headlines such as '1.5 million spinsters in Saudi Arabia' (Ghazi 2006). Arab media reports on the rise in the numbers of unmarried women frame it almost as an epidemic that needs public intervention for the health of the society. One headline from the *Khaleej Times*, for example, read: 'Alarm bells ring as rate of UAE spinsters rises' and the article called for the 'involvement of all segments of the society as well as the authorities to combat this "alarming rate"', given as an entirely improbable 73 per cent of all UAE women (Ibrahim 2004). It is fair, I think, to consider the constitution of this 'crisis' as a form of moral panic (see Cohen 2002) whereby unmarried women are blamed or 'chastised by their societies' (Ghazi 2006) and come to represent social ills and cultural disorder. Media and public discourses also point to an unsettling of long-held cultural assumptions about the universality of marriage and raise questions about whether the 'cognitive frame of marriage' (Friedl 2003) has started to shift.

Although Palestine was late in joining the media (and state) chorus on the single woman 'crisis', the issue has emerged strongly in recent years, inflected by the 'missing men' killed and injured in the second intifada. Islamist political movements (particularly Hamas) and Islamic charities and NGOs have embraced the mission of collective marriage ceremonies, explicitly framed as reducing the social ill of unmarried women and allowing young men to marry cheaply (in an era of prohibitive wedding expenses). In addition, the losses of the second intifada in terms of male death and injury are offered both as an explanation for the crisis and as a justification of public action. The Hamas-led government and/or Islamic charities in Gaza staged ten collective ceremonies in 2008, both for unmarried women (and men) and to remarry war widows. 'There will be more weddings,' said one organizer, 'no one will remain single' (El Khoudary 2008).

Although collective marriages have been staged in the West Bank and sponsored by both Hamas and Fateh (see Jad 2009), Gaza is the main site for them, even though there are actually fewer unmarried women in Gaza than in the West Bank, as we will see below. The 'epidemic' of unmarried women is thus partially socially constructed, reminding us that a moral panic does not imply that 'something does not exist' (Cohen 2002: vii) but does connote a form of cultural politics that crystallizes public anxieties.

Demographic profiles

While, in most of the Arab world, rising numbers of single women are connected with delayed marriage, what is striking in Palestine and requires explanation is that Palestinian women in the West Bank and Gaza appear to have a unique marriage pattern: early but not universal. For Palestinian men, marriage is near universal (Rashad, Osman and Roudi-Fahimi 2005: 2). Palestinian women marry (and bear children) relatively early, with the median age of marriage at 18, but significant numbers of women remain single. Although national-level official statistics are available only from 1995 when the Palestinian Central Bureau of Statistics conducted its first demographic survey, other surveys and research suggest that female singlehood has a longer historical trajectory. There are also significant differences between the West Bank and Gaza and perhaps among regions in the West Bank as well.

There has been a high number of never-married single women, constituting 35 per cent of all women aged 15–49 years in 2000, and, more significant, 12–14 per cent of women aged 35–39 years (PCBS 2002, 2006b). As we can see from Table 6.1, rates of singlehood are consistently higher in the West Bank than in Gaza. Interestingly, in light of the perception among Gaza

Table 6.1 Proportion of never-married women, West Bank and Gaza

	2000		2004	
Age range	West Bank	Gaza	West Bank	Gaza
30–34	14.8	8.5	16.1	9.3
35–39	16.1	8.5	13.2	8.7
40–44	12.3	6.4	11.7	3.5

Source: Halabi (2007: Table 4). Figures are based on calculations from the raw data.

campaigners that the proportion of unmarried women is on the rise, there was only a slight increase from pre-intifada (2000) proportions of single women aged 30–34 years (at 8.5 per cent) to intifada (2004) levels at 9.3 per cent, and there was a sharp decrease among women aged 40–44 years.

Regionally, whereas almost one in ten Palestinian women over the age of 40 is in the never-married category, the proportion was only 1.5 per cent for the same age group in Egypt (in 1996), and about 4 per cent in Jordan. In the Arab region, only Lebanon, Tunis and Algeria have a higher proportion of never-married women, and the first two have considerably higher average ages of marriage for women (see Drieskens 2006 for Lebanon).

Data from the 2000 and 2004 demographic and health surveys in Palestine (PCBS 2000, 2004) make it clear that never-married women are clustered at opposing poles of education. For 2004, almost half of unmarried women over 30 (and thus almost certainly permanently single), had only primary education or lower, while 22.9 per cent had above secondary education. Only 10.7 per cent of married women who were 30 and over had education above secondary-school level. However, the gap widens with age, suggesting that 'educated women had more difficulty marrying in the past' (Halabi 2007: 39). The voices in our focus groups confirm this perception where, at least in combination with other factors such as employment, post-secondary education has become an asset. Coupled with perceived earlier ages of marriage in certain settings (primarily rural), girls with only secondary education find themselves trapped, with diminishing marriage prospects on the one hand and lack of opportunity to earn income on the other.

Is education empowerment? The significance of location and mobility

In an older generation of women, education, particularly post-secondary education, was a key to individual autonomy, public service and social status – but sometimes a detriment to marriage. Educated girls and women were also valued as markers of a desired modernity, and female education was a cause embraced by Arab reformers. For Palestinian parents in the same post-1948 era, education was often seen as a form of portable capital in the insecure conditions of statelessness after the loss of Palestine. From the provision of free education to Palestinian refugees by the United Nations Relief and Works Agency (since 1951) to the founding of Palestinian universities in the West Bank and Gaza in the 1970s, education has been a site of both mobility and security in the highly insecure circumstances of Palestinian life, and female educational levels have increased consistently. Indeed at present, Palestinian young women have slightly higher enrolment rates in post-secondary education than their male counterparts.

For the older generation interviewed in this project, the role of fathers in supporting their daughters' education is prominent. In the early 1960s, Zahera's father, a teacher of Islamic religion and mathematics in Jerusalem, was trusted by his community to take not only Zahera but five other girls to settle them in various universities in Egypt. Parental encouragement of female education was often accompanied by a lack of pressure to marry. The father of Ilham (who later achieved a PhD in Linguistics and became a Birzeit University professor) told her as she was growing up in Nablus during this period: '*Ya binti* [O my daughter]. there is no man in the world that is worth a university degree.' For Zahera, Ilham and others whose university education took place in the 1960s and 1970s, university was inextricably linked to student politics, cultural flowering, and the rise of the Palestinian resistance. Zahera, who was in Cairo during the 1967 war, represented Palestinian students in presenting a petition to the Egyptian government to keep them on in the dormitories when their families were unable to send money. She remembers her Cairo years as 'golden times' and says there were no barriers to prevent women from getting involved in the heady politics of the day.

Given the centrality of education to Palestinian families and their aspirations, it is perhaps not surprising that education and the quest for education figure in these narratives, but it is striking how dominant they are, particularly for women whose education is at risk. Consider Mariam, now 52, a refugee who has lived all her life in Breij camp in Gaza and who finally obtained a degree from Jerusalem Open University at the age of 44 after at least three failed attempts at higher education:

> I received no less than twenty offers [of marriage] in the stages of my life since I was in the second basic class and I refused the subject because Mariam wanted to continue her education and to be necessary to society.

In focus groups with young women today, education remains a central goal, but its perceived utility as an avenue to autonomy and/or public service varies. Unlike the earlier generation, young women today perceive post-secondary education to be a marriage asset if coupled with secure employment. Young women with less education, particularly young women in villages who finished high school education and remained at home, found themselves with diminishing marriage prospects. A young woman in her mid twenties in Beit Fajjar village near Bethlehem, herself 'only' a high-school graduate, observed ruefully, 'Only a Doctora [a PhD holder] can get married at a later age than 18 or 20.'

In our discussions, it was also clear that education must be matched with other attributes to allow mobility. Generally, these attributes are those of a rising urban and increasingly globalized middle class, as well as professional or semi-professional employment, even if found in a rural setting. As one young woman from Sa'ir said poignantly, after describing her own household of 18 people and the restrictions placed upon her: 'There are people in our village who have their freedom. They have small families where everyone is educated and they do things together.' She acutely pinpoints education in the context of changes in family structure and lifestyle that mark the emergence of a middle class, where education, conjugality and 'togetherness, and small nuclear families, lead to an ideal of 'freedom'.

Thus, where education is the sole improvement, the life of a young woman in rural or marginalized settings may not change too much. Sawsan from Yamoun, a remote village in the eastern Jenin district, describes her struggle for a education at the Open University, the difficulties of commuting to Jenin and the greater difficulties of mobility after she completed her studies: 'I finished university after six years. After two weeks, everyone said, "Where are you going?"' Samia, another Open University graduate, from Tubas village in the Jordan Valley, reported similar constraints on her movement imposed by community gossip and pressure: 'I like to go to work. But people say she is not an employee, why does she go? People interfere with everything. If I am walking in the street, they say, "This is not your day to go to work, what are you doing?"'

Both Saswan and Samia, like many of the young women in our groups who pursued higher education, were students at the Jerusalem (Al-Quds) Open University. For young women, the Open University offers an education which can be pursued within the safer confines of home (and village), with only occasional forays into public life and student activity. This also means that the potentially liberating atmosphere of student public and campus life is largely absent. Selwa from the Bethlehem-area village of Beit Fajjar said that she has been going to the Jerusalem Open University for three years but declared proudly, 'I have never spoken to a young man.'

In the conservative southern West Bank Palestinian town of Hebron, we met with female students in the extraordinarily crowded headquarters of the Hebron branch of the Jerusalem Open University, where students were enrolling for the spring semester. Among the group, the students from Hebron city were clearly distinguished from their village counterparts by more fashionable and expensive dress, with stylish headscarves and pastel colours. The several students from villages were poorer, with two in rather drab *jilbabs*, and they felt something of a divide from the city girls. As one girl from the disadvantaged village of Tarqomia said, 'Hebronites won't marry villagers. They are racist.'

Amira, who is on the student council and from a powerful family in the Hebron area, has a confidence in her future that led her to turn down a cousin marriage and to insist on a university education. She expresses her trajectory of education and employment in spatial terms, saying she has 'no borders':

> In my family, I am the only one who entered the university. I am always active, even though people say, 'Why go to the university and get tired?' For me there are no borders. My cousin asked for me but I didn't want. I want to go from the student council to a *wazifeh* [a secure job as an employee].

Whilst Amira is buoyed by her class and family position (and her strong personality), her consciousness of a need to change and move is shared by other young women who may not have her personal and family assets.

Marriage age, staying single and 'change'

An interesting consensus emerged in all the focus groups that the best age for a young woman to marry was in her early to mid twenties when she has her 'own personality', significantly later than the median age of marriage at 18 (over one quarter of Palestinian women are married before that age). However, particularly in village settings, most also agreed that in fact girls usually married at an earlier age, at 18 or younger, and that their own chances of marriage after that age were small. The young women in Sa'ir agreed that families and prospective husbands 'really like a girl who is 15 or 16, 20 maximum'. This gap between the ideals of young women (and often their mothers as well) and the present reality of early marriage is a source of great tension, as well as potential for change. Hadeel, a young unmarried woman in her twenties from Shawawreh, a village on the arid eastern slopes of Bethlehem, is unsuccessfully looking for work. She says there is a change in her village: 'Women are more conscious now. They don't just marry anyone. There is a change.'

This feeling of change is also evident in the more prosperous village of Beit Fajjar near Bethlehem. Basma, an unmarried women in her late thirties who takes loving care of her elderly parents,[6] says that her mother received a house and its land from her parents and will give it to Basma. 'Girls no longer accept everything. They want their rights.'

Yet the combined force of consciousness of rights, pride in education, and family trust does not seem to help these young women with their twin preoccupations of marriage and, almost obsessively, the search for work that yields income. Opportunities are limited, not only by the job market but by what is considered respectable.[7] Being a teacher is OK but a position as a secretary is described as 'difficult', because of the proximity of male employers and staff and the possibilities of sexual harassment. Again, bodies are a source of danger and vulnerability. Two young women in Sa'ir tell similar tales of failed initiatives:

> I took a course in computers for six months and then was forbidden to work.
>
> I took a course in hairdressing, I'm really interested in opening a salon. But I worked for two or three months without wages and then my family wouldn't let me continue.

In terms of marriage, the young women in Sa'ir summed up their bodily situation by saying, 'We are retired.' When we asked why families wanted a young bride of 15 or 16, the answer was proverbial and echoed elsewhere in our discussions: 'They say the husband should raise her with his own hand.'

For a bride to be raised like a child by her husband is of course the stark opposite of the bride with her own 'personality' and education that consistently emerged as an ideal. We asked the young women in Sa'ir, none of whom were able to continue to higher education, if university students graduating at 21 or 22 years might have a chance at marriage. The reply effectively dismissed their own chances as high school graduates (or less) for a suitable marriage: 'Well, if you have a degree and can work, it's OK. If you have only *tawjihi*, there is not much hope. We have "nothing in our hands".'

The young women broadly blame their constrictions on 'the political situation' and the fear it generates among their families. Whether through tales of an Israeli soldier forcing a girl to 'kiss a young man at the Hebron checkpoint', or the murky tale of false pornographic images on mobile phones that led to the 'honour' crime noted previously, the present is full of 'embodied' dangers. Interestingly, the young women look to the past, not the future, for better times. The young women in Sa'ir affirm: 'It wasn't always like this. Things got worse in the Al-Aqsa intifada. Families are afraid for their girls and there is no security.'

Tropes of dis-ease and disorder: customary marriage, old men and young brides

In answer to a number of questions about dangers to, and problems of, young women, many young women – and sometimes their mothers as well – described 'new' and disturbing forms of marriage, rather than the physical dangers and restrictions that surround them. These forms of marriage included both the very old marrying the very young and customary marriage (unregistered marriage without a formal marriage contract). For these young women, most of whose adolescence and young adulthood have been lived in warlike conditions, such dangers and restrictions are the rule rather than the exception. Instead, the pervasive political and security crisis seems to be transmuted into moral disorder, where stories of improper marriages predominate.

Customary marriage is a form of common-law marriage that is unregistered. Although the Islamic sharia allows a form of customary marriage where there is a marriage contract signed by a guardian, *zawaj urfi* has come to have many other forms, including a secret agreement between the couple only, which would constitute an illicit relationship in sharia terms. In other contexts, particularly Egypt, this has led to children without proven paternity (who thus cannot get birth certificates, citizenship, and the like) constituting a subject of great public debate.

In fact, it had not occurred to us to ask about customary marriage, a practice that we thought was not common in Palestine, although its re-emergence and reconfiguration have been subjects of great public concern and debate in other Arab countries, particularly Egypt. It is striking that the subject emerged spontaneously in our discussion twice in groups, in response to our reading of two articles in the local press on youth suicides. In a discussion with university students in Hebron, we read a newspaper clipping in which the police chief of the Hebron district warned of a rise in youth suicides. We asked those present for reasons why a young person might commit suicide. Interestingly, the students assumed the suicides were female although the account described both a male and a female suicide. 'Pressure from families' and 'social and economic reasons' were cited. One girl offered an instance where a young woman was struck by a jinn (a mischievous spirit),[8] and another where a girl was pressured by her brother to marry against her will and stabbed herself in the stomach. All agreed, however, that one reason was 'there are many customary marriages [*zawaj urfi*]' where girls are placed in immoral and deceitful conditions. One recounted: 'One girl was in an urfi marriage and then she got engaged to someone else. She committed suicide.'

Amina, a dynamic young woman who is on the student council at the university, asserted that 'statistics' show that 40 per cent of all marriages are customary. She remained firm in her belief in this very dubious figure, even when its absence in national demographic data was proposed. Her conviction that such marriage is pervasive

– and was not so in the past – is echoed in informal discussions with Birzeit University students, who recount friends and acquaintances as being in such marriages or who are considering the same, partly because of the high cost of an official marriage.

In a focus group with women in Doha and Beit Jala, women responded to another newspaper account of youth suicide (this time in the northern West Bank) with a tale of *zawaj urfi* where a girl in a local high school was discovered to be pregnant at school and it turned out that she was in a customary marriage. 'Girls are tricked,' was the succinct explanation, and it is fair to say that those in 'customary' marriages can also be seen as unmarried women in sexual liaisons.

The extent and forms of customary marriage have not been explored in the Palestinian context, but the discourse circulating in our discussions points to it both as an emerging phenomenon and a trope for other forms of disorder. 'We never had this before,' was a refrain in both groups. Given that marriages (and weddings, as noted by Johnson *et al.* 2009) are a highly resonant symbol for social and political harmony – so much so that democratic Palestinian elections were widely described as a 'Palestinian wedding' – illicit and false marriage is an equally resonant symbol for a world out of kilter.

Another prominent narrative of improper (or unnatural) marriage was that of old men marrying the very young. In Beit Fajjar, Selwa begins to tell a story – with others chiming in – of an elderly man who divorced his wife and married a 14-year-old.[9] This theme emerged several other times in the discussion, including an anecdote of a 70-year-old man who married a 'schoolgirl' and then retired, and she had to open a shop to support them. In the discussion in Sa'ir, the material motives for such marriages were prominent:

> Two old men married sisters of 15 and 16. Their families did it just for the money. The old men were rich.
>
> Another man over 50 married a girl of 15. Now she has a house in her name.

The young women conclude:

> Of course there is force and oppression (*zulm*) in making these matches.

Once again, these stories of the old marrying the young emerged spontaneously as a response to a general question about problems in the village. We can thus position them as narratives of social disorder and moral uneasiness. In the context of Sa'ir, it is interesting that these extraordinary or unnatural marriages were given as pressing problems, whereas no one referred to an actual problem on the day of our meeting. As we walked up the steep hill to the small bare meeting room, an Israeli army jeep entered the village, boys threw stones, and shots were fired. Such an encounter was clearly deemed ordinary, to use one of the most common Palestinian expressions which often has an ironic inflection, '*aadi* (ordinary), which can be used to describe everything from a minor clash with the Israeli army to a full-scale invasion (Johnson 2007b). Yet these tales of old men and teenage brides are also tales of communities and families that have lost their moral compass because of this 'ordinary' situation of war and fragmentation. They use 'force and oppression', significant terms, against girls for material advantage.

Virtual dangers, actual bodies

Another striking version of physical insecurity transformed into moral disorder came in Shawawreh. Entering the meeting shortly after the discussion began, Um Nabil was a tall and imposing woman, draped in black, with a strong square face. The black was not for her widowhood but for her brother, who had been assassinated along with three other militants by the Israeli army in Bethlehem a few weeks earlier. The embraces from everyone in the room were also condolences. Posters of her brother dotted the walls of the village.

With this death on the minds of everyone in the room as a reminder of the insecurity of Palestinian daily life, we were particularly surprised by the unanimous response when we asked what were the main dangers to village girls in their late teens. The answer came quickly: 'Television – but only satellite television. It is a disaster.'

Everyone agrees with this, although they hasten to say that they are not against television or satellite television per se – there are useful educational programmes and they do not even oppose music programmes (thus distancing themselves from some Islamist positions). However, they assert that there are immoral programmes that can disturb young people. Refugee women living in Doha, a suburb just outside Dheisheh refugee camp and nearby Beit Jala, were even more emphatic about the dangers of satellite television. A middle-aged woman with teenage daughters, when asked why a young girl might kill herself, answered, '*Salsalaat*' (soap opera series that are very popular on satellite television) which undermine morals. The notion here is that these series put false ideas about life and morality into the heads of the susceptible young. The women in this particular focus group, most of whom were mothers of unmarried daughters, seemed to cast these lurid virtual soap-opera dangers onto their real streets. As one declared, she trusts her 16-year-old daughter, who is free to say anything she wants, but won't allow her out of the house because 'I am frightened for her. The *shabab* might talk badly to her. They might give her an *acamol* [paracetemol] but it is really drugs.'

Other women chime in with stories of alcohol put in a soft drink and given to a teenage girl, and 'photos' – young men taking photos on their mobiles of girls and then turning them into pornographic pictures and circulating them. While young men – particularly the unemployed and frustrated young men of this period – are certainly sometimes guilty of incidents of sexual harassment, we seem once again to be in the terrain of moral panic, with globalized and sexualized dangers conditioned by satellite as well as by the actual and insecure conditions on the streets of Doha and Bethlehem. The sense of a generation gone astray is of course not particular to Palestine but the contrast made

– with previous generations which stood for national struggle and values – can be striking. One 29-year-old activist in Amari, who had participated as a boy in the popular mobilization of the first intifạda (1988–93), contrasted himself with the teenagers in Amari's youth club: 'We were the generation of intifada, they are the generation of satellite.'

The voices above are countered to some extent by the opinions of young unmarried women themselves about satellite television. Most are eager to distance themselves from its sexualized images. When asked if Nancy Ajram, a very popular and sexy singer on various satellite stations, was someone they admire, young women unanimously rejected her – often with shy laughter. They do note dangers, but often different dangers from their older counterparts. One young woman from Dheisheh refugee camp noted the dangers of believing everything on television:

> There was just a young woman here in her twenties who went on a diet – just a cup of tea a day – because she saw all the images on satellite TV. Her haemoglobin went to 3 and she died.

Young women in the Jenin focus group did note that young men, the *shabab,* are not respectful – 'all they think of is sex, not love'. Their behaviour is blamed on computers and the internet. However, young women found solace in religious and educational programmes on satellite TV, naming several female sheikhs, or religious instructors, whom they greatly admired. These sheikhs addressed issues of family life, bodily comportment and life goals that young women were eager to understand and which they might not have found answers to from their families and communities.

In fact, many of the young women in our discussions were uneasy with their level of knowledge about their bodies and felt that they needed more information. A young woman from Sa'ir said:

> We are embarrassed, we don't know about our bodies. When we ask someone, they say, 'It's wrong to talk like that [*Eib tehki hek*].'

A university student from Dheisheh had a similar complaint:

> Perhaps I shouldn't say, but things happen to my body and I don't know if it is normal or there is illness. Until last year I didn't know that women have three openings. It's like that.

While several young women in Sa'ir and villages near Jenin found it hard to talk to their mothers, another young woman in the Jenin group said the following about menstruation:

> Sometimes the mother puts everything that is needed in the cupboard. Then the girl can be relaxed.

Young women in Beit Fajjar, however, who also affirmed (as noted above) that families like and trust their daughters, found mothers more forthcoming, saying they learned about their periods from their mothers and that, 'It's not like the old days.' And most young women – even those who said they couldn't talk about sex – said such talk was not shameful (*mish eib*) and that girls needed more understanding. Tala, from Dheisheh refugee camp, said, 'I am embarrassed but we need to know about married life.' Manal agreed and added, in an equally embarrassed tone, 'Of course we don't want anything silly, it should be scientific.'

The last remark reflects a feeling that there is a proper, and an improper, way to treat sexual matters, which is also applied to notions of freedom. Fadia, from Jenin refugee camp, after condemning men who tell their wives and daughters that everything is forbidden, hastened to add, 'I am not saying that someone should be just loose and do whatever she wants. There should be a balance.'

Basma, in Beit Fajjar, who agrees that it is not shameful to talk about sexual matters and that families should trust their daughters, states a similar condition when she says, using an interesting spatial phrase, that 'we don't trespass our limits'.

Nonetheless, the desire to understand their bodies is clearly articulated – as are the barriers to such understanding. One young woman in Dheisheh addressed a telling barb at the many NGO activities to 'train' Palestinian youth in democracy. She said: 'Really, we are bored from always having the same subject, communications workshops, democracy. Learning about our bodies would be better.'

Can unmarried women be happy?

While most of the young unmarried women in our discussions continued to see marriage – particularly with a sympathetic partner – as an important good, there were voices of dissent about the happiness of married life and the inevitable misery of unmarried women. When asked if an unmarried woman can have a happy life, the young woman from the Hebron-area village of Tarqumia, had a personal example: 'Yes, my aunt stayed unmarried, she was political and taught school. She was happy and went around. She went to Russia when she liked.'

Her aunt's trajectory – as a professional, a political activist, and an autonomous spirit valuing her independence and movement – is typical of most of the life stories of older professional unmarried women recorded in this project, and indeed of even older generations of unmarried Palestinian women who founded schools and charitable societies, and participated in the nationalist movement (see Fleischmann 2003). An autonomous life was valued both for its own sake and for the opportunity it provided for public service. Zahera reflected on her life course:

> What you want when you are young, you don't when you are older. I value the freedom and space, I don't want to lose it. I am happy with my life. It was my decision [not to marry] and I go with it. If my life was repeated, I will do it again.

Whether young women in both more restricted and more contradictory times can find the same fulfilment in a life without marriage, is of course an open question which the young women in our focus groups addressed in different ways. Most of the young women in Jenin, for example, agreed that, 'If you are not married, you feel weak.' Some limited their aspirations: 'I don't think of love at all. At 27 or 28, it is not one hundred per cent [certain] that I will find someone.'

Yet they did not necessarily locate the source of the misery in their lack of a spouse; rather the problem was the community responses to their unmarried state. Unmarried women could be happy, they opined, in certain circumstances: 'Yes if there was no society to say *awanes* [old maids, spinsters] she could be happy.'

The language is significant: *awanes* (plural of *a'nes*) is a term with a strong negative connotation. Perhaps less negative, but certainly telling, is the common practice of calling unmarried women, whatever their age, 'girls' (*banaat*), a term also meaning daughters. This infantilization and desexualization of unmarried women has a connotation 'of being barred from adult femininity' (Sa'ar 2004).

Nonetheless, in Beit Fajjar, Basma evoked the authority of the Quran, affirming that it says you don't have to get married. And almost all concurred that another key to happiness as an unmarried woman was stable employment. In Shawawreh, a mother defended her two daughters:

> An unmarried *bint* [girl, daughter] can go as she wants. My daughter is 28 years old and she works and buys her clothes and does as she wants. One works in Beit Sahur. There is another one in Abu Dis – an honourable girl [*bint sharifi*]. Girls today do not marry '*min makaan*' [just anybody].

Women in Doha agreed that unmarried women could be happy: 'Yes, if she has good work, like an engineer or a doctor.' Indeed, one affirmed: 'If they are working, it is good to be without a husband.'

There is thus a long (and living) tradition of unmarried women with fulfilled and significant lives that needs to be recovered from the past (see Fleischmann 2003), in the present era when unmarried women are increasingly deemed a locus of moral panic and a trope for social disorder. There are also winds of change, contradictory and frustrated, but embodied in the determination and thwarted desires of a new generation of young women for a productive and meaningful life.

Two short films made by young single women explore these contradictions, desires and determination. In a finely conceived and poetic four-minute video *Rahaf*, the filmmaker, herself from a village, explores the effects of a broken engagement on a young girl who is ostracized and condemned. Fadia El Dein, who made the film, says, 'I passed through this experience and I don't want people to feel sorry for me. People see the girl who has a broken engagement as someone who will be a spinster for life' (Shashat 2008: 16).

In *Remote Control*, Amal, a student at Al Najah University in Nablus, is being teased by her friends about her devotion to her boyfriend, Ahmed, when she hears the news that she has received a full scholarship to the United States. Ahmed demands that she turn it down. Later at home, in her pink fluffy pyjamas, Amal receives a call from Ahmed who thinks she has refused the scholarship; Amal tells him she has to think about it. She turns on her laptop, writes an acceptance letter, and presses 'Send'. In the last shot, Amal has her head back, sad, reflective – and determined to move on.

Acknowledgements

A longer version of this chapter was previously published in the *IDS Bulletin*, Vol. 41, No. 2, and we are grateful to Wiley-Blackwell for their kind permission in allowing a shorter and reorganized version to be published here.

Notes

1 All focus groups with young women were conducted by the author and facilitated by Fadwa Abu Labban, a colleague from Dheisheh refugee camp in the southern West Bank.

2 Under the 1995 Interim Agreement (Oslo agreements) signed between Israel and the Palestine Liberation Organization, the West Bank was carved up into three areas, of which the greatest by far was Area C (about 40 per cent) under sole Israeli security control. Area A (the main Palestinian towns) is under Palestinian control in security matters, while Area B is nominally under joint control, but in fact control is exercised by Israel. The provisions for Area A have been violated repeatedly by Israeli invasions.

3 In 2006, there were 14 recorded honour crimes in Palestine, rising to 18 in 2007 (Palestinian Independent Commission for Citizens' Rights 2007, 2008). Almost all were crimes against unmarried women and committed by male members of the victim's natal family. Johnson (2008) explores cases of honour crimes in the larger context of violence against Palestinian women and girls.
4 A special thanks to Andileeb Udwan for conducting and transcribing two important interviews in Gaza despite the severe conditions in Gaza at the time. These nine topical life stories are examined separately and in more detail in Johnson 2007a.
5 Names and some other identifying details have been changed in order to protect privacy except in the case of the former Minister for Women's Affairs, Zahera Kamal, and Dr Ilham Abu Ghazaleh, both of whom chose not to be anonymous. Names of women in the focus groups have also been changed.
6 While the care of an elderly parent or parents is frequently the duty of the unmarried daughter, Basma has embraced her task and also conducts activities for the elderly: 'I give to people, I don't think of myself at all.'
7 Palestine registers unusually low female labour force participation (at about 12 per cent), largely due to gendered and restricted labour markets. It is also true that participation (and approval of participation) rises when conditions are more secure. At present, insecurity and instability have shrunk both the actual labour market – there are fewer jobs for an ever-growing number of young job seekers – and the perceived market of acceptable jobs for women.
8 In a study of Artas village near Bethlehem, a number of unmarried women blamed their failure to marry on the activities of jinn (Rothenberg 2004).
9 Under prevailing Jordanian law, the minimum marriage age for girls is 15 years and for boys 16 years. However, cases of families presenting false documents are recounted.

References

Butler, J. (1993) *Bodies That Matter: On the Discursive Limits of 'Sex'*, Routledge, London.

Cohen, S. (2002) *Folk Devils and Moral Panics*, Routledge, London.

Csordas, T. (1994) 'Introduction: The Body as Representation and Being-in-the-world', in T. Csordas (ed.), *Embodiment and Experience*, Cambridge University Press, Cambridge.

Drieskens, B. (2006) 'Reasons Not to Marry: Rising Celibacy in

Contemporary Beirut', paper presented at Second World Congress for Middle Eastern Studies, Amman, Jordan, 11–16 June.

El Khoudary, T. (2008) 'For War Widows, Hamas Recruits Army of Husbands', *New York Times*, 31 October.

Fleischmann, E. (2003) *The Nation and Its 'New' Women: The Palestinian Women's Movement 1920–1948*, University of California Press, Berkeley.

Friedl, E. (2003) 'Tribal Enterprises and Marriage Issues in Twentieth Century Iran', in B. Doumani (ed.), *Family History in the Middle East: Household, Property and Gender*, University of California Press, Berkeley.

Ghazi, J. (2006) 'Unmarried Arab Women Chastised by Their Societies', *New America Media*, Pacific News Service, 14 March.

Halabi, H. (2007) 'Profile of Single Women in Palestine', *Review of Women's Studies* 4, Institute of Women's Studies, Birzeit University.

Ibrahim, M. (2004) 'Alarm Bells Ring as Rate of UAE Spinsters Rise', *Khaleej Times*, 16 July.

Jad, I. (2009) 'The Politics of Group Weddings in Palestine: Political and Gender Tensions', *Journal of Middle East Women's Studies*, Vol. 5, No. 3, pp. 36–53.

Johnson, P. (2007a) 'Palestinian Single Women: Agency, Choice, Responsibility', *Review of Women's Studies* 4, Institute of Women's Studies, Birzeit University.

—— (2007b) 'Tales of Strength and Danger: Sahar and the Tactics of Everyday Life in Amari Refugee Camp, Palestine', *Signs*, Vol. 32, No. 3, pp. 597–620.

—— (2008) '"Violence all around us": Dilemmas of Global and Local Agendas Addressing Violence against Palestinian Women, an Initial Intervention', *Cultural Dynamics*, Vol. 20, No. 2, pp. 119–32.

Johnson, P., L. A. Nahleh and A. Moors (2009) 'Weddings and Wars: Marriage Arrangements and Ceremonies in Two Palestinian Intifadas', *Journal of Middle East Women's Studies*, Vol. 5, No. 3, pp. 11–35.

Palestinian Central Bureau of Statistics (PCBS) (2002) *Family Formation in the Palestinian Territory*, PCBS, Ramallah.

—— (2004) *Demographic and Health Survey – 2004: Final Report*, PCBS, Ramallah.

—— (2006a) *Palestinian Family Health Survey, 2006: Final Report*, PCBS, Ramallah.

—— (2006b) *Demographic and Health Survey, 2006: Final Report*, PCBS, Ramallah.

—— (2007) *Palestinian Family Health Survey, 2007: Final Report*, PCBS, Ramallah.

Palestinian Independent Commission for Citizens' Rights (PICCR) (2007) *Annual Report 2006* (in Arabic), PICCR, Ramallah.

—— (2008) *Annual Report 2007* (in Arabic), PICCR, Ramallah.

Rashad, H., M. Osman and F. Roudi-Fahimi (2005) *Marriage in the Arab World*, September, Population Research Bureau, Washington DC.

Rosenfeld, M. (2004) *Confronting Occupation: Work, Education and Political Activism of Palestinian Families in a Refugee Camp*, Stanford University Press.

Rothenberg, C. (2004) *Spirits of Palestine: Gender, Society and Stories of the Jinn*, Lexington Press, Oxford.

Sa'ar, A. (2004) 'Many Ways of Becoming a Woman: The Case of Unmarried Israeli-Palestinian "Girls"', *Ethnology*, Vol. 43, No. 1, pp. 1–18.

Scheper-Hughes, N. and M. Lock (1987) 'The Mindful Body: A Prolegomenon to Future Work in Medical Anthropology', *Medical Anthropological Quarterly*, Vol. 1, No. 1, pp. 6–41.

Shashat (2008) 'Women's Film Festival in Palestine', Shashat, Ramallah.

Weiss, M. (2002) 'The Body of the Nation: Terrorism and the Embodiment of Nationalism in Contemporary Israel', *Anthropological Quarterly*, Vol. 75, No. 1, pp. 37–62.

Weizman, E. (2007) *Hollow Land: Israel's Architecture of Occupation*, Verso, London.

PART III
Changing Institutions?

7

Narratives of Egyptian Marriages

Mulki Al-Sharmani

A number of new family codes have been introduced in Egypt since 2000. Local and international media at the time hailed these new laws as a significant achievement for women. In this chapter, I will argue that despite the significance of the new reforms, they have not been able to transform the gendered and hierarchical legal construction of marriage in which a husband is obligated to provide for his wife and consequently acquires the right to her obedience (that is, her physical and sexual availability).

First, I will briefly outline marital relations and roles as defined by classical schools of Islamic jurisprudence. I will also examine the model of marriage espoused by contemporary Egyptian family laws, shedding light on how the present codes have drawn on and modified the *fiqh*-based (Islamic jurisprudence) construction of marriage. Second, I will recount a narrative of marriage as lived by an Egyptian woman. Third, I will examine how these narratives of marriage – institutional and lived – are validated or contested through courtroom practices. My aim is to show the reader: (1) how the contradictions and tensions inherent in the institutional narrative of marriage are played out in the real lives of women; and (2) the ways in which the institutional narrative is maintained, reinforced or displaced by new legal reforms, such as mediation-based family courts and *khul*.[1] In recounting these narratives, my focus will be on constructions and contestations around the marital roles of husbands and wives, and their connections to female sexuality and rationality.

The analysis in this chapter is based on 12 months of fieldwork conducted in 2007 in four governorates in Egypt (Cairo, Giza, Gharbeya, and Alexandria). In the course of this fieldwork, interviews were conducted with 53 female litigants, 11 male litigants, and 30 court personnel. In addition, two focus group discussions were conducted with lawyers. Court proceedings and mediation sessions were observed once a week over a period of six months, and 25 court records were analysed.[2] Furthermore, 11 interviews were conducted by the author with key members in women's rights organizations, members of the legislative committee at parliament, and the National Council of Women,[3] prominent lawyers and judiciary, and public thinkers. All these persons were involved in the process of lobbying for, debating, and legislating the new laws (namely, the Personal Status Law (PSL) No. 1 of 2000 and PSL No. 10 of 2004).

First narrative: the institutional construction of marriage

Fiqh-based marriage

Egypt, like all other Middle Eastern countries, with the exception of Turkey, adopts family laws that are based on the doctrines of classical schools of Islamic law. The main schools are *Shafii, Hanafi, Hanbali, Maliki, and Twelver Shia.* Adherence to the Hanafi school of jurisprudence, which was decreed in the Ottoman period, has been maintained in the legal system of the modern Egyptian state. However, the newly codified law borrowed rulings from the other Islamic schools of jurisprudence, particularly the Maliki with regard to judicial divorce. Still, the legal system requires the judge to apply the dominant opinion of the Hanafi school unless there is an explicit text in the Egyptian legislation on the personal matter being reviewed.[4]

It is inevitable that any reform efforts have to engage with the model of marriage that is sanctioned by Islamic legal schools. Islamic law makes an intrinsic connection between marriage and sexuality. Men and women's heterosexual drives and desires are acknowledged and accepted, but both sexes are only allowed to fulfil these needs and desires through the institution of marriage. So, one of the main functions of Islamic marriage is to make sexual relations between the married couple licit. But how does sexuality (both male and female) feature in *fiqh* constructions of marital roles? And is the *fiqh*-based model of marriage inherently discriminatory against women?

Abu Odeh (2004) argues that Islamic schools of jurisprudence share a gendered model of marriage in which the relations between husbands and wives tend to be hierarchical. In this model, Islamic marriage is based on a contractual agreement between a man and a woman in which the husband has the duty to provide for his wife and their offspring, and in return the wife puts herself under his authority and protection. The husband's exclusive right to his wife's sexual and reproductive labour is earned through, and conditioned upon, his economic role. This model of marriage does not recognize shared matrimonial resources. Whatever possessions and assets the wife brings to the marriage remain hers. Likewise, apart from maintenance for herself and her children, the wife cannot make claims to resources acquired by the husband during marriage. In addition, the husband has a unilateral right to repudiation and polygamy.

However, the schools of Islamic *fiqh* differ on some of the rights that they grant to wives. For instance, according to the Hanafi school, a woman at the age of maturity can contract her own marriage and does not need a male guardian to represent her. This is not the case in the other schools. Yet, in Hanafi *fiqh*, women's divorce rights are greatly restricted, whereas the Maliki school accords women the right to seek divorce on multiple grounds, such as harm, abandonment, and lack of maintenance. Interestingly, in all schools of jurisprudence a wife is entitled to seek *khul* divorce, although jurists of different schools disagree on the financial compensation that a husband is to receive from the wife in this case.

Ziba Mir-Hosseini (2003) also argues that the *fiqh*-based model of marriage is hierarchical, with gender forming the basis of this hierarchy. The author divides Islamic legal discourse on gender into three types: classical, neo-traditional, and reformist. The first, which she traces to classical Islamic legal schools, conceives of gender relations and roles as unequal and women as inferior to men. These gendered notions, the author points out, were shaped by the prevailing metaphysical and philosophical views of the time, in which women were thought of as sexual beings who 'are made of and for men' (Mir-Hosseini 2003: 10). This discourse promoted a model of marriage that could be traced to a pre-Islamic form of marriage called 'marriage of dominion'. In this type of marriage, women were considered the property of their husbands. Similarly, the model of marriage that was espoused by the classical *fiqh* was one based on the notion of sale. That is, marriage was conceptualized as a contract in which women exchanged their sexual and reproductive labour for the husband's financial support. Mir-Hosseini argues that it is important to understand classical *fiqh* as a contextualized human endeavour on the part of learned religious scholars to interpret the rules of the sacred texts on how Muslims should live their lives in accordance with the teachings of their faith. That is, the religious knowledge that was produced by these schools was shaped by the historical and social contexts of the time.

With the establishment of modern nation-states in Muslim countries, family laws were codified. In most of the countries in the region, these modern laws continue to be based on the doctrines of Islamic *fiqh*. Thus the *fiqh*-driven hierarchical gendered model of marriage was maintained, but was further strengthened through state institutions and governing practices. Mir-Hosseini refers to the gender discourse that was reflected in those modern personal status laws as neo-traditional. This discourse introduced some reforms but continued to maintain and justify unequal rights of husbands and wives through the idea of complementarity of gender roles.

Mir-Hosseini (2003) argues that towards the end of the twentieth century, a third discourse emerged, which she calls the reformist discourse. This new discourse revisits the gender inequalities inherent in the classical *fiqh*-based model of marriage and tries to illuminate the contradictions between the gendered interpretations of sacred texts produced by classical *fiqh* and its subsequent scholarship, and the universal values of the Islamic faith (namely equality, justice, and freedom).

It is notable, though, that the *fiqh*-based model of marriage has been put into practice with a lot of fluidity and diversity which did not necessarily assert male dominance or negate women's rights (Sonbol 1996; Brown 1997; Tucker 1998; Moors 2003; Esposito and DeLong-Bas 2001). For example, contrary to the privileging of male sexual rights that is implicit in classical *fiqh* constructions of marital roles, courtroom practices and jurists' *fatwas* (legal opinions) throughout many pre-codification eras affirmed wives' sexual agency and right to consensual pleasurable marital sex (Tucker 2008). Furthermore, through the practice of inserting stipulations in their marriage contracts, women were able to restrict their husband's right to polygamy and repudiation; they were able to negotiate a wide range of rights such as adequate support for themselves and their children, maintaining their economic activities after marriage, choosing their place of residence, pursuing education, and so on (Hanna 1996; Sonbol 2005).

In fact, some of the historians who studied the development of Islamic legal schools and modern Muslim family laws point out that gender inequality and biases against women that are found in present-day family codes are not simply consequences of their religious foundations. Historians such as Abdel-Rehim and Sonbol have also traced the discrimination against women that is embedded in modern family laws to modernist notions of building cohesive nuclear families that are to be disciplined and controlled by modern nation-states (Abdel-Rehim 1996; Sonbol 1996; Sonbol 2005). Sonbol (2005), for instance, points out that the process of codification of Muslim family laws was based not only on the doctrines of one or several Islamic legal schools but also on borrowings from colonial European laws.[5] She shows that the project of subject-making and nation-building that was undertaken by modern Muslim nation-states in the 20th century incorporated modernist European notions of nuclear families as the essential blocks for progressive and well-governed societies.

This discourse shifted the purpose of marriage from regulating a contractual relationship between a man and a woman to creating nuclear families and maintaining their cohesiveness. Modern nation-states saw the nuclear patriarchal family as the institution in which individuals were reproduced as citizens and dutiful members of the nation. To enable families to fulfil their roles in the process of subject-making, these states devised family laws that regulated the rights and duties of family members. Husbands were bestowed with the responsibility of heading the family and providing for its family members. In return for the protection and financial support that women and children received from the husband/father, they owed him obedience and submission.

Other scholars such as Tucker (2008) also argue that modern family laws are in fact more discriminatory and disempowering of women than the doctrines of classical Islamic jurisprudence because of the centralized and intrusive power of the modern nation-state, which is reflected in its rigid and gendered codes and procedures. For instance, up until 1967, modern Egyptian personal status laws stipulated that married women who were found to be 'disobedient' by the court should be returned forcibly to the conjugal home by a state enforcement agent. This practice never existed in sharia courts in pre-codification eras. In addition, judges in sharia courts, drawing on the flexibility and pluralism of juristic doctrines, did not confine the notion of 'disobedience' to wives but also extended it to husbands whom they found to be the cause of marital conflict and abuse against their wives. Yet in modern family laws, the notion of 'disobedience' has been limited to wives.

Marital roles and rights in Egyptian personal status laws

Egypt's codified personal status laws adopt a model of marriage that is traceable to the one constructed by Islamic *fiqh*. Article 1 in PSL No. 25 of 1920 defines a husband's main role as being the provider for his wife, while the role of the latter is to be sexually available to the husband. The law, furthermore, makes a wife's right to her husband's financial support conditional on her fulfilment of her sexual role. To fulfil her sexual role, the wife is expected to be physically available in the conjugal home. Article 11 in PSL No. 25 stipulates that a wife who is found by the court to be disobedient *(nashiz)* loses her right to her husband's financial support. Disobedience is defined by the law as a wife's refusal to reside in the conjugal home with her husband.[6] This legal narrative of marital roles and rights is maintained in subsequent codes (PSL No. 25 of 1929 and PSL No. 100 of 1985). In addition to assigning different and gendered roles to husbands and wives, these laws also grant both spouses unequal rights and are discriminatory against women in many respects. Men have an unfettered right to unilateral repudiation and polygamy, and they enjoy full guardianship over their children. Women, on the other hand, have highly restricted access to divorce and cannot be the legal guardians of their children even when they are the custodial parent.[7]

In 1979, the late President Sadat decreed PSL No. 44 of 1979, which included revolutionary reforms. PSL No. 44 protected working women from obedience ordinance suits brought by their husbands on the grounds of their leaving the conjugal home to work, and it affirmed their right to spousal financial support. Other reforms included a wife's automatic right to judicial divorce if her husband entered into a new marriage, without her having to prove injury first. It also included her right to the conjugal home in the case of divorce, if she had custody of the children. The new law also granted *mut'a* (indemnity) to women divorced by their husbands without their desire or fault (Fawzy 2004). To avoid opposition from the religious establishment, from Islamist groups and from other conservative factions in society, President Sadat decreed the law at a time when the parliament was not in session. PSL No. 44 of 1979, however, was later annulled by the High Supreme Court in 1985 because the process through which it was passed was ruled to be unconstitutional. President

Sadat had passed the law without presenting it first to parliament for review by using his presidential power to issue decrees during times of emergency. The High Supreme Court, however, ruled that at the time the law was decreed, there was no emergency that would legally justify the President's use of that power.

Thus, contemporary marriage as constructed by Egyptian legal doctrine is one in which a husband supports his wife and children, provides for them an adequate and safe conjugal home, and is considered by the legal system as the guardian and the leader of this family unit. In exchange, a wife is expected to fulfil the sexual needs of her husband, to be physically available in the conjugal home, and to care for the children (but she cannot claim guardianship over them). In other words, her sexual role, unlike her husband's, is objectified and her rights are unequal to his. But is this institutional narrative of marriage lived by Egyptian women and men? How does it fit with the realities of their daily lives and the socio-economic conditions of their society?

Second narrative: lived realities of marriage

Marriage continues to be an important social institution in which young men and women as well as their families invest heavily. Men and women seek marriage for stability, independence, social acceptability and, of course, the fulfilment of their sexual and romantic desires. Their families invest in their marriages to help their children, to forge alliances, and to maximize family resources. On the other hand, the costs of marriage have become a monumental economic burden for many young Egyptians and their families. The Egypt Labour Market Panel Survey of 2006 showed that the nominal national cost of marriage between 1995 and 1999 was LE25,705, and in the subsequent five years, it rose to LE32,329 (Singerman 2007).

Young men work for many years, migrate, and solicit the assistance of their families in order to save for the costs of marriage. Women and their families also have to strategize in order to save for their share of the costs of marriage.[8] Young women from the low and middle classes work and join savings pools (*gam'iya*) in order to save for the costs of their marriage (Amin and Al-Bassusi 2003). A husband with financial assets becomes the most desirable marriage partner for daughters. The most important of these assets are a job with a regular source of income, an apartment, and the ability to cover the costs of marriage. This strategy of seeking a husband with adequate financial assets, however, does not always work. In the first place, not many men are able to shoulder the financial responsibilities and costs of marriage without having to work for many years and delay marriage or depend on the assistance of their families. Sometimes when the husband's family contributes to the establishment of the new conjugal home, the family makes claims on the resources of the new couple and wants to have a central say in the use and management of these resources.

The economic burden of marriage, coupled with the great social need to get married, creates a lot of stress and strain on single women and men. Thus, women and men often go through the process of getting married with a lot of caution and fear. Women in particular feel vulnerable because of the asymmetry between their marital rights and those of their husbands. With the help of their families, women generally seek a number of financial guarantees from their bridegrooms in order to protect themselves from the husband's abuse of his legal right to unilateral divorce. What is sometimes lost in this process of negotiation, however, is an effort to create a marital relationship on the basis of mutual respect, trust, and shared ownership of the new conjugal life.

The women interviewees in this study sought marriage for the social acceptability and sense of personhood attached to the role of wife and mother. Economic factors also motivated the interviewees' pursuit of marriage. Some got married to escape the life of economic hardship that they led in the household of their extended family, others to relieve their families from the responsibility of having to support them; some of the women were pressured to marry in order to escape the stigma that their community and the larger society attach to being an older unmarried woman.

The process of pursuing marriage entailed finding a partner, negotiating each partner's share of the marriage costs, and entering into marriage with adequate protection against divorce and abandonment. However, these different aspects of the process are not necessarily congruent with one another. Negotiations and compromises have to be made. Some women strategize better than others, but still many enter into marriages that are based on highly precarious foundations. These weak foundations include reliance on meagre resources that are shared with in-laws, the husband's precarious employment status, and discrepancy between the husband's and the wife's perceptions about their financial roles in the marriage and the realities of their economic needs. Additional dimensions include the pursuit of partners with economic assets at the expense of emotional and educational compatibility as well as the unequal and hierarchical legal rights and obligations of husbands and wives.

Nadia, one of the interviewees, is a 29-year-old woman with a 16-month-old daughter.[9] She had been married for three years, and had been in a legal conflict with her husband for a year at the time of the fieldwork. She filed for judicial divorce and child alimony on the grounds of harm. Nadia had been living with her in-laws in their apartment building. She lived in a separate apartment, but she had to share meals with her in-laws in their apartment, where she was expected to do the cleaning and cooking every day. Her in-laws had a key to her apartment and accessed it freely to use the washing machine and the bathroom heater. Her husband, who worked as an air-conditioner repair man in Kuwait, sent monthly allowances to his family but no separate money for his wife since he expected her to share meals with his family. Nadia suffered from the lack of privacy and independence, leading to constant fights with her mother-in-law. She asked her husband for an apartment in a separate building, but he and his family refused. The problems with the in-laws, however, were not the only cause of the marital rift between Nadia and her husband. Her husband was emotionally and sexually abusive; he repeatedly put her down and she thought this was perhaps due to the gap in their educational level. She recounted the pain she experienced numerous times when her husband demanded to have sexual intercourse with her shortly after he had insulted her. She felt that their sexual relations were his right and her duty. This resonates with the legal discourse that defines marital roles in terms of a husband's financial provision in exchange for a wife's sexual availability.

In one of several family-initiated mediations, it was agreed that Nadia would continue to live in her in-laws' building, but that her husband would send her LE200 a month so that she could cook her meals separately and manage her daily expenses. This agreement only lasted for a month; the husband's family objected because they were concerned that he would cut down on the monthly sum of money he sent them to pay for the annual taxes of the family-owned auto repair shop.

Nadia's own family background and the strategies she used to make decisions about her marriage partner and to cover the costs of marriage shed light on the difficulties and contradictions of the politics of marriage. Nadia's father, a non-literate manual labourer, worked in Libya for several years until he had saved enough money to purchase a small apartment in a poor urban area in Giza. Because the family made little money from their small convenience store and her father's health was getting frail, Nadia started working when she was 16. Every summer, she worked in service jobs such as a sales assistant in a pet shop or a cleaner in a hairdresser's. She used her income to cover her own personal expenses. When she joined a two-year vocational institute after high school, she got a full-time job working as a sales person in an upscale make-up and lingerie store. She worked 12 hours a day and made LE500 a month in addition to LE100–150 commission from the sales profits. Nadia focused on her job and stopped going to the vocational institute. Still, she managed to sit for her final exams and successfully graduated. During the six years she worked before getting married, she had two goals: to save enough money to buy her trousseau (*gehaz*), and to help her family. She managed to buy the furniture for the living room, the washing machine, the kitchen stove, some chinaware, carpets, bed sheets and kitchen utensils. She also paid for the costs of painting her parents' apartment and changing the upholstery of their living-room furniture. In addition, she was able to save LE5,000.

Nadia's criteria for choosing a marriage partner are indicative of the socio-economic challenges confronting young men and women who wish to marry as well as of the limitations of women's legal rights and obligations in marriage. She wanted a partner who was able to provide for her and had enough financial assets to cover his share of the costs of marriage. From her late teens onwards, Nadia turned down a number of suitors who had enough cash to cover the costs of marriage but who earned income from informal and intermittent work (*arzagi*).[10] Before getting married, she had been engaged to her co-worker's brother. He held a government job, was of a similar educational level, and had an apartment. Moreover, she liked him and thought that he was good-looking. But the marriage plans fell through because they could not agree on the marriage costs. Her fiancé wanted her to pay half the costs of the wedding party. But since she had already paid for the engagement party, she and her family thought that they should not contribute to the wedding party. Therefore, they broke the engagement but her fiancé came back a few months later and wanted to revive the marriage plans. This time, he agreed to pay for the wedding party but said that he would not be able to buy her a jewellery gift (*shabka*). She agreed, but once again the marriage plans failed because they disagreed on what to write in the *qayma*, the record of items and furniture in the conjugal home which the wife claims in the event of the dissolution of marriage. Although Nadia wanted to marry him, she decided that if she were to compromise on the *qayma* and give up her right to *shabka*, she would enter into the marriage with insufficient leverage and thus less protection from divorce or the financial vulnerability associated with it.

Although her job as a salesperson in a fancy store was financially lucrative, the working hours were too long. So Nadia decided that it would be very difficult to juggle her job with married life and child-rearing. Also, she was fearful that if she continued working after marriage, her future husband would forfeit his role as the primary provider for the family. She recounted the experiences of several of her friends whose husbands expected them to contribute all their salaries to the household expenses. She pointed out that these husbands feared that their wives would become defiant because they had their own source of income, and accordingly they put too many financial demands on their wives. Yet the financial obligations on these working wives were not matched by any support from husbands in housework or child-rearing responsibilities. The experiences of Nadia and her friends regarding the tensions created in the marriage because of their work (or giving up work) are partly related to the contradictions created by the failure of existing family law, as enacted by the state, to acknowledge married women's economic contributions to their nuclear families. This was despite the fact that many families were, in current times, financially dependent on the income of the wife.

After her first engagement failed, Nadia was even more convinced that the financial assets of a future husband were the crucial criteria for the choice of a partner. Her present husband, whose parents and siblings lived in the same street as her family, proposed. His education level was lower than hers; he had dropped out of elementary school. She did not feel an emotional attachment to him as she did with her previous fiancé. But the present suitor had an apartment in his family-owned building and held a well-paying job as an air-conditioner repair man in Kuwait. In addition, unlike her previous fiancé, he agreed to buy her a LE5,000 *shabka* and sign the *qayma* that she and her family proposed. Nadia felt that she did the best she could in light of the inherent difficulties and challenges of pursuing a stable marriage. Her insistence on receiving a *shabka* served her well when the marriage fell apart. She sold her jewellery and used the money to pay for the costs of her Caesarean section when delivering her daughter. In addition, she was able to reclaim the furniture in the conjugal home because of the *qayma* and was able to sell some of these possessions in order to have an income while her court case was in process.

Nadia's experience illustrates the contradictions that arise from the incongruence between the institutional construction of marital roles and the realities of many Egyptian women and men. The spousal financial protection that the law promises to Nadia is unattainable in real life. Nadia had to work and save money in order to be able to contribute to the establishment of the marital household. Unlike the institutional narrative of marriage, hers was one in which she did not receive the advance portion of the dower.[11] Her husband provided the apartment and she helped with the furnishing. In addition, she failed to collect the deferred portion of the dower because of the ineffective enforcement mechanisms of the legal system. Because the law does not recognize her financial contribution to her nuclear family or grant her any rights because of this role, Nadia was reluctant to continue to work after marriage. Moreover, the lack of workers' benefits and protection in her job made it difficult for her to juggle work and the marital roles which she was legally and socially expected to fulfil.

The tensions inherent in the gendered marital relations constructed in family laws have also shaped the process through which Nadia sought marriage, her expectations from married life, and her disappointments. Her pursuit of a husband who would be more likely to commit to his role as a provider and willing to concede more financial assets to her in the marriage negotiations are tied to the rules underlying the legal model of marriage. That is, women like Nadia pursue the partner/provider not only because of the difficult socio-economic conditions of their times but also because they realize that their strongest claim in the legal discourse is a husband's financial provision. At the same time, Nadia was cognizant of other things that she wanted but lacked in her marriage, namely her husband's respect, his affection, and his appreciation of her as a person and partner.

Procedural reforms: are they transforming marriage?

Since 2000, Egyptian women's rights activists have sought gender-sensitive reforms in family law through the piecemeal, cautious but safe approach of procedural changes. An alliance of women's rights organizations, prominent legal figures, government officials, and members of parliament successfully lobbied for PSL No. 1 of 2000. The goal of the law was to simplify and improve the procedures through which personal status cases are to be reviewed and adjudicated.[12] For the women's rights organizations, this procedural law was a vehicle through which they sought to expand women's access to divorce by the inclusion of Article 20, granting women the right to no-fault divorce known as *khul*.[13] PSL No. 1 of 2000 also includes Article 17 which gives women in unregistered marriages (known as *urfi* marriage) the right to file for divorce. But these legal gains were not made without some concessions. During the contentious parliamentary debates about the *khul* article, the legislators agreed to insert a number of additional procedures to be followed in each *khul* case with the aim of restricting women's quick access to *khul*. It was agreed that in every *khul* case, the disputants are obligated to go through two reconciliation efforts undertaken first by the judge and then by two arbiters within a period of time not exceeding three months.

Another procedural reform is the establishment of family courts through the promulgation of PSL No. 10 of 2004. The aim of the new family courts is to establish a specialized, affordable, accessible, non-adversarial, and family-oriented legal system. The new courts handle all personal status (that is, family) cases. Each case is reviewed by a panel of three judges who are assisted by two social and psychological court experts. These experts, one of whom should be a woman, are obligated to attend court sessions, meet with disputants, and submit reports to the court. In addition, a specialized public prosecutor's office dealing solely with family law cases has been established. And to shorten the litigation process, the appeal of cases at the Court of Cessation has been abolished.

The most significant feature of the new system is the compulsory pre-litigation mediation. Before a disputant can file a suit, she/he is obligated to file for mediation. Mediation offices are housed in the family court, and mediation is carried out by three mediation specialists who have training in law, psychology, and social work. Mediation sessions are conducted over a period of 15 days. Upon the consent of the two parties, the mediation period can extend to two more weeks. If mediation fails, disputants can file a court case within a week. However, if a settlement is reached and approved by disputants, it is legally binding. Furthermore, mediation services are free for all disputants.

The idea behind abolition of adjudication at the Court of Cessation and the establishment of alternative mechanisms of dispute resolution is to address the problems of lengthy and expensive litigation processes. These are problems which predominantly female litigants tend to encounter, being the majority of the litigants in family courts. Moreover, the inclusion of female mediation specialists and psycho-social experts among the court personnel is meant to make the legal process more sensitive to women's experiences. But implementation shows that a number of problems impair the effectiveness of the new court system and accordingly affect women's access to justice.[14]

But perhaps it is mostly the gendered legal process – manifested through the discourse and practices of the court personnel – which is playing out in contradictory ways for individual litigants, thereby complicating the goal of achieving gender justice through the current legal reforms. In court sessions, case records, and lawyers' briefs, one can trace a particular discourse on female rationality, female sexuality, the sexual rights and obligations of husbands and wives, and the interplay of these rights and obligations with spouses' financial rights and obligations. In this discourse, women are considered emotional and hasty, and therefore incapable of making rational decisions about dissolving their marriage and obtaining divorce. Marital sex is predominately seen as a husband's right and a wife's duty, and this notion in turn leads to a narrow understanding of spousal sexual abuse of wives. In what follows, I will elaborate further on each of the above-mentioned points.

Some of the interviewed mediation specialists and court experts were of the opinion that women, particularly the young, resort to *khul* hastily and over petty reasons such as the husband's refusal to buy them the kind of shampoo they prefer or because of a disagreement over the colour of the upholstery for the furniture in the conjugal home. This perspective is in sharp contrast with the reasons for filing *khul* that were reported by the interviewed female litigants. Of the female litigants we interviewed, 13 of the 53 filed for *khul.* All of them had grounds for filing prejudicial divorce but opted for *khul* in order to shorten the litigation process and to save on costs. A similar finding has been reported by a study commissioned by the Center for Egyptian Women's Legal Assistance (CEWLA) (Halim *et al.* 2005). The grounds included spousal abuse, the husband's failure to provide spousal maintenance, the husband's abandonment, the wife's lack of sufficient livelihood, and her need to apply for state welfare.

The scepticism on the part of the court personnel about women's rationality, particularly when it came to decisions about divorce, was also accompanied by practices that were used by some mediation specialists and judges to pressure female litigants to reconcile with their spouses. A common practice was to warn the female disputant of the difficulties and stigma that awaited her if she became a divorced woman. In one of the observed court sessions, for instance, the senior judge tried to persuade a plaintiff to reconsider her divorce claim by warning her that her young daughter would probably have a difficult life with limited prospects for marriage and respectability if her mother became a divorcee.

Court discourse and practices also tend to depict female sexuality as the object of the husband's protection. A common legal practice observed among lawyers and judges was for lawyers to make legal claims on the grounds of a husband's role as the protector of his wife's sexuality and for judges to accept these claims. For example, in the court records of one of the researched prejudicial divorce cases, the wife's lawyer argued that the husband was not fulfilling two of his fundamental duties as a husband, which are supporting his wife and protecting her sexuality. He pointed out that the husband did not maintain his wife, and that he frequently travelled and left his 'young beautiful' wife alone with his brother who was living with them. The fact that the husband entered into a second marriage and concealed it from the first wife was mentioned in passing in the brief. But the latter reason, unlike the husband's failure to support the wife and guard her sexuality, was not stressed as the main form of 'harm' which was the basis for the plaintiff's right to claim divorce. Again, the court based its judgment to grant divorce on the grounds of the husband's failure to support and guard his wife's sexuality. This seems to be an instance in which legal practice and discourse are shaped by social norms. According to social norms, men have an obligation to guard the sexual honour of their wives, but written texts of family laws do not assign this role to husbands (although they link their financial role as a provider to their right to sexual relations with their wives).

Another important dimension of the gendered discourse that shapes the legal process is related to the sexual rights of husbands and wives. Court personnel emphasized the sexual rights of husbands and the sexual duties of wives, but not necessarily vice versa. According to them, a woman's main duty in marriage was to be sexually accessible to her husband. However, a woman's right to have sexual relations (or satisfying relations) with her husband, while not disputed by court personnel and disputants, was never mentioned by them as one of her basic rights. Rather, what was stressed was her right to be supported by her husband.

Furthermore, what constitutes spousal sexual abuse was a contentious notion between court personnel and female disputants. Mediation specialists, court experts, lawyers, and judges defined spousal sexual abuse in narrow categories, namely if husbands had anal sex with their wives or if they abstained from having sexual relations with them for a long period of time. Female disputants who were interviewed for this study, on the other hand, identified forced sexual intercourse and sexual relations that were accompanied by emotional maltreatment as a serious form of spousal sexual abuse. Furthermore, 11 of the interviewed female litigants considered it as one of the reasons why they wanted to end their marriage. One of the interviewees, for instance, suffered from severe bleeding because her husband forced her to have sexual intercourse with him, against the orders of the obstetrician, shortly after she delivered their child in a difficult Caesarean section. However, this interviewee, as well as the others who suffered from similar forms of spousal sexual abuse, chose not to make their legal claims on these grounds. They thought it was humiliating to recount such experiences to the court personnel; moreover, they did not think that their experiences of spousal sexual abuse would be taken seriously by the mediation specialist and judiciary. Thus, these women opted instead for gendered but more guaranteed claims such as the husband's failure to support despite the wife's obedience and sexual availability.

Notably this gendered legal discourse and practices pertaining to women's sexuality and sexual roles in marriage do not always hinder female plaintiffs' access to the legal redress which they are seeking. Some plaintiffs (for example the disputant seeking divorce because her husband had remarried) succeed in securing prejudicial divorce precisely by making use of the gendered aspects in this discourse. Others also strengthen their legal claims to maintenance by making the case to the court that they have fulfilled their sexual duties towards the husband and that they have guarded their sexual fidelity although the husband is estranged from them and/or has forfeited his roles as provider and protector of his wife's chastity.

The manoeuvring of these litigants, their strategies (and those of their lawyers), and the success of some in achieving their goals within a legal system that objectifies their sexuality raises interesting questions about empowerment. How do we understand empowerment in these cases? It is true that some of these women obtain the judicial divorce or the alimony they seek. But in the course of reaching their goals, they participate in the performance and the perpetuation of a legal narrative in which their sexual roles and rights and those of their partners are differentiated and essentialized (that is, gendered). Yet the institutional power that this narrative holds – through its repeated performance in courtroom practices and its interplay with the social norms governing gender relations and rights within marriage – continues to disempower women collectively and individually. This is because the institutional narrative partly enables husbands to commit abuses against their wives in the first place, under the pretext of being the partner entitled to 'obedience'. And again, this narrative continues to re-enforce the sexual agency and rights of husbands, on the one hand, and, on the other, the sexual objectification of wives.

Concluding thoughts

Marital relations in contemporary Egyptian personal status laws are based on the notion of the husband's maintenance of his wife in exchange for her obedience. The latter is defined by physical availability in the conjugal home and enabling sexual relations with the husband. This model of marriage is incongruent with the socio-economic conditions of many married couples, and it is disadvantageous and unjust for women. In real life, many Egyptian women (and their families) contribute to the costs of the wedding and the setting up of the conjugal home. Women also contribute to the maintenance of their conjugal family. Thus, women suffer from legal inequality, as well as the contradictions between the legal construction of marriage and the lived realities of their married lives.

Moreover, this legal construction of marital roles implicitly renders sexual relations between spouses as a husband's right and a wife's duty. The privileging of husband's sexual rights is reflected in courtroom practices which depict a wife's sexuality as the object of the husband's control and protection, and define sexual abuse in narrow terms that are detrimental to wives. Even existing personal status laws that give women the right to claim divorce on the grounds of sexual harm do not seem to offset the dominance and power of this underlying legal narrative of the husband as the sexual agent and the wife as the sexual object.

It is true that the new procedural laws that have been introduced since 2000 have expanded women's rights to judicial divorce and introduced alternative mechanisms of family dispute resolution with the goal of making access to the legal system and justice easier and less costly. But the benefits of these changes for women are diminished by legislative and implementation gaps. Most of all, these procedural reforms have not transformed the gendered and hierarchical model of marriage that continues to be espoused by the substantive personal status laws.

Currently, efforts are underway on the part of women's rights organizations and the government to introduce a new comprehensive family code that would address substantive issues such as the definition of marriage and marital roles, polygamy, spouses' rights to divorce, maintenance, child custody, and so on. Women's rights activists, in particular, are seeking a law that would adopt a model of marriage that is just to women. But what would such a marriage look like for Egyptian women who – despite their shared legal inequalities – are differentiated by social class, education, and their sensibilities and desires? For one thing, doing away with the sexually objectified and financially dependent role for wives has implications for the financial relations between the spouses. A wife may no longer enjoy the exclusive right to her own financial assets, which she may be obligated to contribute to the family if there is need. It may follow that she will not be able to file for divorce on the grounds of lack of maintenance, if she is financially able. Will this model of marriage be just and desirable to all Egyptian women? Many women contribute significantly to the financial support of the family but unlike their husbands, they do not acquire any legal rights from their financial role. Some women, nevertheless, may be ambivalent or even opposed to being legally obligated to support their conjugal family and to give up their claim to the financial support of the husband in exchange for equal marital and parental rights. What about women who are not earning a living but are shouldering all the responsibilities of childcare and housework? How will their labour be measured and taken account of, in legal terms?

In particular, a big challenge confronting those pushing for a new model of marriage is to redefine the sexual roles and rights of spouses. How can the right to marital sex be delinked from the financial role of the husband (or for that matter of either spouse)? What reforms (in legal doctrine and practice) are needed in order to affirm and uphold equal rights for both spouses to healthy, pleasurable, and consensual sexual relations with the other partner? And what would be the multidimensional grassroots changes that are needed to create an enabling and supportive societal environment for such reforms?

Notes

1 *Khul*, in Islamic jurisprudence, is divorce initiated by a wife, which does not require a reason, and where the wife agrees to pay the husband a specified sum for her freedom.

2 Interviews were conducted by the author with two research assistants, Sawsan El Sherif and Fayrouz Zaki. The author also conducted the observation of mediation sessions and court proceedings, the focus group discussions, interviews with 12 judges, and the analysis of court records.

3 The National Council for Women was established by the government in 2000. The council aims to promote policies to strengthen women's rights and enhance their development as well as monitoring the government's efforts to reach these goals.

4 See Article 6 of Law 462/1055, Article 280 of Law 78/193, and the current procedural Law No. 1 of 2000, Article 3.

5 Scholars such as Mayer (1996) also show how the model of marriage that is based on the husband's financial and protective role versus the wife's obedience was adopted in the Napoleonic Code of 1804, in English

Victorian laws and in German legislation of the 19th century. Mayer traces this gendered notion of marriage in the Tunisian Family Code of 1956, the Moroccan Family Code of 1958 and the Algerian Family Code of 1984. The central point that scholars such as Mayer and Sonbol are making is that it is misleading to attribute the gender inequalities that are found in modern Muslim family laws to a sharia-based model of marriage. See Mayer 1996, Sonbol 2005, and also Wright 2007 and El Sadda 2006.

6 The law stipulates that the conjugal home has to be adequate and safe for the wife and that the court needs to ascertain that the wife's desertion of the conjugal home was not because of reasons that are sanctioned by social norms (*urf*). However, the law does not spell out what these reasons are. But it is commonly understood that some of the acceptable reasons would include leaving the conjugal home to visit members of the extended family or to seek education or health care. Whether a wife's leaving the conjugal home for work is considered a socially acceptable reason has been contested by litigants and judges. PSL No. 100 of 1985 stipulates that if a wife has written in her marriage contract that she holds a job, a husband cannot bring an obedience ordinance case against her on the basis of her going out to work.

7 The new Egyptian Child Law, which was passed in June 2008, grants custodial female parents educational guardianship over their children. However, existing personal status laws are still silent on this issue.

8 According to the Egypt Labour Market Panel of 2006, the bride and her family contribute 31 per cent of the costs of marriage, while the groom and his family contribute 69 per cent. Although the share of the bride and her family is less than that of the groom and his family, it is still a considerable percentage, particularly for the lower and lower-middle classes (Singerman 2007).

9 The real names of interviewees have been changed for the purpose of confidentiality.

10 Examples of such jobs are street vendors, construction workers, and vocational workers who are employed on a temporary basis.

11 Because many men cannot afford to pay a dower, it has become a custom among many Egyptian families for women to forgo their right to the advance portion of the dower. Thus, men provide the conjugal home, and the couple share the costs of furnishing the marital home. In the marriage contract, a symbolic figure such as LE1 or PT25 is often written as the advance portion of the dower. The wife is entitled to the deferred portion of the dower in the event of divorce or the death of the husband.

12 Law No. 1 of 2000, for Reorganization of Certain Terms and Procedures

of Litigation in Personal Status Matters, cut down the 318 clauses of previous procedural laws to a mere 79. The law replaced Law 78 of 1931, Part 4 of the Civil and Commercial Code, Articles 868–1,032 of Law No. 77 of 1949, and some of the procedural articles included in the substantive personal status laws.

13 According to the *khul* law of 2000, the female plaintiff is granted divorce in exchange for returning to the husband the dower that is recorded in the marriage contract. Normally, the advance part of the dower is paid by the husband at the time of drawing up the marriage contract, whereas the deferred part is expected to be paid to the wife at the time of the husband's death or in the event of divorce.

14 For a detailed analysis of these implementation problems, see Al-Sharmani (2009).

References

Abdel-Rehim, A. R. A. (1996) 'The Family and Gender Laws in Egypt during the Ottoman Period', in A. A. Sonbol (ed.), *Women, the Family and Divorce Laws in Islamic History*, Syracuse University Press, Syracuse, NY.

Abu Odeh, L. (2004) 'Modernizing Muslim Family Law: The Case of Egypt', *Oxford University Comparative Law Forum*, No. 3. www.ouclf.iuscomp.org.

Al-Sharmani, M. (2009) 'Egyptian Family Courts: Pathway to Women's Empowerment?', *Hawwa*, Vol. 7, No. 2, pp. 89–119.

Amin, S. and N. Al-Bassusi (2003) *Wage Work and Marriage, Perspectives of Egyptian Working Women*, Population Council Working Papers No. 171, Population Council, New York.

Brown, N. (1997) *The Rule of Law in the Arab World*, Middle East Studies, No. 6, Cambridge University Press, New York.

El Sadda, H. (2006) 'Gendered Citizenship: Discourses on Domesticity in the Second Half of the Nineteenth Century', *Hawwa*, Vol. 4, No. 1, pp. 1–28.

Esposito, J. and N. DeLong-Bas (2001) *Women in Muslim Family Law*, Syracuse University Press, Syracuse, NY.

Fawzy, E. (2004) 'Muslim Personal Status Law in Egypt: The Current Situation and Possibilities of Reform through Internal Initiatives', in L. Welchman (ed.), *Women's Rights and Islamic Law: Perspectives on Reform*, Zed Books, London.

Halim, N., A. Sultan and W. Morcos (2005) 'The Social Effects of *Khul*: A Comparative Study of *Khul* and Prejudicial Divorce', unpublished manuscript (in Arabic), Center for Egyptian Women's Legal Assistance (CEWLA), Cairo.

Hanna, N. (1996) 'Marriage among Merchant Families in Seventeenth-Century Cairo', in A. A. Sonbol (ed.), *Women, the Family and Divorce Laws in Islamic History*, Syracuse University Press, Syracuse, NY.

Mayer, A. E. (1996) 'Reform of Personal Status Laws in North Africa: A Problem of Islamic or Mediterranean Laws?', in *Women Living Under Muslim Laws Occasional Paper No. 8*, pp. 1–20.

Mir-Hosseini, Z. (2003) 'The Construction of Gender in Islamic Legal Thought and Strategies for Reform', *Hawwa*, Vol. 1, No. 1, pp. 1–25.

Moors, A. (2003) 'Public Debates on Family Law Reform: Participants, Positions, and Styles of Argumentation in the 1990s', *Islamic Law and Society*, Vol. 10, No. 1, pp. 1–11.

Singerman, D. (2007) *The Economic Imperatives of Marriage: Emerging Practices and Identities among Youth in the Middle East*, Middle East Youth Initiative Working Paper No. 6, September, Wolfensohn Center for Development and Dubai School of Government, Washington DC and Dubai.

Sonbol, A. A. (1996) 'Law and Gender Violations in Ottoman and Modern Egypt', in A. A. Sonbol (ed.), *Women, the Family and Divorce Laws in Islamic History*, Syracuse University Press, Syracuse, NY.

—— (2005) 'History of Marriage Contracts in Egypt', *Hawwa*, Vol. 3, No. 2, pp. 159–96.

Tucker, J. (1998) *In the House of the Law: Gender and Islamic Law in Ottoman Syria and Palestine*, University of California Press, Berkeley, CA.

—— (2008) *Women, Family, and Gender in Islamic Law*, Cambridge University Press, Cambridge and New York.

Wright, D. C. (2007) 'Legal Rights and Women's Autonomy: Can Family Law Reform in Muslim Countries Avoid the Contradictions of Victorian Domesticity?', *Hawwa*, Vol. 5, No. 1, pp. 33–54.

8

Gender and Sexuality Activism in Beijing

Negotiating International Influences and National and Local Processes

Susie Jolly

In January 2008, Beijing, a couple of days after my arrival, I struggled to get out of bed in a fog of jet lag, vaguely aware of the radio in the background. The radio reported on young women training to become hostesses for the Olympics. Part of their look was a 'Chinese style smile', which showed only eight teeth and expressed China's warm welcome to the world. All the hostesses met minimum height requirements. There were no fixed weight requirements but 'of course they are not too fat', in order to fit all the clothes ordered for them. One woman described how her feet hurt from wearing the high heels, but she felt it was so worth it, and with great enthusiasm practised her smile for an hour every morning in front of the mirror.

This was just one example of the preparation for the Olympics in full swing, providing an opportunity for celebration of national identity as well as international exchange. Chinese women whose bodies fitted the costumes (and the gendered norms of beauty), and whose smiles fitted the national ideology, presented their eight teeth each to the foreign visitors.

The Olympics also meant many other things, as people I interviewed reported. Yan Yuelian (of Zi Teng sex workers' rights organization) described to me a crackdown on sex workers (interview, 2008). Girls from Zhejiang province selling sex in Beijing shared a rumour that if you were pregnant, police would release you immediately and this seemed to work for a while.

Some got pregnant for up to a few months before aborting, but even that strategy seemed to be wearing thin. Beijing was being cleared of sex workers. One year later, a survey of 200 sex workers in Beijing found that over 40 per cent had left the city several months before the games because of fear of a crackdown or low demand. However, those that stayed reported an increased income due to high demand (Aizhixing Institute of Health Education 2009). The months before the games started were also not a good time for sexuality-related workshops or get-togethers. Meetings of large groups of people on any issue were considered more sensitive during this period. Some sexuality NGO websites were closed down during the games.

Beijing is a globalizing city, well connected with international markets and media, and the Olympics were just one part of this. Many factors, both domestic and foreign, influence China's changing practices around sexuality and the related agendas pursued by activists and policymakers. This chapter traces the ways in which Chinese activists, particularly in Beijing, have negotiated international forces as well as national and local processes in their efforts to push for change. I will be exploring how this confluence of forces has enabled the many shifts that have come about and how the work of activists, government actors and donors around discourses of gender relates to new narratives of sexuality.

This chapter draws on relevant literature in Chinese and English, on my experience working and consulting for international donors in China over the past 15 years, and on my engagement in feminist and queer activism. In January 2008, I interviewed 17 activists, donors, researchers and staff in governmental organizations.[1] The activists and academics are among the leading people working on these issues in China today, having been centrally involved in policy work and activism over a number of years. The donors are generally on the more progressive side, and engage with work on gender, HIV and AIDS and/or sexuality. Many of the interviewees I had known for many years, so openness and trust were already established and interviewees were relaxed in sharing information. I had subsequent exchanges with some interviewees by email and by phone. None of the activists wished to remain anonymous. However, one of the interviewees from a government agency, and three donor staff preferred to do so. Those who were happy to be cited are named in the text, the others are given pseudonyms. Everyone was happy to have their interview recorded on tape.

The following section explores the changing relationships between donors, government and activists. First, I show how these spheres are in fact overlapping rather than distinct, before considering the domestic policy context and international influences, and how these are negotiated. The second section explores relationships between gender and sexuality work, including schisms between the two. I examine how strategic efforts to introduce gender to China played into these schisms and how these were manifested in organizing against domestic violence. The third and final section considers what the changes mean, how they have come about, and the implications for women's empowerment.

Changing relations among donors, government and activists

Donor, government, activist: overlapping spheres of work

There are huge overlaps among donors, government and activists. Some NGOs are now functioning as donors, and managing umbrella funds to distribute resources, such as Wan Yanhai's Aizhi Foundation. Wan Yanhai described his relationship negotiations with particular funders as being similar to those with his grantees (interview, January 2008). And many donor staff come from activist backgrounds and are still involved in activism, and themselves need to raise funds to distribute or support programmes (for example Guo Ruixiang in UNIFEM).

Some national staff in donor agencies previously worked for government agencies. Ms Y from a UN agency previously worked for the National Family Planning Commission, and

Zhou Kai in UNAIDS previously worked for the Centre for Disease Control. A position in a governmental organization can be completely compatible and even complementary to activism, as Du Jie demonstrates by combining her position in the Women's Research Institute, affiliated to the All China Women's Federation (one of the mass organizations set up by the party/state), with membership in the Gender Training Group and many other NGOs. Even Wan Yanhai, an activist who has been detained several times, formerly worked for a government-run health institute in the 1990s.

In many ways we are talking about a common professional scene, rather than institutions in opposition. The overlaps facilitate relationships among donors, government and activists, even if they do not automatically overcome divergent interests. Two interviewees both used the same phrase – 'the bottom decides the brain' (*pigu jueding naodai*) – to make the point that people's views change according to where they sit institutionally. Yan Yuelian referred to the few sex workers who became health trainers for the Centre for Disease Control starting to act more like patronizing health professionals than sex worker allies (interview, January 2008).

Policy context: increasing space for gender and sexuality work and for living diverse desires?

> On the one hand, police still raid the Beijing gay film festival and parade sex workers and clients through the streets in Shen Zhen city; on the other hand, health officials work with gay communities to prevent HIV/AIDS in many cities; sex workers are increasingly accepted by the general public; transgender people can change sex in hospitals and on their birth certificates; and an agent for 'Asexual Marriages' has appeared on the Chinese market.[2] The current government's 'human centred' policies allow certain desires to be expressed. (Interview with He, 2008)

The policy environment has changed enormously over recent decades, creating more space for progressive work around sexuality, particularly in relation to HIV and AIDS, but perhaps more generally also, with new commitments such as to being 'people-centred' (*yi ren wei ben*). The overall message I was getting from interviewees was that things are getting better but remain mixed and contradictory. Since the interviews in 2008, however, restrictions on civil society have in many ways increased, in terms of what can be stated publicly, online, to the press, if and how meetings can be organized, and possibilities for accepting international funding. However, the longer-term trajectory since the founding of the People's Republic of China in 1949 has still been towards greater possibilities for civil society mobilization on sexuality or any other issue, and there has been a remarkable increase in space since the 1980s for openly living out diverse sexual relationships.

The first law issued by the Communist Party in China after taking power in 1949 was the 'Marriage Law', which forbade forced marriage and proclaimed husbands and wives equal in marriage. However, freedom to look for relationships other than marriage, and to divorce or stay single, were circumscribed by social pressure as well as government policy.

> China's communist regime ... initially espoused an 'official' ideology of equality between women and men, outlawing concubinage and prostitution and mobilizing women into the workforce. Yet ... the project of equality entailed the desexualization of women, while tight controls on personal life severely restricted sexual freedom and access to sexual knowledge. The only acceptable form of sexual activity was within monogamous marriage. (Jackson *et al.* 2008: 8)

Sexual equality went hand in hand with the 'desexualization of women' and to some degree of men, in the moralistic ideology of the Communist Party. This was because ardour was expected to be revolutionary rather than sexual, and because the emphasis was on preventing sexual exploitation rather than enabling sexual freedoms.

In the 1980s, nongovernmental organizations did not exist in China, university students were banned from dating, and laws against 'hooliganism' were used to justify the harassment of gay men. 'Homosexuality does not exist in China' was a common refrain, in spite of cruising areas in such central locations as Tiananmen Square in Beijing, where men could enter liaisons with other men. People who tested positive for HIV in the late 1980s and early 1990s reported that the clinics often directly informed the local authorities to report on their status, ensuring exposure and stigma.

Nowadays, a vibrant civil society includes gender and development networks, *lala* (lesbian) and *tongzhi* (LGBT) telephone help lines, sex worker groups, groups of people living with HIV and AIDS, and an organization of women married to gay men. Every other summer, the Institute of Sexuality and Gender in the People's University of Beijing brings together about a hundred people from throughout mainland China, as well as a handful from Taiwan, Hong Kong and further afield, for a conference on Chinese sexuality research.

Injustices do continue. Police paraded sex workers and their clients through the streets of Shenzhen in 2006 to shame them. The consumerist market economy has spawned a new emphasis on femininity, with images of scantily clad women used to sell things. Urban women working in sales have to tread a fine line, presenting themselves as pretty and appealing but not too sexually free, at the same time as dealing with high levels of sexual harassment (Liu 2008). Activists who criticize government too directly may be detained. And government tolerance of NGOs – whether on sexuality or any other issue – is limited. Indeed, from 1996 to 2002 the total number of registered 'social organizations' fell by 18 per cent due to more restrictive registration requirements and the closure of some organizations (Saich 2004). Nevertheless, the massive economic and social changes in China since the 1980s have included greater space for a diversity of expressions of love and desire, and for organizing to increase such space.

Negotiating domestic policy spaces

The ambivalences and tensions implied by Chinese policy on

sexuality over the years have created spaces for the expression of, and organizing around, certain desires and relationships whilst circumscribing others. Different parts of government may take different approaches. For example, the Ministry of Health system generally endorses/facilitates health education initiatives for sex workers and drug users at a local level, while the Public Security Bureau (PSB) may be more likely to obstruct and arrest people. Sometimes there are tensions between the PSB and the health system, but in some cases they work together. Mr A (from a government HIV/AIDS advisory body) (interview, January 2008), explained how the health bureau gradually built trust among initially suspicious sex workers, when the latter realized that the health bureau would not pass on any information to the PSB. Ms Q and Ms Y (from the same UN agency) reported how more sympathetic local PSBs may give names of 'entertainment venue' (brothel) owners to the health bureau to facilitate safer sex initiatives, and may even endorse these initiatives (for example in Wuhan). However, when there are periodic crackdowns by some PSBs, health bureaus do not try and interfere in these (interview with Ms Q and Ms Y, January 2008).

The tensions between different understandings of sexuality on the part of state institutions located in the different spaces of 'health' or 'security' are illustrated below.

> Last year ... Heilongjiang Centre for Disease Control (CDC) trained sex workers on how to protect against HIV, but then the local PSB said CDC seems to be accepting the sex industry. CDC said we are only recognizing reality and making efforts to prevent the HIV/AIDS epidemic, as sexual transmission in China has been increasing rapidly. (Interview with Guo Ruixiang, UNIFEM, January 2008)

The political sensitivity of an issue is determined less by its disturbance of conventional moralities than by its offence to government priorities. For example, Confucian ideology has it that a daughter-in-law should be filial by producing many sons. But family planning, that is, the One Child Family Policy, is a policy priority, so opposing this is very sensitive. This is of course a very emotive issue, and on visits to rural areas I have heard stories of violence between those implementing the family planning policies and couples angry at forced abortions or sterilizations (which are now far less common than in the 1990s). Yet almost no civil society groups work in this area. The UN Population Fund (UNFPA) and the Ford Foundation have engaged with government bodies on providing more client-centred services, and increasing informed choice for couples about which contraceptive method to use, but they do not challenge the quota for the number of children that couples are allowed to have.

Currently, the imbalanced sex ratio (more boy babies being born than girl babies due to sex-selective abortions) is a concern for government, in part because of fears that a significant number of the next generation of men will not be able to find wives. Now, active measures are being taken to prevent abortions of female foetuses. Pre-natal sex testing is illegal. Reproductive health services are provided which also serve a monitoring role of identifying which women are pregnant, and whether or not they exceed their quota for permitted children. If within their quota, and subsequently found to have had an abortion because the foetus was female, the women may then be fined or penalized in other ways. Some feminist organizers are capitalizing on official concern with this issue to encourage government action which more fundamentally challenges gender inequality and makes girl babies more welcome.

Exceeding the quota for numbers of children is illegal and punished by fines, the parents losing their jobs, and the child being excluded from state education and health systems. By contrast, homosexuality is not illegal. And even though drug use and sex work are illegal, organizing in relation to HIV and AIDS, by 'minority' groups such as homosexuals, drug users and sex workers, is probably less controversial than married couples protesting family planning restrictions. Relations with state agencies are more likely to be shaped by whether or not the action defining the group is considered illegal or a policy priority. This is less likely to be a critical feature for non-state actors in society. Xiaopei He (Pink Space NGO) found that as drug use and sex work are illegal, it was actually easier for government to work with homosexuals. Socially however, as Mr A (government HIV/AIDS advisory body) pointed out when analysing social attitudes, stigma against homosexuals was the greatest. He felt that people can understand sex workers, because their goal is making money, something not so hard to relate to. From a government perspective, Mr A said that methadone treatment for drug users was supported by the PSB because it reduces crime.

In relation to HIV and AIDS, work with drug users, men who have sex with men, and with sex workers is in some ways less sensitive than work with people who have contracted HIV through blood transfusions or selling blood. This is because lack of government regulation was responsible for the latter, so the groups affected try to call government to account and demand compensation, whereas people who have contracted HIV through sex can be blamed themselves. Work on many sexuality or gender issues tends to be positioned as 'social issues', in contrast to more obviously political work such as calls for more accountable government.

Negotiating international forces and 'Chinese-ness'

A sense of national identity can be particularly strong around sexuality. On one occasion I was working with a Chinese consultant on an HIV and AIDS programme in China. We visited a brothel and interviewed the boss, among others. For every question we asked, he preceded his answer with, 'We Chinese …' (*zanmen zhongguo ren*). I was seeking to understand his specific experience and ways of working in one Chinese brothel. But staring at my white face and high nose, he felt his story was explaining China to me. Ironically, after the visit my co-consultant declared, 'It surprises me that Chinese people are having so much sex, when I don't even like having sex with my husband.' I was intrigued that her sense of national identity was so strong that she expected her sexual experience necessarily to have something in common with that of over 1 billion other Chinese people. In this instance, the sense of Chinese identity was assumed and internalized.

At other times, people are pressured to prove that they are indeed 'Chinese enough' and not tainted by foreign influences. Taiwanese scholars Ding Naifei and Liu Renpeng (1998) describe how this works:

> There must certainly be a 'Chinese-ness' different from 'the west' that is … found to reside in Taiwan, Hong Kong, China, Malaysia, even in Chinese America, or even in Taiwan queers and licensed prostitutes. In such discourses, 'Chinese/Western' differences become a trope whereby feminism, gay and lesbian movement [sic], or the study of (dissident) sexualities are seen to have originated in 'the west'. In relation to which 'China' and 'Chinese-ness' provide an idealized and romanticized contrast, or, take on the attributes of a 'student' working hard to progress in the face of the challenges from 'the west'. (Ding and Liu 1998: 27)

Ding and Liu explain how 'Chinese-ness' is required to prove either that one is not too Western, or that one is seen as inferior and needing to catch up with the West. They echo Martin Manalansan (1995), in relation to lesbian and gay movements in the South. He states that faced with the pervasiveness of Western gay and lesbian identities, and the US framing of the gay movement as an international standard, southern queers may be caught in a binary of two possible reactions: 'the "authentic" nativist search for primordial "gay and lesbian" phenomena', or a collaboration with 'the imposition of international egalitarianism' (Manalansan 1995: 426).

Ding and Liu's article itself uses a Taoist framework to challenge the pressure on sexual dissidents to prove that they are Chinese enough. In their article, they draw largely on Chinese references, mostly critiquing the few Western resources to which they refer. In protesting against pressure to demonstrate 'Chinese-ness', they refrain from placing Western knowledge in a position of superiority. In this way, they escape the dichotomous trap they pose, making their argument even more convincing.

Several interviewees referred to facing objections to non-Chinese frameworks for thought and action. Du Jie (All China Women's Federation) described resistance from staff in a governmental organization for whom a team of trainers of the Gender Training Group were running a gender training workshop. The workshop had been organized by the United Nations Development Programme (UNDP) a few years earlier.

> They said why do we need gender? We have [the concept of] 'equality for men and women' (*nannu pingdeng*). They thought Chairman Mao had already brought in 'equality for men and women'. Sometimes we say 'equality for men and women' and gender are the same, but they are not. Gender is new. 'Equality for men and women' does not include sexuality and sexual orientation. They were very resistant. They said, 'What's the need for Western feminism?' [laughs] ... but people don't say that so much anymore. And we learnt to use examples from Chinese history and today's gender statistics. (Interview with Du Jie, All China Women's Federation, January 2008)

Mr A described arguments opposing the introduction by the World Health Organization (WHO) of a programme of condom promotion with sex workers, which had been successful in Thailand.

> We started in four pilot cities here, and there was a huge media debate. People said 'Thailand is capitalist, we are socialist. We cannot let our girls sell their flesh.' But they were just empty words. People [who were] saying that weren't providing any alternatives for sex workers. And seeing as buying and selling sex is everywhere, pragmatism won out. (Interview with Mr A, government HIV/AIDS advisory body, January 2008)

For some, the Chinese–foreigner division led them to reflect on other differences. Li Xiaojiang, a leading feminist activist, is famous for advocating that Chinese feminism should find its own path rather than following the West. She has written about her relationship with Mary Ann Burris (Bai Mei), Ford Foundation Programme Officer on Reproductive Health during the early and mid 1990s, and she published an exchange of letters between them (Li 1997). Li describes how

> Burris, a foreigner, specially emphasized 'listening to the real voices of Chinese woman' but nevertheless specifically wanted to assign a 'Foreign expert' to consult on our programme. I resisted the foreign expert, but in fact I secretly lacked confidence that we 'Chinese experts' actually knew much about the reproductive health of women in our own land. Luckily we all had a common goal: to understand the real situation and improve Chinese women's health. (Li 1997: 3)

Li goes on to observe that having thought that as Chinese women they knew best about Chinese women's health, they soon realized that as urban Han women they knew very little about rural or ethnic minority women. She pointed out that an open, non-judgemental research approach which started from the assumption of their own ignorance was key in making the study effective and building solidarity between different groups of women. Xiaopei He described how the 'Beijing sisters' lesbian group debated whether or not to allow men into their group in the late 1990s. Having already admitted 'foreign imperialists' (that is, non-Chinese), however, they decided they could not exclude Chinese men (He 2001).

In the next section, I continue to explore these negotiations of domestic and international forces, more specifically at the interactions between gender and sexuality activism in China. I start by examining the schism between gender and sexuality work in China, and then consider how the journey of the concept of gender – from English to Chinese – has contributed to this division, particularly in work on HIV and AIDS. I then examine conceptions of gender and sexuality in efforts to combat domestic violence, around which considerable mobilization has taken place. Finally I look at the limits of this mobilization, and the possibilities for moving beyond violence. The aim is to open up space for women to pursue their desires rather than just protect against that which they do not desire.

Gender and sexuality activism in China

Gender–sexuality schisms

Innovative work on HIV in the late 1990s in China opened up spaces for mobilization by men who have sex with men (MSM) and, to some degree, sex workers. However, this happened parallel to, rather than in collaboration with, women's rights activism. Several interviewees across donor, government, activist, and researcher spheres identified a lack of communication among gender and sexuality scholars and activists:

> Gender studies tends to look at equality between women and men, but not diversity issues. Pressures to be a 'proper man' or 'proper woman' can in themselves be damaging, aside from issues of inequality. Transgender in particular will suffer from this, but not only transgender. Taking into account diversity issues and theorizing homosexualities would strengthen feminist studies in China. Intersex is also an issue, let's respect their natural sex. Homosexuals don't have sex differences [from each other] but many have gender differences. We start from homosexual relations which orients our gender perspective. (Interview with Guo Yaqi, January 2008).

Guo Yaqi identifies a weakness in discourses which focus only on equality *between* women and men and leave out issues of how people are pressured into *becoming* 'proper' women or men. Popular media in China and a range of new publications on parenting express anxieties that the current generation of single children are becoming more androgynous because parents want them to be everything that both a daughter and son would have been. According to the parenting texts and popular media, girls might become too boyish and aggressive, but at least they would be strengthened, whereas boys were at real risk of being weakened and becoming effeminate. For many, the key 'gender' issue is how to restore normative gender roles. Ironically, these are historically quite recent, as during the Cultural Revolution of 1966–76, women and men were both supposed to be primarily revolutionary workers with similar gender roles, rather than sexed or sexual beings. 'Gender awareness' (*xingbie yishi*) is now often taken to mean encouraging girls to be 'aware of' and comfortable with femininity, and boys with masculinity. Connected with the fear of boys becoming more effeminate is the greater awareness that homosexuality exists in China, and a realization that one's children might become homosexual. Dealing with equality between women and men in the public realm but failing to take on gender diversity and sexuality issues leaves space for such heteronormativity.

While Guo Yaqi critiqued the limitations of 'gender studies', Du Jie focused on the limitations of sexuality research. According to Du Jie, Chinese sexuality research had ignored power relations and gender dynamics, focusing on the psychological and medical aspects rather than social issues. Some sexuality scholars emphasize sexual fulfilment but take a psychological and biological perspective, not so much addressing social issues or gender. 'What about power relations and a woman's right to say no? You can't address sexual fulfilment without looking at these too' (interview with Du Jie, 2008). Du Jie saw the gap in sexuality research as being about power and gender inequality. She felt this gap partly resulted from the women's movement in China focusing on social and economic development issues, and sidelining sexuality and other more personal aspects. Two factors were important here: the sensitivity of issues concerning sexuality, and the lack of funding in this area. She suggested, as did Eve Lee (Ford Foundation), that an exchange between gender and sexuality scholars and activists would be hugely helpful (interview, 2008).

Lesbian activism may also have suffered from the women's movement's lack of attention to sexuality. While there is a thriving lesbian bar scene in many Chinese cities, and some lesbian hotlines and activist groups, the level of activism by lesbians falls far behind that of gay men. Funding priorities are also relevant here: HIV and AIDS funding has supported organizing by MSM but not lesbians.

Gender's journey into China

The gender–sexuality divide comes in part from the history of how gender was translated and used in Chinese, to fit into Chinese official discourses of 'Marxist conceptions of women'. Min Dong-chao narrates how the concept of gender travelled to China and was translated into Chinese, ending up emphasizing poverty reduction and development rather than personal issues such as sexuality (Min 2003). While the terms 'gender' and 'gender theory' appeared in a few academic publications in the 1980s, they did not gain prominence until the early 1990s. Min marks out the 1993 training on 'Women and Development' in Tianjin Normal University as a key turning point. The concept of gender was introduced at the training by the Chinese Overseas Women's Research Association and became a major point of discussion. From this moment, gender began to gain ground as both concept and category in mainland Chinese women's studies. The United Nations 1995 Fourth World Conference on Women in Beijing, and associated international funding, further extended the term to be incorporated into official discourse and more grassroots activism.

In 1996 Huang Qicao, then vice-chairwoman and secretary of the party committee of the All China Women's Federation (ACWF), the national machinery of women, called for 'an integration of gender concepts [*xingbie guandian*] into the mainstream of policy' (Min 2003: 18). And Chen Minhua of the ACWF explained gender in language similar to that used to define Marxist feminism, thus making 'gender' acceptable to official Chinese audiences. At the same time, this opened up some possibilities for new action on gender, and relabelled Chinese official discourse in ways more acceptable internationally (Min 2003: 18). However, such an understanding of the concept did lose some of the newer content of gender. It also influenced the debate in Chinese women's studies on how the term should be translated. The dominant terms have now become '*She hui xing bie*', literally 'social sex difference' for gender, and '*shengli xingbie*', literally 'physiological sex' for sex. Both were newly created terms, and within their meaning express the division inherent in the Western constructionist view of gender as a social category and sex as a physiological one.

Min describes the impact of these framings as reinforcing the Marxist feminist emphasis on macro development, economic and social issues, whilst losing the personal and sexual dimensions of liberal feminism.

> After the 1995 Women's Conference, the Latin American Women's Movement used a translation of gender to start a struggle with the Catholic church, among which was a struggle for … legalization of abortion, recognition of homosexuals and single-parent families etc. But in mainland China, gender was translated to mean … women's social political rights (e.g. poverty among women, rural women's land rights, gender equality in rural elections, girls' education, etc.). (Min 2003: 21)

> After the concept of 'gender' travelled to China in the 1990s, it became a common term in women's studies. Often you could see the expression: Biological sex cannot be changed, social sex can be changed. But very rarely did anyone ask: why can't biological sex be changed? How does the discipline of biology express sex and the body? ... The emphasis [in the way the term was translated] on the social aspect of gender, and the separation of sex and gender, neglected the discussion of many years in the locations where the concept of gender originated, as to the relation between the two concepts of sex and gender, and the criticism and reflection on the separation. As a result, Chinese women's research did not fully discuss the relation between the two, or discuss sex and women's individual selves … Because the 'natural' dimensions of sex and the body were abandoned, several research areas were dropped. So now we can see: in mainland China the study of sex has been left to the medical world, and to male-centred sexology, 'the body' has been left to authors on women's beauty etc. …Recently we have often heard male sexologists calling for feminist research on sex. At last we are beginning to see women's research scholars beginning to notice this gap, and starting to explore the host of theoretical and practical problems brought about by this division of sex and gender. (Min 2003: 22)

Min cites the Latin American movement's inclusion of sexuality and body issues in activism around gender. However, the Chinese lack of attention to sexuality in relation to gender is reflected in international gender and development (GAD) discourses. The understanding of sex as biological, and gender as social, remains a foundational concept in GAD, erasing questions of the body (Friedman 2006). The GAD mantra that 'sex is biological, and gender social' is repeated in numerous contexts, Western and non-Western, and is a common element of gender training.

Gender, sexuality and HIV and AIDS

Another example of sexuality being partitioned from gender appears in international work on HIV and AIDS, and the effects of this partition make such work less effective. International development discourses on HIV and AIDS (in most non-African contexts) include MSM. However, MSM tends to disappear off the agenda in 'Gender and HIV and AIDS work', even though MSM is a manifestation of highly gendered processes. Gendered HIV and AIDS work is often considered to be specifically about the 'feminization of HIV and AIDS', that is, the increasing proportion of women among people living with HIV and AIDS. In all regions other than sub-Saharan Africa, however, the total number of men living with HIV still exceeds that of women. Powerful gender stereotypes about macho men link seamlessly in with homophobia, and homophobia is one of the forces that encourage men who have sex with men to marry women, thus putting their wives at risk of HIV.

A different divide exists within work on 'women and HIV and AIDS'. This is the divide between 'good' women, such as married women, and 'key populations' such as sex workers, even though sex workers in most countries are mostly women. This can be seen in the division of remits between UN agencies in relation to HIV and AIDS, with UNIFEM's focus on women (meaning married and 'normal' women, not sex workers), UNAIDS's focus on MSM, and UNFPA taking the lead with sex workers. This division of responsibility takes place not only at headquarters but in country-level offices, including China's, with the result that people are boxed into particular categories that do not reflect the realities of their overlapping identities. At the same time, considerations of women's rights, sexual orientation and sex work are institutionally separated, although there have been some recent efforts by UNIFEM and UNAIDS in China to overcome these divisions (see Bu and Liu 2010).

It is not only UN agencies that may separate key populations from the general population in ways which prevent mutual learning and exchange. A programme of the UK's Department for International Development (DFID) included fun and ribald training for sex workers, with tricks such as how to put condoms on using your mouth. Yet the same programme included information campaigns targeted at migrants arriving in railway stations, which taught people to 'Be chaste and respect yourself' (Jolly with Wang 2003). Of course, sex workers and migrants may need different messages and approaches, but not that different! Such programming contributes to a silo effect with each initiative running on separate tracks.

The NGO Pink Space tries to break down such divisions, by organizing exchanges among different groups. One example is that between women sex workers and HIV-positive women from rural areas with a high prevalence of HIV (transmitted through blood sales and transfusions). Another is between women married to gay men, and lesbians and gay men themselves. These different groups may not be natural allies – HIV-positive women have a lot invested in emphasizing blood as the route of infection, so as not to be seen as 'sluts', and sex workers may not want to be tainted by suspicions of HIV. Women married to gay men might be hostile to the lesbian and gay population. Yet such exchanges have generated frank conversations and budding solidarity (interview with He, 2008).

Organizing against domestic violence

Tensions over how far sexuality and personal desires should be on the gender agenda emerge again in organizing against domestic violence. In spite of the Marxist feminist conception of women in macroeconomic and social terms, and the legitimacy sought for gender by associating it with these frameworks, the ACWF has always engaged in 'family' issues, for example by holding 'model husband competitions' and providing marital counselling at a local level to encourage couples in conflict with one another to reconcile. This was less a politicization of personal issues than a treatment of 'women's issues' as matters of the domestic realm. As an organization, the ACWF has been characterized as a 'semi-private, semi-public' institution (Bu and Milwertz 2007: 5). The ACWF has always had ambivalent functions: dealing with family issues at village level and helping implement policies such as family planning, while representing women's interests at the Communist Party level and bringing women in line with Communist Party priorities.

Complaints about 'wife-beating' would be addressed by local women's federation bureaus in their marriage counselling remit. 'Wife-beating' was generally perceived as a problem of backwardness, of underdevelopment, and of lagging behind reforms (Bu and Milwertz 2007). This rubric meant that survivors and victims, as well as perpetrators, were sometimes blamed for the violence. This resonated with the tendency to view wife-beating largely in terms of relations between husband and wife.

The 1995 Fourth World Conference on Women and the preparations beforehand were instrumental in bringing about changes in understandings of domestic violence in China (Bu and Milwertz 2007; Zhang 2009). Bu and Milwertz (2007) trace the change, looking at how domestic violence was 'discovered' and 'explored' by activists. Domestic violence came on to the radar after the lawyer Pi Xiaoming started to receive women who had been subjected to such violence, and the Maple Women's Hotline started to document complaints. In spite of government reluctance, the women's hotline succeeded in presenting their work at an NGO forum workshop at the UN Fourth World Conference on Women. The exchanges in the preparation process and during the conference instigated a new view of domestic violence as a widespread social phenomenon. As such, it was more an issue of gender inequality and men's abuse of women than simply one of soured relations between spouses.

This shift in approach made possible the foundation of the anti-domestic violence network of NGOs. Ge Youli explains how the idea for the network came out of a lunch meeting with the Ford Foundation in the 1990s. Violence against women was gaining attention internationally, but not yet in China: 'at the time domestic violence was in the position sexuality is today in the Chinese women's movement' (interview with Ge Youli, 2008). Ge Youli thought that establishing a network against domestic violence was a great idea and took it forward with feminist allies. In the late 1990s, Ford funded six key women activists (including Ge) to take part in a regional conference in India on violence against women. This gave further impetus to the establishment of a Chinese network against domestic violence. Energetic mobilization by the individual programme officers in Ford helped secure funding for the initiative from Ford, Sida, Oxfam Novib and the Norwegian Centre for Human Rights at the University of Oslo.

In 1998, the UNDP convened a gender training workshop for women's rights advocates, who then put together a Chinese gender training manual (with the support of Sarah Cook at the Institute of Development Studies, UK). The women's rights advocates subsequently established a Chinese 'Gender Training Group', in which I initially participated. Now, gender training has become one of the methods used by the anti-domestic violence network to change understandings of domestic violence. The network encourages members employed in party/state institutions to take part in gender training. Gender training courses are tailored for groups involved in their initiatives, such as the police, media, medics, and the judiciary.

Further progress was made in 2001, when the revised Marriage Law was adopted – its reference to 'domestic violence' was the first time the phrase had been used in national legislation. The ACWF set up women's shelters in some locations. The anti-domestic violence network developed a clear and transparent governance structure and the ability to distribute grants to member organizations. With further funding from Ford and others, they put out a call for proposals, all in Chinese. The end result of the process was that a whole different set of non-Beijing organizations, including local women's federation and community groups, received grants rather than the more established NGOs in big cities with more experience in fundraising. However, recent constraints on civil society organizations have circumscribed the work of the anti-domestic violence network.

Between violence and pleasure: limits to change?

While it has been possible to politicize what was previously seen as an issue of marital relations, the connections between violence against women (VAW) and sexuality have not been much discussed, and links with other sexuality movements have not been made. Guo Ruixiang did believe that some domestic violence has its origins in poor sexual relations and men's desire to dominate in sex. However, the UNIFEM-supported work does not make these connections. While VAW has become possible to mobilize around, and has entered national legislation, more positive aspects of sexuality remain neglected in research and organizing.

In a review of Chinese studies of women's sexuality, Pei, Ho and Ng (2007) cite how the emphasis in Chinese women's studies in the 1990s, and since, has focused only on the negative aspects of women's sexuality:

> Women's sexual experience per se remained a sensitive topic … It is only in the context of discussions of topics such as rape, domestic violence, and prostitution that women's voices could legitimately be heard. Therefore, research that claims to focus on (all) women's sexuality was actually carried out on certain groups, such as rape survivors and victims of sexual violence or sexual harassment … Such studies, however, served to reinforce the perception that women are weak and lack control of their own lives, bodies and sexuality. As a

> result, female stereotypes remained firmly rooted and constructed in a male-centred culture, and their self-initiated choices ignored, their resistance interpreted as a challenge to the predominant values in culture and society. Women's pleasure, desire and autonomy, topics central to contemporary feminist discourse, were still searching vainly for their language of expression. (Pei *et al.* 2007: 207–8)

There have been a few exceptions, for example in the work of the celebrity academic Li Yinhe on women's sexuality, which has featured in-depth interviews with a variety of women. This narrated women's perceptions of sexuality, including the pleasures and ambivalences of non-normative relations, such as sex outside marriage, and sex beyond menopause. Another leading researcher, Pan Suiming, in his extensive documentation of the lives of women sex workers, has described how they negotiate and gain power in their interactions, depending on the context and conditions.

The difficulty in addressing women's desires, pleasures and fulfilment is echoed in development agency initiatives in China. UNIFEM focuses on sexuality mainly in relation to violence against women and HIV and AIDS. I asked Guo Ruixiang, of UNIFEM, if there was potential for more positive approaches. She replied:

> Already sex education in school is becoming less judgmental. Sex is something everyone is doing, but not many people talk about it in public. But how to operationalize a positive approach to sexuality is not obvious. A very careful approach is needed. Repression is not healthy, I've read work by Pan Suiming, we do need a positive attitude to life. Public education is important but it's difficult due to Chinese gender stereotypes. For example, a girl should not know much about sexuality so that she can be seen as chaste.

Guo told the story of a woman whose husband was having an affair and stopped having sex with her. In a workshop on domestic violence, this woman described her husband's denial of sex as a form of violence. This account implies a recognition of women's desire for sex, and an understanding of sexual violence as being more than the imposition of unwanted sexual interactions on women. However, it also suggests some conception of sex as a duty within marriage. I asked Guo if women denying their husbands sex could count as violence. She said you had to consider the gender power relations to understand what was actually going on.

Ms Q described her UN agency philosophy as including advocacy on some positive sides of sexuality in young people's sexuality education, but 'we haven't got that far in practice' (interview, 2008). Ms Q herself had participated in the session run by the Pleasure Project at the International Conference on AIDS in Asia and the Pacific in 2007, and would like to put some of these ideas into practice in China but is not sure how it would work. When scholar Pan Suiming was invited to a UN workshop on sex work in Beijing in 2007, he talked about people's rights to sexual pleasure, so these issues can be heard in such arenas.

Some initial efforts have been made, such as the DFID China–UK HIV/AIDS Prevention and Care Project 2000–6. Some parts of the programme included innovative approaches, such as a discussion of sexual pleasure and desire. The *Healthy Angels* magazine targeted at female sex workers featured a quiz entitled 'Are you prepared for a safe sex life?' This included questions such as 'Can I let my sexual partner know what kind of touching I like, and where I like to be touched?' 'Can I experience sexual pleasure without using drugs or drinking alcohol?' Information targeted at MSM featured sexy photos with explicit references to enjoying safer and non-penetrative sexual interactions. But these more positive representations were a small part of the overall programme, and messaging was inconsistent.

At the same time, the booming Chinese market has enabled commodification and commercialization of sexuality, particularly women's sexuality, affording new spaces for both fun and exploitation (Liu 2008). Sex shops have transitioned from advertising 'marital aids' and being staffed by older (hence married) women in medical uniform, to being staffed by younger women and men. The medical facade has been dropped. One woman blogger, Mu Zimei (her pseudonym), became famous by having numerous one-night stands with different men and writing a disparaging and graphic account of each. She portrayed her blog as a form of revenge, 'girl power' style, against men for their vanity and illusions of superiority to women. The blog generated extensive discussion. Mu Zimei's followers include women's movement activists, some of whom thought she must have been psychologically damaged by male exploitation in the past, while others have been inspired by her audacity.

What space for women's empowerment?

In this concluding section, I consider how the changes have come about and what they mean for sexuality and for women's empowerment. Following the 1949 revolution, the official storyline regarding women and men was that they were equal, with similar gender roles, and that they expressed ardour for the revolution – not for sex, romance or even for marriage. Sexual impropriety – which could mean any kind of sex outside marriage – could lead to severe penalties, such as public criticism and losing one's job. Since the post-Cultural Revolution era, from the early 1980s onwards, more space has been allowed for the admission and expression of individual subjectivities. At the same time, government policy has called for 'modernization', and 'opening the door' to international exchange, and has shifted towards a market economy. This has included more freedom for some kinds of gender and sexual expression. Women are allowed to be feminine, men to be masculine, and young people even – in some instances of fashion and popular culture – are allowed to be a bit androgynous. And now there are more possibilities for sex without marriage, even with someone of the same sex, without making huge sacrifices in life. In spite of the tensions of the current political climate, the last few decades have also seen more possibilities for civil society organizing around both gender and sexuality.

How have these changes come about? Different linkages,

pushes, and connections, including brave and creative organizing by activists; the growth of the economy and the internet; a shift from moralistic to pragmatic policymaking by government; engagements with international media and donors – all these have had a role in paving the way for new narratives of sexuality to unfold.

Activists tactically engage with media new and old, with and without donor support, exploiting policy openings and flexibilities to advocate as effectively as they can. Access to the internet has enabled new exchanges of information – both within and beyond China, as well as new forms of organizing. Around 80 per cent of young people in China now have some kind of access to the internet. International donor support for civil society and government has also had some impact. Total development aid contributes minimally to the national economy and the government sets parameters for action. Nevertheless, donors were influential in supporting the emerging civil society in the 1990s and they still play a role today.

Perhaps the larger impact has come from domestic policies. Family planning policies and the One Child Family policy (introduced in 1979, in practice mostly in urban areas) meant that sex could no longer be framed as primarily about reproduction (interview with Pan Suiming, Institute of Sexuality and Gender, People's University, 2008). The generation of only children that followed are more individualistic, no longer conceiving of choices around love and marriage as being about filial piety and duty to one's parents but seeing them as more about pleasing oneself. This can explain young people's greater acceptance of sex before marriage and of homosexual relationships; for them, pursuing individual desire seems reasonable (interview with Huang Yingying, Institute of Sexuality and Gender, People's University, 2008).

The government has responded pragmatically to international growth trajectories of HIV and AIDS, and evidence of their spread in China, shifting from initial punitive measures for people living with HIV and AIDS (PLHA) and those considered at risk, to a more pragmatic and humane approach. The experience of SARS in 2003 made it clear that suppressing information can exacerbate ill health as well as economic and social instability (Wu *et al.* 2007). Concern with the sex ratio imbalance and predictions of a generation of unmarried bachelors have led to new institutional concern for gender equality.

A major policy change which has enabled a whole new landscape is the shift from a planned to a market economy, including a more globalized economy. With this change, the impact of the economy on gender and sexual relations has also changed. For example, until a few years ago, urban Chinese residents working in the formal sector would be allocated free or heavily subsidised housing by their employers. However, that housing was often a dormitory bed until marriage made one eligible for a flat of some kind. Many work units only allocated housing to male employees on the assumption that women would get access to housing through their husbands, thus reinforcing heteronormative gender and sexual relations. Now, under a more marketized economy, employers far more rarely provide housing of any kind to employees, with new implications for gender and sexual relations. Given the expectation for urban middle-class couples that the man will provide housing upon marriage, and the rising price of real estate, many men are left unable to attract wives.

The market economy has brought with it huge economic growth as well as new possibilities for gender exploitation, new pressures to fit normative gender roles, and generally greater gaps between rich and poor. Women have to present themselves as attractive according to gender stereotypes in order to work in sectors such as service industries and sales (Liu 2008). Economic dependence on family networks can mean poorer lesbians succumb to the pressure to marry once in their twenties (Suda 2010). In rural areas, poor men find it harder to get married due to increasing bride price.

New industries have emerged around cosmetic surgery, sex work, marriage ceremonies, maternity and baby equipment.

Pain-free abortion is advertised on billboards by hospitals making money from these operations, with no incentive to advise people who seek their services how to make sure that this is their last abortion. LGBT people risk discrimination, but at the same time a small-scale pink economy exists and is likely to grow.

Lisa Rofel (2007) argues that in post-economic-reform China, the idea of the socialist citizen has been replaced by the neoliberal subject; 'the desiring subject … who operates through sexual, material and affective self-interest' (Rofel 2007: 3). Pursuing individual desires around sexuality or gender expression is legitimated but the same is not true for protesting structural inequalities which limit who can pursue these desires, and how. In some ways, this generates tolerance for diverse individual trajectories but less space for tackling structures of inequality, whether sexual, gendered or economic.

The globalizing economy is part of this – with international business investing heavily in China and engaging with gender norms in their search for profit. A McDonalds advertisement taps into people's resentment of gendered pressures, asking, 'What do you think happiness is?' A young man replies, 'Not having to pay the mortgage, long live renting!' One young woman says, 'Happiness is not having to look for a partner, being single feels good,' and another declares, 'Being able to go out without putting make-up on.'

While advocacy has focused on the socialist state, now the capitalist economy is just as relevant. Some LGBT groups have suggested working on international companies in China, asking them to abide by equal opportunities commitments they have made in their headquarters or other country offices. Some civil society groups collaborate with or seek sponsorship from private companies, while others fear such moves will compromise their independence. Women now gain the freedom of consumer choice but face market pressures. The struggle for empowerment must shift to encompass this arena as well.

Notes

1 Field research for this chapter was completed in 2008 and the writing of this piece was completed in summer 2010 when I was convenor of the Institute of Development Studies Sexuality and Development Programme.

2 In Changsha, a commercial marriage bureau (dating service) was set up in 2007 for those seeking affectionate but sex-free marriages with someone of the opposite sex because they are either asexual, impotent, homosexual, have lost interest in sex due to their old age, or have had bad experiences (www.wx920.com).

References

Aizhixing Institute of Health Education (2009) *Research Report on Behaviour, Rights Protection and Service Needs of FSW*, Aizhixing Institute of Health Education, Beijing.

Bu, W. and X. Liu (2010) 'Report on Gender and HIV/AIDS in China', sponsored by UNIFEM and UNAIDS, New York.

Bu, W. and C. Milwertz (2007) 'Non-Governmental Organising for Gender Equality in China – Joining a Global Emancipatory Epistemic Community', *International Journal of Human Rights*, Vol. 11, Nos. 1–2, pp. 131–49.

Ding, N. and R. Liu (1998) 'Reticent Poetics, Queer Politics', English version of 'The Penumbra Asks the Shadow: Reticent Poetics and Queer Politics', *Gender Research*, Vol. 3, No. 4 (Queer: Theory and Politics Special Edition), pp. 109–55.

Friedman, A. (2006) 'Unintended Consequences of the Feminist Sex/Gender Distinction', *Genders Online Journal,* Issue 43, www.genders.org/g43/g43_friedman.html.

He, X. (2001) 'Chinese Women *Tongzhi* Organising in the 1990's', in P. Hsiung, M. Jaschok, and C. Milwertz (eds.), *Women Activists in Contemporary China*, Berg, Oxford.

Jackson, S., J. Liu and J. Woo (eds.) (2008) *East Asian Sexualities*, Zed Books, London.

Jolly, S. with Y. Wang (2003) 'Gender Mainstreaming Strategy for the China–UK HIV/AIDS Prevention and Care Project', www.siyanda.org.

Li, X. (1997) 'Why Do We Start from Cultural Anthropology?' in X. Li (ed.), *Reproduction: Tradition and Modernization* (in Chinese), Henan People's Publishing House, Zhengzhou.

Liu, J. (2008) 'Sexualized Labour? "White-Collar Beauties" in Provincial China', in S. Jackson, J. Liu and J. Woo (eds.), *East Asian Sexualities*, Zed Books, London.

Manalansan, M. (1995) 'In the Shadows of Stonewall: Examining Gay Transnational Politics and the Diasporic Dilemma', *GLQ*, Vol. 2, Duke University Press, Durham, NC.

Min, D. (2003) 'Fragments of the Gender Travel in China', *Collection of Women's Studies*, September, 5th Series, No. 54 (in Chinese).

Pei, Y., S. P. Ho and M. L. Ng (2007) 'Studies on Women's Sexuality in China since 1980: A Critical Review', *Journal of Sex Research*, Vol. 44, No. 2, pp. 202–12.

Rofel, L. (2007) *Desiring China: Experiments in Neoliberalism, Sexuality and Public Culture*, Duke University Press, Durham, NC.

Saich, T. (2004) *Governance and Politics of China*, Palgrave Macmillan, New York.

Suda, K. (2010) 'Chinese Lesbians Organizing in Urban Public Space: 1995–2010', paper presented at the 'Chinese Women Organizing: Looking Back, Looking Forward' international symposium, Beijing Foreign Studies University, 5–6 July.

Wu, Z., S. Sullivan, Y. Wang, M-J. Rotheram-Borus and R. Detels (2007) 'Evolution of China's Response to HIV/AIDS', *The Lancet*, Vol. 369, No. 9,562, pp. 679–90.

Zhang, L. (2009) 'Chinese Women Protesting Domestic Violence: The Beijing Conference, International Donor Agencies, and the Making of a Chinese Women's NGO', *Meridians: Feminism, Race, Transnationalism*, Vol. 9, No. 2, pp. 66–99.

About the Contributors

Mona I. Ali is a professor in the English Department and director of the Centre for Humanities and Interdisciplinary Studies at Cairo University. She is a member of the board of trustees of the New Woman Foundation, where she is also the editor-in-chief of the theoretical magazine *Tiba*. Ali is also a writer, storyteller and member of the 'I am the Story (Ana el-Hekkayya)' storytelling group. She has published on the theory and practice of translation, travel literature, women's writing and postcolonial literatures.

Mulki Al-Sharmani is an Academy of Finland research fellow and lecturer at the Faculty of Theology, Study of Religion Unit, at the University of Helsinki. From 2005 to 2010, she was a joint research/teaching faculty at the American University in Cairo, at the Social Research Center. Mulki's research interests and work are in Muslim family law, gender, Muslim feminist engagements with Islamic textual tradition and religious discourses, and transnational migratory family life. She is the co-editor of a volume in this series, *Feminist Activism, Women's Rights, and Legal Reform.*

Bibi Bakare-Yusuf is a publisher based in Abuja, Nigeria. She has a PhD in gender studies from the University of Warwick. Her research areas of interest are embodiment, memory, sexuality and cultural production.

Deevia Bhana is a professor in the School of Education, University of KwaZulu-Natal. She is known for her work on childhood sexualities, gender and violence, AIDS, schooling, and health promotion in South Africa. She is a co-author of *Towards Equality? Gender in South African Schools during the HIV/AIDS Pandemic* (2009) and a co-editor of *Babies and/or Books: Pregnancy and Young Parents at School* (2012).

Samia Huq is an anthropologist and associate professor at the Department of Economics and Social Science at BRAC University, Dhaka. Her areas of interest include religious revival, religious identity, religion, politics, social movements, and secularism. Publications from this research are ongoing, appearing in several international peer-reviewed journals and as book chapters. Huq is currently involved in research tracing the cultural history of the Bengali Muslim woman as she lived in and created the world of Bengali performance arts in the context of partitions and the emergence of Bangladesh. Concurrent research includes Islamist women and their contribution to public debates and public policy issues, and education for women, religious and secular, and its effects on gender norms, faith and development.

Penny Johnson is an independent researcher who works closely with the Institute of Women's Studies at Birzeit University, where she edits the *Review of Women's Studies*. Her recent writing on gender dynamics in Palestine has focused on weddings during the two Palestinian intifadas, unmarried women, young Palestinians' talk about proper and improper marriages and, most recently, wives and mothers of Palestinian political prisoners. She is an associate editor of the *Jerusalem Quarterly* and a member of the Arab Families Working Group. A former coordinator of the Human Rights Committee at Birzeit University (1982–93) and a founding member of the Institute of Women's Studies, Johnson lives in Ramallah.

Susie Jolly is a hybrid activist/researcher/communicator/trainer and is currently also a donor. From her different positions she consistently seeks to challenge the 'straitjacket' of gender and sexuality norms that disempower so many people. She currently leads the Ford Foundation sexuality and reproductive health and rights grant-making programme in China. Previously, she founded and led the Sexuality and Development Programme at the Institute of Development Studies. She has had extensive engagement with gender and development issues internationally, with six years' experience at the BRIDGE gender information unit, IDS, as well as a lifetime of feminist activism. She is the co-editor of a volume in this series, *Women, Sexuality and the Political Power of Pleasure*.

Cecilia M. B. Sardenberg is a Brazilian feminist activist and since 1982 has been a member of the faculty of philosophy and human sciences of the Federal University of Bahia (UFBA). She is also a visiting professor at the Institute of Development Studies. She was one of the founders of UFBA's Nucleus of Interdisciplinary Studies on Women (NEIM), where she teaches feminist theory and where she helped create the masters and PhD programmes on interdisciplinary studies on women, gender and feminism. She has worked in the area of gender and development in Brazil, both as a practitioner and researcher, and has published several articles in Brazil and abroad on feminist and gender studies. She is the convener of the Latin American hub in the Pathways of Women's Empowerment research consortium, and national coordinator for OBSERVE – the Observatory for the Application of Maria da Penha Law, the new domestic violence legislation in Brazil.

Index